1997

LITERATURE, NATURE, AND OTHER

LITERATURE, NATURE, AND OTHER
Ecofeminist Critiques

Patrick D. Murphy

STATE UNIVERSITY OF NEW YORK PRESS

Production by Ruth Fisher
Marketing by Dana E. Yanulavich

Published by
State University of New York Press, Albany

© 1995   State University of New York

For information, address State University of New York Press,
State University Plaza, Albany, N.Y., 12246

Library of Congress Cataloging-in-Publication Data

Murphy, Patrick D., 1951–
      Literature, nature, and other : ecofeminist critiques / Patrick D.
   Murphy.
         p.   cm.
      Includes bibliographical references and index.
      ISBN 0–7914–2277–1 (alk. paper). — ISBN 0–7914–2278–X (pbk. :
   alk. paper)
      1. Feminist literary criticism. 2. Ecofeminism.   I. Title.
   PN98.W64M87   1995
   801'.95—dc20   93–8733
                                                                        CIP

10 9 8 7 6 5 4 3 2 1

*For Marikochan
and her possible futures*

Contents

✌ Acknowledgments ∿

Many people have contributed to my thinking, writing, and teaching over the past several years, and while I cannot thank all of them here I would like to single out a few. The anonymous reviewers and editor Eugene C. Hargrove of *Environmental Ethics*; Karen Warren for encouraging my work and providing exceptionally detailed and insightful critiques of my writing. Peter Quiqley, who spurred my own interest and theoretical questioning through his sophisticated questions and analyses; Cheryll Glotfelty who early on expressed interest in my work and has engaged me since in valuable dialogue and has helped with the realization of some dreams; Gretchen Legler for arranging my participation in panels at M/MLA and Minnesota and sharing her work with me; Susan Jaret McKinstry, Dale Bauer, Helen Wussow and Karen Hohne for facilitating my writing through their editing projects; Peter Narusewicz, Michelle Toohey, and Lidija Tonic, who have not only provided me with diligent research assistance but have also served as insightful conversation participants, as well as the other students a IUP who have educated me when they thought they were being educated; Nancy Lang, whose study of Native American women authors initiated the work that led to my writing on Joy Harjo; Michael Hoffman, Dave Robertson, and Jack Hicks at UC Davis who have been invaluable to my intellectual development; Katsunori Yamazato and Eric Paul Shaffer, who have stimulated and educated me in many ways; the anonymous reviewers for SUNY Press and the members of the SUNY Press staff who have turned this manuscript into a book; finally, Izumichan, who needs no explanation, and Gary Snyder, who has been the pivotal figure in all of this for me. They have all endeavored to save me from myself at times, but any mistakes found here indicate that they have not always succeeded, and the responsibility for learning what the shortcomings of this book reveal remains my own.

The following chapters have been revised, several extensively, from previously published essays, and I would like to acknowledge those original publications. "Prolegomenon for an Ecofeminist Dialogics" originally appeared in *Feminism, Bakhtin, and the Dialogic Voice*, edited by Dale Bauer and Susan Jaret McKinstry, published by SUNY Press, 1991, 39–56. "Ground, Pivot, Motion: Ecofeminist Theory, Dialogics, and Literary Practice" originally appeared in a special issue of *Hypatia: A Journal of Feminist Philosophy* 6 (1991): 146–61, on ecological feminism, guest edited by Karen Warren and is reprinted with the permission of Indiana University Press. "Voicing Another Nature" first appeared in *A Dialogue of Voices: Feminist Literary Theory and*

Bakhtin, edited by Karen Hohne and Helen Wussow, copyright 1994 by the Regents of the University of Minnesota, and published by the University of Minnesota Press. "Sex-Typing the Planet: Gaia Imagery and the Problem of Subverting Patriarchy" was originally published in *Environmental Ethics* 10 (1988): 155–68. "Somagrams in An/Other Tongue: Patricia Hampl's 'resort,'" was originally published in *Women's Studies* 19 (1990): 45–54. "'A Mountain Always Practices in Every Place': Climbing Over Transcendence" originally appeared in Chinese in *Proceedings of the Fu Jen University, Taiwan, Second International Conference on Literature and Religion: Poetry and the Transcendent,* edited by Nick Koss and published by Grand East Enterprise, Ltd., Hong Kong, 1994. A portion of "Centering the Other: Trickster Midwife Pedagogy" originally appeared as part of "Coyote Midwife in the Classroom: Introducing Literature with Feminist Dialogics," published in *Practicing Theory in Introductory College Literature Courses,* edited by James M. Cahalan and David B. Downing, NCTE, 1991, 161–76. A version of "The Present is to Nature as the Past is to Culture as the Future is to Agency" was originally published as "Rethinking the Relations of Nature, Culture, and Agency" in *Environmental Values* 1.4 (1992): 311–20, published by White Horse Press, Knapwell, Cambridge, UK.

∽ Preface—By Way of Memoir ∽

As I began revising material for the chapters that follow and considered other chapters that I might write, I realized that I needed to situate myself for their readers. Not in order to demonstrate a right to speak, or an experiential authority, but to clarify my changing position, my stance and ground. At first, I thought I would write that "Sex-Typing the Planet," originally a conference paper for a California American Studies Association meeting held at Davis, where I was working on my doctorate, was the starting point. But that is not really accurate, although its publication did mark a broader self-recognition of my work as ecocritical than my earlier essays on Gary Snyder did. Then, I thought that it was my master's thesis, written at California State University, Northridge, comparing the attitudes toward place expressed in the writings of Gary Snyder and Wendell Berry, a piece of which became my first critical publication. But that wouldn't have come into existence without my having been introduced to Jack Kerouac's *The Dharma Bums* in one of the undergraduate courses I was required to take in order to gain admission to the Northridge M.A. program in English (I had a B.A. in History). I kept backing up until I reached my childhood.

I did not get all the way back to a primal scream or anything, but I did begin to recall the scenes of my engagement with the nonhuman in the small Illinois town that was my first home. And I think that these memories have become more poignant for me of late for two reasons. One, our daughter is two-and-a-half years old, and building a skyfort and a sandbox for her, and taking her for walks, and pointing out butterflies, crows, grasshoppers, rabbits, and one deer in the yard this past summer have reminded me of the positive moments of my childhood. Two, in November of 1992 we moved across town from a skinny little lot—but wonderful old house—a block from campus, to a two-acre parcel and a rundown two-story house, just across the borough line. At the dead end of one street and with a house number on another street that exists only on city maps, we constitute a gap in the urbanization around us, so that we still legally have well water and a septic system. Like the second house I lived in as a child, also at the edge of town, our property abuts a Catholic cemetery. We are now near a couple of golf courses and some woods, and the rabbits burrow on the hillside in a tangle of raspberry, sumac, poison ivy, and the remains of several old apple and oak trees. There is a sense that so much of the noise of the rest of our lives recedes as we walk the small rectangle of land that has been entrusted to us by deed. The quiet reminds me of how the world changed when my brothers and I used to cross the condemned stone bridge,

with the holes in its floor, over the creek that separated the World War II hous-
ing tract in which we first lived from the farmland on the other side; or the
change in sounds when at our next house I would cross the road and the corn
or soybean field and enter the woods along the Kankakee River, with the long
abandoned barge locks still standing, beached until their final crumbling by
the changes in transportation technology late in the nineteenth century.

   I was neither an environmentalist nor an ecologist, in the senses in which
Peter Berg distinguishes these;[1] just a boy connecting with the nature of the
place that was home, the flat farmland fringed by woods and creeks and roads
illuminated late at night by summer lightning. Growing up in a family headed
by a functioning alcoholic, I felt always on the outside of things, always less
than something I ought to be; but not when I was alone in the woods walking
and climbing, or alone in the cemetery overlooking the millrace reading and
reading, my back against the cool granite of a tombstone. My concerns as I
entered my teens were not with nonhuman nature but human nature. At fourteen I entered a seminary for a brief period of time.

   Then I hoped that literature might cure people of their ignorance and stu-
pidity, and planned to major in English at UCLA. But there was Vietnam and I
became an anti-imperialist antiwar activist, and abandoned the "irrelevancies"
of English for the relevance-generating discipline of History. And then I
moved on to Marxism, specifically Maoism, and for seven years made revolutionary propaganda my career. Now I'm a postmarxist, after having actually
been, unlike many, a practicing Marxist. On the other side of that, I began to
think that many of the most fundamental contradictions were not resolvable,
only mediatable. I think that is why, when I finally made it to doctoral study,
Bakhtinian dialogics became so significant a critical *method* for me: dialectics
without the millenarian revolutionary teleology, without the rush to the preordained synthesis.

   Reading *The Dharma Bums*, while I was stocking grocery shelves at night
and taking classes in the daytime, introduced me to an image of Gary Snyder
that led me to his poetry, and that did really produce a chronotope for my academic direction. But there was also a nonacademic moment before that, which
deserves recognition. I began dating the woman with whom I am now married
when we both worked in a supermarket in downtown Los Angeles. We went
on a picnic to Zuma Beach, and during the course of the day she initiated a
conversation about whether or not rocks had souls—a topic that initially did
not square well with my materialism. Yet I attempted to come to terms somehow with what I later realized was an animistic spiritual naturalism, a kind of
metaphysical materialism in that the spirituality is immanent and innate
rather than extrinsic and transcendental. That conversation and subsequent
related ones actually prepared me for coming to terms with Snyder's Buddhist
ecology. Shinto seems to have been a mode of apprehension inculcated in

Bonnie as a child in Japan, which appeared in the rocks-have-souls argument. Such apprehension has helped me move beyond the reductionism of instrumentalist materialisms, whether of the Marxist or the bourgeois scientific varieties. Such moving beyond has in turn helped me to open up to the ecological dimensions of the life philosophies represented in literary works by contemporary Native American writers.

While one pundit has written that everything he needs to know he learned in first grade, I feel that most of what I need to teach today I learned after graduate school. Although I had some encounters with feminism, mainly involving other students in my classes, I learned dialogics on the side and worked on Snyder and Berry and a few other environmental writers largely on my own. I was hired by IUP to teach modern American poetry, with the assumption that the focus would be on modernists, such as Eliot, Stevens, and Crane, who had appeared in my dissertation along with Jeffers and Masters. Little did I realize when I accepted the position that six years later I would be teaching almost exclusively contemporary writers, focusing on critical theory, multiculturalism, and environmental literature, with continuing attention in all cases to women writers. I had not planned to develop formal expertise within any of these areas but found myself feeling the need to teach them, and to develop at least some minimal level of authority to justify my selection of topics, whether for my advanced doctoral seminar in American multicultural literature or the senior synthesis course on gender, ecology, and culture.

My critical and pedagogical emphases have grown within and through me over the years since I arrived in Indiana, Pennsylvania, and the chapters of this book, consisting of revised essays and papers written almost entirely during that period, reflect this growth and the defining of a focalization that interrelates them. For several years my work seemed to occur in disparate areas. But in the course of writing the "Prolegomenon" they began to look more like a structure than a pile of lumber, and with the recent work on Native American and Chicana writers and the notion of "ecological multiculturality," I think I have my house framed, with the founding of *ISLE: Interdisciplinary Studies in Literature and Environment* demarcating the living room. The amount of theoretical and critical "finishing" that remains to be done would be daunting, however, if we weren't doing the same thing with this physical house in which I key this preface—in one of the few rooms that is more or less done, although the kitchen is shaping up nicely and this spring I hope to put in the dining room ceiling. Like the back stoop that I enclosed to create an airlock/mudroom and a place for our longhaired cat named Leguin to ride out the winter, there is always new work to be done along with the remodeling of the old rooms. A case in point is a recent ecofeminist analysis of Disney animation, a project I had not envisioned concerning a medium I had not anticipated critically working up, although I couldn't refuse the request for it any more than I could have turned down Bonnie's for the mudroom. Anyway, the house is framed; I don't know what the next addition will be, only that it will be connected to the rest, one way or another.

I have organized these chapters into three sections. Part One presents a set of theoretically driven chapters in which the examples serve to elaborate the argument, rather than the argument's being developed from the examples. In terms of the chronology of their original versions, they are mixed up, with the earliest one actually appearing last. I think this is appropriate, since much of the preceding theorizing prepares for and articulates what I either presumed or intuited in "Sex-typing the Planet," the basic argument of which spurred me to evolve an articulatable theory for the sensibility that I was just developing. Part Two consists of chapters focusing on individual authors, and presents extended applications of the theoretical position, or some component of it, developed in Part One. Part Three primarily addresses pedagogy, as well as nature writing canon formation, and the task of male practice in response to feminism within the ecology movement. "Simply Uncontrollable" is probably the only chapter in this book specifically directed at the men in the audience. I have also added an Appendix and provided at its beginning a rationale for its inclusion.

I

Chapter One

Prolegomenon for an Ecofeminist Dialogics

I

Pluralistic humanism has run its course. What may have once encouraged individual growth and intellectual diversity for some components of the culture is now producing a *laissez-faire* attitude that truncates the debate over cultural values through nonjudgmental or "undecidability" postures.[1] As Gerald Graff has trenchantly suggested, "real disagreement has become rare, for the multiplicity of tongues leads not to confrontation but to incommensurability and talking at cross-purposes" (*Literature* 190). The various cataclysms of the twentieth century that dethroned the idealist humanism that posited the linear progression of western civilization did not dethrone the anthropocentrism of religious and secular humanism, nor did they disrupt the androcentrism that arises from the patriarchal base of western culture. Similarly, the theoretical projects that arose to challenge humanism have produced an energetic skepticism and a shifting of foci of theoretical and critical attention, but they have not promoted neither a world view that enables any kind of affirmation of new values nor a praxis that enables the application of such values in the physical world. In marked contrast to the critical maladies of enervated humanism, solipsistic skepticism, and paralytic undecidability, a triad of (re)perceptions has appeared, which, if integrated, can lead toward an affirmative praxis: the Bakhtinian dialogical method, ecology, and feminisms.[2]

Dialogics enables the differential unification of ecology and feminisms, which is to say a conjoining that does not conflate particularities or subordinate one to the other. Such an integration can produce a new perception of the relationship of humanity and world, and a praxis that works toward the decentering dealienation of andro/anthropocentric humanism and the reintegrative, affirmative dissolution of the intellectual isolation of radical skepticism. Dialogics encompasses Marxist dialectics by emphasizing the unity of opposites and their interanimating dynamic tension (see Lenin 192–238 and 359–63; Mao 117–25).[3] At the same time, it reveals that the most fundamental relationships are not resolvable through dialectical synthesis: humanity/nature, ignorance/knowledge, male/female, emotion/intellect, conscious/unconscious. And these paired terms are not even actually dichotomous or dyadic but only indicate idealized polarities within a multiplicitous field, such as that of planet, thought, sex/gender, perception, and mind. Bakhtin's conception of centripetal/centrifugal tension provides a means of countering totalization, so that any totality is continuously recognized as already a relativized, temporal centripetal entity in need of centrifugal destabilizing. While human forces are always at work centralizing, quantifying, and coding phenomena, other human forces are always challenging and breaking up such reductions and constructions in order to sustain themselves.

II

Ecology and feminisms provide the groundings necessary to turn the dialogical method into a livable critical theory, rather than a merely usable one applicable only to literature, language, and thought. As Gayatri Chakravorty Spivak candidly observes, "one must fill the vision of literary form with its connections to what is being read: history, political economy—the world. And questioning the separation between the world of action and the world of the disciplines. There is a great deal in the way" (95). And one of the "deals" in the way consists of critical theories that can be represented as critical discourses in the classroom but cannot be implemented as transformative pedagogies or applied in the rest of our interpretive behavior, by means of which we act in the world.

Ecology as a discipline means, fundamentally, the study of the environment in its interanimating relationships, its change and conservation, with humanity recognized as a part of the planetary ecosystem. Ecology, then, is not a study of the "external" environment which we enter, or a management system for the raw materials at our command, although some misperceive it in these ways; it is a study of interrelationship, place, and function, with its bedrock the recognition of the distinction between things-in-themselves and things-for-us. The latter entities result from intervention, manipulation, and transformation. And, as a corollary, if we can render other entities things-for-us, the reverse also exists: other entities can render us things-for-them. Ecology can be a means for learning how to live appropriately in a particular place and time, so as to preserve, contribute to, and recycle the ecosystem (see Rolston 14–27). As Adrienne Rich expresses it, "I need to understand how a place on the map is also a place in history, within which as a woman, a Jew, a lesbian, a feminist, I am created and trying to create" (8; see also Snyder, *Old Ways* 63–64).

In a very basic way, the recognition of the difference between things-in-themselves and things-for-us, and the corollary of us-as-things-for-others leads directly into feminisms, particularly in their interrogations of gender. Only by recognizing the existence of the "other" as a self-existent entity can we begin to comprehend a gender heterarchical continuum in which difference exists without binary opposition and hierarchical valorization. And the "male" and "female" that constitute the dyad are not absolute gender categories but species generative distinctions in reproduction carried over into conceptualizations of the cultural formation of gender. Those feminisms committed to exposing, critiquing, and ending the oppression of women, overthrowing patriarchy and phallocentrism, demand male recognition of the other as not only different in more ways than binary configurations can recognize, but also of equal ontological status. And this would mean recognizing the concepts of both self and other as interdependent, mutually determinable, constructs; it would also mean female recognition of a woman not only as an other but also as a self. As the poet Sharon Doubiago dramatically states it, "because of sexism, because of the psychotic avoidance of the issue at all costs, ecologists have failed to grasp the fact that at the core of our suicidal mission is the psychological issue of gender, the oldest war, the war of the sexes" (4).

But that first recognition of the other as self-existent entity is just that, a first step. It enables the further recognition of interrelationship and interanimation, but on a heterarchical basis rather than on a hierarchical use-value or exchange-value basis, both of which would define autonomy from the perspective of individualism as a strength, rather than as a lack. Barbara Johnson notes that only a romantic androcentrism can phallaciously raise autonomy over all other relationships: "Clearly, for Thoreau, pregnancy was not an essential fact of life. Yet for him as well as for every human being that has yet existed, someone else's pregnancy is the very *first* fact of life. How might the plot of human subjectivity be reconceived (so to speak) if pregnancy rather than autonomy is what raises the question of deliberateness?" (190; see Keller 106–7). Such a question arises only as a result of feminist interrogation. It not only interrogates autonomy but also affirms relationship, and privileges nurturing over engendering to the degree that these two wholly interrelated phases of the parent/offspring relationship have been separated in Western culture since the time of the Greeks, with engendering having more status than nurturing. Thus, while slaves have always been thought capable of nurturing, they have never been officially delegated to engendering the wealthy classes. Johnson's privileging provides a necessary corrective to the androcentric-based difference between the definitions of "fathering" and "mothering," which in themselves have significant ecological implications, the former of begetting and unlimited expansion and the latter of sustaining and cultivating, as Annette Kolodny discusses at some length in *The Lay of the Land.*

But heterarchy does not reductively return us to pluralism. Hazel Henderson, in explaining heterarchy, speaks of such a viewpoint as meaning subset plurality within a system without dominant/subordinate ranking, and argues that "hierarchy is an illusion generated by a fixed observer" (212). Thus we can recognize that biogender differences exist, can occur in both genders, and should not be comparatively evaluated to determine which are more useful or superior. Rosemary Radford Ruether makes the case that "without sex-role stereotyping, sex-personality stereotyping would disappear, allowing for gen-uine individuation of personality. Instead of being forced into a mold of mas-culine or feminine 'types,' each individual could shape a complex whole from the full range of human psychic potential for intellect and feeling, activity and receptivity" (210). At the same time, such a heterarchical viewpoint would necessarily challenge any effort to maintain and cultivate sociogender differ-ences because these would limit subset plurality and serve oppressive and exploitative purposes. This viewpoint would lead to specific political practices that would subvert existing social structures and participate in the process of evolving new structures. Such evolution in turn serves a basic ecological func-tion: "A healthy, balanced ecosystem, including human and nonhuman inhab-itants, must maintain diversity" (King, "Toward" 119). Aldo Leopold's "land ethic" is also often invoked in this regard: "A thing is right when it tends to preserve the integrity, stability, and beauty of the biotic community. It is wrong when it tends otherwise" (262). Diversity will occur within ecosystem homeostatis, i.e., dynamic balance, which is "an achievement and a tendency. Systems recycle, and there is energy balance; yet the systems are not static, but dynamic" (Rolston 14). It is the capitalist myth of unlimited expansion that is actually a static ideal no different from the dream for a perpetual motion machine.

Using the health of the ecosystem as the fundamental criterion for judg-ment enables us to introduce a new conception of value to oppose those that dominate capitalist and state capitalist economies. In opposition to either use value or exchange value as the criterion of worth, we need to develop a crite-rion of ecological value, which emphasizes interrelationship, maintenance, and sustainment (or "carrying capacity"). Diversity would be recognized as a necessary dimension of individual species survival, both within itself—as sub-species and cultural multiplicity—and within its ecosystemic relationships. I would argue that just such heterarchical differentiation explicitly, and a sense of ecological value implicitly, guides much of Carol Gilligan's In A Different Voice. As she suggests, "through this expansion in perspective, we can begin to envision how a marriage between adult development as it is currently por-trayed and women's development as it begins to be seen could lead to a changed understanding of human development and a more generative view of human life" (174). The triad of dialogics, feminisms, and ecology, in that order, appear in this remark concluding her book.

In terms of judgmental criteria, feminists have criticized Marxists for sub-ordinating the struggle against women's oppression to the class struggle, and for emphasizing the conditions and relations of production over those of reproduction. Such criticisms are directed against the limitations of a determinist interpretation that privileges the history of class struggle over the larger history of human inequality based on gender oppression and reproductive exploitation. Oppression and exploitation, gender and class, are intimately and inseparably linked, although with a significant difference. Specific conditions and relations of production and the classes that arise from them are historically transient. But sexual difference, like pigmentation, will exist with any relations of production, and will continue to produce a dynamic tension born of difference that can potentially result in oppression, particularly in terms of the power of cultural constructions of gender. The relations of reproduction, unlike those of production, are necessarily more dialogical than dialectical (see Spivak, "Feminism and Critical Theory" in *In Other Worlds*). And the struggles to end both patriarchy and capitalism need to be placed in an even larger context: the relationship of humanity within nature. The recent development of an ecological feminism (ecofeminism) has begun this process of explicitly intertwining the terrains of female/male and nature/humanity, which have been artificially separated by philosophical linearity for far too long.

The weaknesses regarding gender oppression and sociogender differences in "Deep Ecology" demonstrate the inability of environmentalism on its own to produce a sufficient livable theory.[4] Feminist thought must be employed to bring to consciousness and thus enable the breaking of patriarchal habits of perception. But environmentalists have not initially recognized the identity of interests. Ynestra King noted only a few years ago that

> For the most part, ecologists, with their concern for nonhuman nature, have yet to understand that they have a particular stake in ending the domination of women because a central reason for woman's oppression is her association with the despised nature they are so concerned about. The hatred of women and the hatred of nature are intimately connected and mutually reinforcing. ("Toward" 118)

King argues that domination of man over woman is the prototype for other forms of domination, but it is unlikely that they can be chronologically separated since they are founded on the same conception of reality. More important, however, are the four principles that King establishes as the basis for ecofeminism: one) the oppression of women and the building of "Western industrial civilization" are interrelated through the belief that women are closer to nature; two) life on earth is heterarchical, "an interconnected web"; three) a balanced ecosystem of human and nonhuman "must maintain diversity"; four) species survival necessitates a "renewed understanding of our relationship to nature, of our own bodily nature and nonhuman nature around us" ("Toward" 119–20).

Ariel Salleh critiques Deep Ecology in terms of its failure to make the paradigm shift necessary to achieve its professed goals. Specifically, she argues that it takes an anti-class posture, but ignores oppression, and that it remains trapped in a "tacit mind-body dualism" that downplays the significance of ideology as a material force in the world. "The feminist consciousness," declares Salleh, "is equally concerned to eradicate ideological pollution, which centuries of patriarchal conditioning have subjected us all to, women and men" ("Deeper" 342; see also Salleh, "Class," and Salleh, "Ecofeminism"). She concludes that the proponents of Deep Ecology remain locked in the old dualistic paradigms because they have not as yet denounced and sought to overthrow "the suppression of the *feminine*." And this "is not just a suppression of real, live, empirical women, but equally the suppression of the feminine aspects of men's own constitution which is the issue here" ("Deeper" 344).

Karen J. Warren begins her discussion of ecofeminism with this very problem of dualism, and for her the strength of ecofeminism is that it "encourages us to think ourselves out of 'patriarchal conceptual traps,' by *reconceptualizing* ourselves and our relation to the nonhuman natural world in nonpatriarchal ways" ("Feminism and Ecology" 7). Much of Warren's essay is given over to a critique of liberal feminism, Marxist feminism, radical feminism, and socialist feminism, and their shortcomings which necessitate a "transformative feminism," that will "make a responsible ecological perspective central to feminist theory and practice" ("Feminism and Ecology" 18; see also Warren, "Power").

But how are all of these interrogational and transformative strands to be woven into a meta-philosophical net with a self-conscious method of critique and affirmation? Ecofeminism needs a critical method not only to link its fundamental aspects but also to enable it to remain an active, developing critique guiding practice, a meta-philosophy, rather than a monological political dogma or an abstract interpretative instrument. That method is dialogics. And the emphasis on consensus decision-making, as observed for decades in feminist and ecofeminist groups and communities, indicates that dialogical practice is already well underway and that, as usual, social practice precedes and generates the conditions that require theorizing (see Estes on "consensus").

III

The Bakhtinian dialogical method is becoming widely recognized across academic disciplines, but some character traits are less well known and more neglected than others. It seems no accident that *Freudianism, A Marxist Critique,* published under Vološinov's name, is the last Bakhtinian text to be reissued and appear in paperback, although it was one of the earliest works published. Except for its appendix, it is the text least related to literature and literary theory per se, but one of crucial importance for the Bakhtinian concept of "utterance," particularly in terms of the "inner word" and in terms of a larger conception of the dialogic method as reaching beyond aesthetic texts.[5]

In opposition to what was perceived as Freudian psychoanalysis, *Freudianism* presents dialogical conceptions of the self, the psyche, and the "content of consciousness," which initiate recognition of the constitution of the individual as a *chronotopic relationship*, that is, a social/self construct developing within given social, economic, political, historical, and environmental parameters of space and time (Bakhtin, *Dialogic* 85). Thus, the other, in its various manifestations, including *parole*, culture, place, class, race, and gender, participates in the formation of a self. The individual occurs as chronotope within the story of human interaction with the rest of the physical world, but that narrative is only a historical fiction organized by means of a limited perspective through which beginnings, middles, ends, and motivations are substituted for the non-human-centered, contiguously structured universal story that allots us only episodes—the self in and as part of the other (perhaps one of the most dangerous of these fictions currently in theoretical circles is the Lacanian claim of human "prematurity" and the necessity of a lifetime of "lack" and frustration, based on Lacan's claims in "The Mirror Stage"). Conceptualizing self/other as interpenetrating part/part and part/whole relationships rather than dichotomy is fundamental for apprehending the mutually constitutive character of the dialogics-ecology-feminisms triad. Both ecology and feminisms are deeply concerned with the conception of the other as part of effecting crucial paradigm shifts in human understanding.

Just as the other participates in the formation of the self, so too does the self as individual-in-the-world participate in the formation of the other in its various manifestations. And, just as the self enters into language and the use of *parole*, so too does the other enter into language and have the potential, as does any entity, to become a "speaking subject," although centripetal structures and cultural forces hinder such a realization. The implications of this other as speaking subject need to be conceptualized as including more than humans, and as potentially being constituted by a speaker/author who is not the speaking subject but a renderer of the other as speaking subject (Bakhtin, *Problems* 47–57). The pivotal questions here will be the degree to which language is recognized as one type of sign system, the degree to which volition is assumed as a prerequisite for becoming a speaking subject, and the degree to which the other speaking subjects who do not use the *parole* of human beings can "speak" in a sign system that can be understood by humans.

In *Freudianism*, Bakhtin attacks Freudian psychology as being based on "a sui generis fear of history, an ambition to locate a world beyond the social and the historical, a search for this world precisely in the depths of the organic" (14). In contrast, he claims that "outside society and, consequently, outside objective socioeconomic conditions, there is no such thing as a human being. Only as a part of a social whole, only in and through a social class, does the human person become historically real and culturally productive" (15). All this is true in contradistinction to the ahistorical biologistic bent under attack, but it is true only insofar as we are talking of a person as a sociocultural historical entity. Yet a human being is also a biologically developed entity. As Holmes Rolston III has expressed it, "kept in its environmental context, our humanity is not absolutely 'in' us, but is rather 'in' our world dialogue" (59). In his effort to reinsert the human being into history and culture, Bakhtin artificially removes that being from the environment. It has been the value of both feminist and postmarxist psychoanalytic study that the psychological dimensions of the individual are being analyzed as an integral part of the whole being, and not as a narrowly defined originary center, but the tendency remains to isolate qualitatively that being from the rest of the world.

From the opening of *Freudianism*, Bakhtin emphasizes the significance in psychology of the conflicts between inner and outer speech and various levels of inner speech, that communication between the conscious and the unconscious consisting of specific utterances that have a speaker and a respondent, a "self" and another "self," which are not identical but are parts of the same mind (23–24). Jacques Lacan views the unconscious as being "structured like a language," and some French feminists, such as Hélène Cixous, also view it as having language at least as it is constituted by means of the "Imaginary." But Bakhtin points out that this use of language always appears in the form of utterances made by the conscious speaking subject, even when mediating messages from the unconscious.

As Bakhtin insists, "every utterance is the product of the interaction between speakers and the product of the broader context of the whole complex social situation in which the utterance emerges" (*Freudianism* 79; see *Speech Genres* 71). Even the articulation of the unconscious is a social interrelationship by virtue of its minimal dynamic of being an utterance (79). This point is reinforced by Bakhtin's claim that "any speaker himself is a respondent to a greater or lesser degree" (*Speech Genres* 69). Thus, the other is always implicated in psychical activities, and indicates that the self itself is not singular, unified, or total, but is multiple, through the non-identity of the conscious and unconscious and self-conceptions and drives (see Paul Smith, Ch. 5). It is precisely this recognition of non-identity and the need for inner dialogue, specifically between masculine and feminine aspects of the psyche, that Salleh sees as missing from the propositions of Deep Ecology and seriously impairing its subversion of patriarchy's hegemony. As Cixous's attempts to write the Imaginary indicate, as in "The Laugh of the Medusa," all efforts to articulate the mind involve social interaction. Even as she seeks to "break" the language, she does so in a sociohistorical context and through orienting her ideas toward an audience that is expected to participate actively in the constitution of meaning ([Bakhtin]/Volosinov, *Marxism* 102; see *Speech Genres* 111).

In like manner, as Freud recognized, "the unconscious speaks more than one dialect"; that is, it uses a variety of sign systems, verbal and nonverbal, to communicate (see Bruss 132–33). To the degree that we are able to articulate verbally the mental activities of our unconscious as well as the conscious parts of our mind, these articulations are oriented toward the rest of the world, and our position in that world. And they are articulated by means of words that always already introduce that other world to us as a result of the historicity of *parole*. But this also applies to articulation by means of other semiotic stuctures, which are also either culturally or naturally constituted so that the audience for them has the potential for responsive understanding (see [Bakhtin]/Volosinov, *Marxism* 10–12). I would argue that, like the unconscious, the nonhuman also articulates itself by means of various "dialects," and that neither requires volition to do so.

In addition, Bakhtin argues for calling "the inner and outward speech that permeates our behavior in all its aspects 'behavioral ideology.'" He goes on to say that "this behavioral ideology is in certain respects more sensitive, more excitable and livelier than an ideology that has undergone formulation and become 'official.' In the depths of behavioral ideology accumulate those contradictions which, once having reached a certain threshold, ultimately burst asunder the system of the official ideology" (*Freudianism* 88). Here one sees implicit the fundamental tension between centripetal and centrifugal forces, with the centrifugal privileged for its desystematizing power. The upshot of all this is that even at the level of the articulation of the unconscious the individual is already socially interacting, laying the basis for an impact upon the world that has been impacting on that individual.[6] What is suggested here is the role of the individual, through self-reflection and self-conscious articulation of thought, in transforming ideology (*Freudianism* 90). This occurs as a result of the individual's undergoing, reflecting on, and articulating the differences between experiences in social reality and the natural world that do not square with the official ideology, and then developing subject-positions through the playing-off and adaptation of non-dominant ideologies that enable resistance (Paul Smith, Ch. 1).

If, indeed, psychoanalysis and self-analysis involve a dialogue of the conscious and unconscious, which together constitute the life of the mind, then conscious/unconscious form an unsynthesizable dialogical relationship. Freud, recognizing that the unconscious could not be abolished, attempted to keep it in check through the Superego. Others before Freud attempted a similar maneuver in the realm of the intellect/emotion dichotomy construct, believing that rationality and reason, products of enlightenment, would enable one to overcome the emotions. Emotions, of course, were the province of the feminine. Suprisingly enough, despite the obviously oppressive character of this hierarchical assignation of reason and emotion to the differing genders, we see its repetition in the attempted Lacanian identification of the unconscious with the female (see Jardine, "Gynesis," for a critique of this position). And yet again, we have both within each of us, emotion and intellect, conscious and unconscious, and at various times one serves us better than the other in our worldly encounters. Dialogics lets us recognize the mutually constitutive character of these dyads, with each aspect at specific times constituting a center of mental activity and requiring the other to act as centrifugal force to prevent the solidification of that center into dogma. If emotion and instinct arise from historical natural influences upon the evolution of the species, then their impact on our behavior, their entry into consciousness, are a form by which the nonhuman world speaks to us through signs that our conscious renders verbally. To deny emotion as feminine and/or instinct as primitive nature is to reserve the role of speaking subject only for the ego and to deny a voice to the other, which is in reality a part of ourselves.

The dialogical relationships of intellect/emotion and humanity/nature, conceptualized as complementary dyads rather than dichotomies, can be ascertained only by attempting to facilitate the coming into verbal being of both sides of the slash (/). And here one of the limitations of Bakhtin's formulations reveals itself, in his restricting the conception of the other to participants in human society. Ecology must be brought to bear, to break dialogics out of the anthropocentrism in which Bakhtin performs it (see, for example, "Discourse in Life" 95). The limitation he imposes renders it impossible for any aspect of the nonhuman to be rendered as a speaking subject, whether in artistic texts, other texts, or human behavior. Although he does argue that the object of the utterance is a living participant, a third constitutive factor of the utterance, which can be the external/nonverbal world to which the speech act is oriented, it remains an object ("Discourse" 101–2). And yet, does not instinct itself, which arises from outside of or prior to society, become a speaking subject through the unconscious and the emotions, which themselves create electrochemical changes in the human body?

Numerous authors and artists have attempted to render nature as a speaking subject, not in the romantic mode of rendering nature an object for the self-constitution of the poet as speaking subject, but as a character within texts with its own existence. I think here of the efforts of such writers as Dorothy Wordsworth, Robinson Jeffers, Mary Oliver, John Haines, Ursula Le Guin, Gary Snyder, and Linda Hogan. I think these attempts are most successful when they include human characters as well, enabling the differential comparison of self and other. An ecofeminist dialogics requires this effort to render the other, primarily constituted by androcentrism as women and nature (and actually as the two intertwined: nature-as-woman and woman-as-nature), as speaking subjects within patriarchy in order to subvert that patriarchy not only by decentering it but also by proposing other centers. Speaking at the Center for the Study of Democratic Institutions, Gary Snyder called for establishing "a kiva of elders" to represent the nonhuman within democratic institutions:

> Historically this has been done through art. The paintings of bison and bears in the caves of southern France were of that order. The animals were speaking through the people and making their point. And when, in the dances of the Pueblo Indians and other people, certain individuals became seized, as it were, by the spirit of the deer, and danced as a deer would dance, or danced the dance of the corn maidens, or impersonated the squash blossom, they were no longer speaking for humanity, they were taking it on themselves to interpret, through their humanity, what these other life-forms were. That is about all we know so far concerning the possibilities of incorporating spokesmanship for the rest of life in our democratic society. (*Turtle Island* 109; see also Rodman and Silko, "Landscape")

That may have been about all we knew fifteen years ago, but feminisms have taught us much since then about incorporating at least part of the rest of life into our discourse, constituting women as speaking subjects. The point is not to speak for nature, but to work to render the signification presented us by other elements of nature into a verbal depiction by means of speaking subjects, whether this is through characterization in the arts or through discursive prose. To quote Snyder again:

> What we must find a way to do, then, is incorporate the other people—what Sioux Indians called the creeping people, and the standing people, and the flying people, and the swimming people—into the councils of government. This isn't as difficult as you might think. If we don't do it, they will revolt against us. They will submit non-negotiable demands about our stay on the earth. We are beginning to get non-negotiable demands right now from the air, the water, the soil. (*Turtle Island* 108)

I don't share his optimism about the facility of this move, but I believe in its necessity, and applaud Le Guin's depiction of it in *Always Coming Home*. This takes us back to the question I raised earlier, whether or not volition is required for a speaking subject, for the existence of signs that can be transmit-

ted by a nonhuman speaking subject and that can be understood and interpreted by humans. When a person cries out in pain, is it volitional? Does the
scream signify? When selenium poisons ground water, causes animal deformi-
ties, and reduces the ability of California farmers to continue to overcultivate
through irrigation land with little topsoil, are these signs that we can read?
And in reading such signs and integrating them into our texts, are we letting
that land speak through us or are we only speaking for it?

Nonhuman others can be constituted as speaking subjects, rather than
constituted merely as objects of our speaking, although even the latter is
preferable to silence. The analogy I would use is that of men adopting feminist
theories, practices, or interpretations. Far too often men continue to attempt
to speak *for* women, with the following result: "when male theorists borrow
the language of feminist criticism without a willingness to explore the masculinist bias of their own reading system, we get a phallic 'feminist' criticism
that competes with women instead of breaking out of patriarchal bounds"
(Showalter 127). It is possible, however, for men to render women as speaking
subjects by means of their application of feminist theories, criticism, and
scholarship (Heath 8–9, 27–28). The feminists who have constituted themselves as speaking subjects have enabled some men to render that voicing.
Such rendering will always occur within the limitations of the author's/
speaker's refractive mediation, and there will always be two voices there, the
feminist speaking subject and the rendering male author, just as there will be
in the case of the nonhuman speaking subject and the rendering human
author, but in neither instance does this remove the need to wage a struggle for
such rendering. Richard Ohmann makes the point that

> If [men] are "in" feminism at all, we were dragged into it kicking and
> screaming, and now that we're there we should think of ourselves as
> on extended probation, still learning. What we do there with our
> experience, our competence, and our gender and class confidence, is
> a matter to be negotiated through caution, flexibility, improvisation,
> listening, and often doubtless through a strategic fade into the wall-
> paper. But I don't see drawing back from the knowledge that femi-
> nism is our fight, too. (187)[7]

"Caution, flexibility, improvisation, listening" are certainly attributes of
the best ecological and feminist work to date practiced by both women and
men, and imply a strongly dialogical orientation toward critical work. And yet,
how does one maintain such a stance and avoid tendencies toward dogmatism
and totalization? Dialogical rigor.

IV

At the end of each of the preceding parts of this chapter, I have emphasized application of the dialogic method to avoid interrogative sclerosis and ideological calcification. Bakhtin himself presents a dyad that both explains the need to oppose dogmatism and totalization—that clarifies the heterarchical yet partisan character of dialogics—and provides a conceptual framework for being able to critique and affirm without absolutes. That dyad is centripetal/centrifugal, a mutually constituted relational unity of opposites: "Alongside the centripetal forces, the centrifugal forces of language carry on their uninterrupted work; alongside verbal-ideological centralization and unification, the uninterrupted processes of decentralization and disunification go forward" (*Dialogic* 272). In language and ideology this dyad continuously manifests itself as "center" and "margin," and has been a crucial basis for the development of deconstruction. Yet, deconstruction has found itself unable to affirm much beyond pleasure and play—hardly sufficient for the process of reconstruction that occurs following the overthrow of any outmoded system of thought, government, culture, or community. A paradigm shift requires not merely the scuttling of the previous paradigm but the institution of a new one, which in its turn will also need scuttling. In response to the Derridean critique of feminism, Cary Nelson makes the point that despite the valuable warnings against the dangers of totalization and essentialism:

> What is needed is a commitment nonetheless to real social change, a recognition that monological and militantly certain discourses are often strategically necessary if people's lives are to be better. On some local fronts, we need to believe that there are wrongs to be righted and real forms of progress to be achieved. Derrida does actually acknowledge this, but he tends to put his reservations first. (168)

And what is put first tends to be what is privileged. To effect change, commitments need to be made and risks taken. As deconstructionists recognize, centers continuously appear and form. The struggle is not to abolish any type of centering, but to recognize the relative nature of centers and their dynamic relationship with margins. Given the cultural and ideological hegemony of capitalism in the United States, ecofeminists must necessarily comprise part of the margin, serving as a centrifugal force which attempts to break up and fragment the totalizing discourse that perpetuates business as usual. At the same time, those working within the margins must recognize that at any given moment they are forming a center from/on which to work. But there are centers and there are centers. One type serves as foundation, cast in stone and rendered immovable, on which to stand; the other serves as pivot, a base on which to step and from which to move on to another center-as-pivot. The distinction here is between dogmas or beliefs and perspectives or hypotheses (see Fuss on the limits of both essentialism and constructivism).

Defending Deep Ecology, George Sessions suggests the problems associated with failure to distinguish between dogmas and perspectives. He recognizes and opposes the way some forces within the ecological movement in the United States have become misanthropic due to an ecocentrism that requires an absolute "Earth First" position. At the same time, Sessions argues that "the Age of Ecology involves a major 'paradigm shift' to an ecocentric mode of understanding the world. . . . The ecocentric perspective involves a biological, as well as a cultural, understanding of the human species resulting in a new awareness of the place of humans in the ecological web and of the ecological limitations of humans in the Earth community" (66). It seems to me that this definition of an "ecocentric mode of understanding" is far more dialogical than the beliefs of many adherents of ecocentrism, including some whom Sessions cites. Yet he himself is caught up in a non-dialogical nostalgic conception of ecocentrism that would render its present-day formulations essentially identical with ancient and primal ones: "When we realize that over 99% of all humans who have ever lived on Earth have been hunters/gatherers, then it is clear that ecocentrism has been the dominant human perspective throughout history" (66). Here Sessions confuses conditions of existence with beliefs about that existence and overlooks the philosophical and experiential distances between our ancestors and ourselves.

Substitution of ecocentrism for anthropocentrism does not constitute the significant paradigm shift that Sessions, as well as many of the rest of us, wish to see occur, because it allows belief in and promotion of static absolutes to be perpetuated. We have seen this same problem arise in Marxism, with the establishment of the dialectic not as a method but as a blueprint in which the "synthesis" is idealistically preordained. Nostalgia is another dimension of the absolutist tendencies of dogmas, which reinforces static idealizations. If ecocentrism or androgyny existed once long ago in a virtually unblemished state, as some clearly claim, then we need only get back to that state and find the answer that has already existed, rather than to create a contemporary, relative answer that will invariably be flawed and inadequate to the complexities of the question that required it. The recognition of such inadequacy provides the skeptical self-interrogation necessary to maintain any answer as a pivot rather than a foundation, to be metaphilosophical even during the process of philosophizing. In like manner, different elements within the feminist movement have set specific goals and principles for themselves that need to be revisioned continuously if participants are not to end up asking "is that all there is?" in the absense of any method for projecting the next step.

Not long before his death Bakhtin wrote that "there is neither a first nor a last word and there are no limits to the dialogic context" (*Speech Genres* 170). The dialogic method is a way to incorporate that decentering recognition of a permanent *in media res* of human life and a constantly widening context for human interaction and interanimation within the biosphere and beyond. Coupled with the two basic pivots outlined here, ecology and feminisms, dialogics provides a method by which we may yet effect one of the paradigm shifts necessary to break down the dualistic thinking of patriarchy that perpetuates the exploitation and oppression of nature in general and women in particular. At the same time, it warns us that once we do succeed in dismantling patriarchy and its socioeconomic systems, a new host of problems and contradictions will arise, as yet unenvisioned, that will require new debates, new answers, and new pivots. Ecofeminist dialogics provides a place and method by which to step and dance, but not to stand.

Chapter Two

Ground, Pivot, Motion:
Ecofeminist Theory, Dialogics, and
Literary Practice

Cheryll Burgess Glotfelty, in issuing a clarion call for an "ecological literary criticism," observes that "while other social movements, like the civil rights and women's liberation movements of the sixties and seventies, have had a significant impact in shaping literary studies, the environmental movement of the same era has not" (1). Having gathered momentum throughout the 1980s, the environmental movement, particularly as it is manifested by ecofeminism, will not only make its existence felt in literary studies in the 1990s but has the potential to alter such studies irrevocably. Does this mean, then, that since literary theory and criticism is coming belatedly to ecofeminism that the educational exchange must occur in a single direction? I do not think so. I would like to suggest that, first, certain areas of literary theory, such as Bakhtinian dialogics as developed by feminist critics, can be immensely beneficial to the further development and elaboration of ecofeminist philosophy; and, second, that a more forceful and integrated recognition of the role and place of literature as one element of ecofeminist activism can be gained.

Multivocality Rather Than Pluralism

As I indicated in Chapter One, the development of an ecofeminist dialogic method requires significant adaptation of the ideas of Bakhtin, since neither he nor his colleagues ever concerned themselves with ecology or feminism. Further, Bakhtinian dialogics provides a method for entertaining debate and consideration of conflicting viewpoints without lapsing into liberal pluralism. Dale Bauer, by distinguishing between pluralism and "multivocality" in *Feminist Dialogics* (xi), persuasively argues that for disagreement to accomplish anything, it requires genuine dialogue that leads to altered understanding rather than a verbal smorgasbord of perspectives. To date, Ellen Rooney in *Seductive Reasoning* has provided the most devastating critique of pluralism not only as a popular myth of U.S. politics and foreign policy, but also an academic form of critical discourse that seeks to recuperate all other critics into a circle of unchanging chitchat. While allowing various constituencies to voice their objections, pluralism disavows any need for change other than minor reforms and eschews any theorizing "that would expose the systematic and concrete affiliations that bind critical and political pluralism together as the elements of a heterogeneous yet hegemonic discourse" (33–34). It is also important to note that pluralism has never included everybody: "our cultural discourse is a totality which does not contain everything—did not, for example, contain women, who were decisively not *only* the relative creatures the culture had imagined them to be" (Tarantelli 180; see Marinit 150). And pluralistic humanism continues to dispute whether to include in its purview nature as a subject rather than simply an object of its attention.

Feminists have been utilizing Bakhtin's ideas for some years now, and Bauer makes numerous references to such work. But the critical theory in which *Feminist Dialogics* is grounded develops beyond a view of Bakhtin's various dialogic essays as mere source material. Bauer understands Bakhtinian dialogics as a method by which to orchestrate and direct feminist theories of culture and literature. Repeatedly, her literary analysis telescopes out from the aesthetic text to larger questions of cultural community and political and ideological power under patriarchy. That is not surprising, for anyone employing dialogics as a method must find herself constantly shuttling back and forth between text and context, discourse and community, and personal and political (see Díaz-Diocaretz 136; Zavala, "Bakhtin and the Third" 58). Bauer argues that "what is missing from the dominant mode of Bakhtin scholarship is any interest in gender theory or sexual difference in a materialist-feminist practice" (xiii). Yet what remains missing from Bauer's analysis is any attention to ecological issues.

In *Honey-Mad Women*, Patricia Yaeger has passionately depicted some of the means by which women writers have employed "emancipatory strategies" within the boundaries of patriarchal norms and imposed exclusion, not only to give voice to the muted but also to challenge the illusion of "norms" that patriarchy persistently generates. It is time that literary critics more systematically begin to search for the "emancipatory strategies" that have been giving voice to ecological narratives, and to recover those works that have realized such strategies, while critiquing the rest of the literary canon in terms of these strategies as they appear or fail to appear in heretofore canonized "major" works. At the same time, feminist criteria must be brought to bear on the rapidly evolving "canon" of nature writing and environmental literature, which is being structured by some critics in a way that nature becomes a province clearly dominated by white male authors. Feminist criteria for canonical debates, including conflicting ones, have been offered by numerous theorists; ecological criteria remain partial and dispersed, with efforts toward relative codification just under way (see Burgess, Campbell, Kolodny, Meeker, and Waage).

Marxism, Dialogics, and Ecofeminism

The influence of Marxism on feminism has led to much attention to dialectical synthesis as a critical praxis. Dialogics, however, can take praxis further because it can encompass Marxist dialectics while at the same time correcting its mechanical progressivism by emphasizing the unity of opposites and their interanimating dynamic tension (see Zavala, "Bakhtin and the Third"). And it does so without an idealist belief in the immediacy and facility of synthesis and without privileging class contradictions as invariably primary. In both instances, Marxist practice has shown itself utterly insensitive to ecological issues and human/nonhuman relationships.

In the past few years, the journal *Capitalism, Nature, Socialism* has attempted to bridge the gap between the "reds" and the "greens." But even in their labelling there appears a tendency to define fundamental socioeconomic change in narrowly "political" terms, rather than in terms of larger cultural behavioral transformations, particularly as they might be modelled by immediate epistemological reconfigurations, with their attendant ontological implications. Take, for example, articles in Number Fourteen (June 1993). Half of the volume is given over to three articles on "Red-Green Politics." Of these, "Women and Waste" breaks out of the arena of simplistic electoral politics that determines the analysis of the preceding two articles; nevertheless, it relies on identifying class conflict as the fundamental determinant of accurate critical analysis. According to Irmgard Schultz, the German Women's Movement has only two responses to curbside recycling: reject it as more unpaid labor or accept it as ecologically responsible behavior. The latter is defined as exclusively reformist and equated with false consciousness. "Ecological ethics" is defined as being based on "women show[ing] their notorious guilty conscience regarding children" (62). There is no suggestion that applications of anti-consumer mentality practices that are not class-based can contribute to a radical critique of capitalism if formulated according to alternative epistemologies, such as an ethics of caring. Women in this analysis are reduced to a single subject position, that of unpaid proletariat, while identification with their subject position as nurturers is considered a false sense of responsibility, because it is analyzed only in terms of the relations of production and not in terms of the relations of reproduction and attendant ethics-generating practices. The idea that one should let the environmental crisis worsen until it lays bare the contradictions of capitalism and leads to revolution remains squarely within a tradition of linear, teleological thinking that perpetuates capitalism and the illusion that exchange value is the only value that counts.

The degree to which "socialist ecology" remains locked in the paradigms of the capitalism it claims to oppose is suggested by article the "Marx and Resource Scarcity" by Michael Perelman, which refers to the role of Marxism in "future debates about the political economy of *natural resource utilization*" (79; my emphasis). Ecological theory, and ecofeminist theory in particular, have already revealed the bankruptcy of continuing to think of the rest of our biosphere in terms of the instrumentalist reasoning accepted in the use of that emphasized phrase. Surprisingly enough, this point is made in the same issue of *CNS*: "Feminists maintain that we can no longer afford to think in terms of reductive frameworks that overlook the fact that we *are* the environment for one another" (125). Unfortunately, this remark appears only as part of a brief "conference report" by Hilde Hein, and the articles published in this issue in no way indicate general agreement with this recognition on the part of the contributors to *CNS*.

Other, Another, and the Problem of Biospheres

When integrated with ecofeminism, dialogics can enable philosophy to move beyond the limitations of the distinctions between use value/exchange value and things-in-themselves/things-for-us where Marxist theory tends to stop, and to recognize and celebrate the corollary concept of us-as-things-for-others, or mutually constitutive value (re. Bakhtin's "I for another," see Morson and Emerson 23). We need to recognize the existence of the other as a thing-in-itself (see Jung 8–9). And let me clarify this term by saying that it has nothing do with Kant's idealist anthropocentrism (see Morson and Emerson 8, Holquist, *Dialogism* 39); rather, "thing" for the purposes of my argument here means any material entity, including humans, animals, and ecosystems. At the same time, only by recognizing that humans are not only things-in-themselves and things-for-us but also things-for-others, including the stable evolution of the biosphere, can we begin to understand our appropriate ecological niche and attendant practices.

This is certainly an extremely complex process, and any rush to claim such understanding likely reveals only our own propensity toward reductionism. Such is the case with Dorion Sagan's *Biospheres: Reproducing Planet Earth*. Sagan replicates the imperialist and masculinist ideology of late capitalism when he claims that our ecological purpose is to reproduce "biospheres," which on other planets "would act as a sort of settling propagule to establish an Earthlike environment" (207). He conceives of earth as a white European, with the right to replicate itself anywhere it chooses. He also assumes that we need not fundamentally reorganize human interaction with the environment, as technology will provide all necessary solutions (206). Not suprisingly, neither capitalism nor feminism is listed in the index, and no ecofeminists, or for that matter any kind of feminists, are referred to in the text.

A dialogical orientation reinforces the ecofeminist recognition of interdependence and the natural need for diversity. This recognition, then, requires a rethinking of the concepts of other and otherness, which have been dominated in contemporary critical theory by psychoanalytic rather than ecological constructs. If the recognition of otherness and the status of other is applied only to women and/or the unconscious, for example, and the corollary notion of anotherness, being another for others, is not recognized, then the ecological processes of interanimation—the ways in which humans and other entities develop, change, and learn through mutually influencing each other day to day, age by age—will go unacknowledged, and notions of female autonomy that have been useful to women in thinking through the characteristics of their social oppression will end up complicitous with the traditional American, patriarchal beliefs in autonomy and individualism. Although the United States has been a culture that champions individualism as an ideology, it has consistently demonstrated an unwillingness to tolerate individuality whenever such behavior threatens "national security" or "the American way of life" (King, "Ecofeminist Imperative"). An ecofeminist dialogics would suggest that, rather than trying to imagine liberatory notions of autonomy, feminist theoreticians might more productively imagine responsible human behavior by working out the implications of a theory of *volitional interdependence* among human and nonhuman alike.

Finally, Bakhtin's conception of centripetal/centrifugal tension provides a means of countering tendencies toward totalization that can arise within any effort at systemic analysis and critique. The centripetal tendency is toward centralizing, homogenizing, and rulebinding; the centrifugal toward decentering, differentiating, and innovating. That is to say, a dialogic method can expose the false dichotomy of center and margin that is utilized by oppositional groups notwithstanding that such use codifies the existing power structure's claims to centrality, legitimacy, and authority. There are unequal power relationships and structures that are spun out of such relationships, but if the ecological model of mutual interdependence has any validity, there can be no real margins except as ideological constructs. Nor can there be any centers; rather, there exist cultural and physical pivots that may or may not resist the inevitability of a next step.

Stories and the Voicing of Other Subjects

As I have argued in Chapter One, the individual occurs as one chronotope within the story of human interaction with the physical world, insofar as the individual has a particular perspective that is communicated to others through language and behavior. One can see the connection here between this concept of an individual life as chronotope, and a reorientation of understanding about the relationship of that chronotope to the contextual world in which it occurs, and Jim Cheney's statement that "narrative is the key then, but it is narrative grounded in geography rather than in a linear, essentialized narrative self" ("Postmodern" 126; cf. Quigley). Although Cheney emphasizes local geography in "Postmodern Environmental Ethics," a study of the ways in which narrative can contribute to developing a sensitivity to an ecofeminist bioregional ethics, I think he would agree that such geography participates in a larger, longer story extending beyond this one planet's biosphere.

Minimally, such a reconsideration of the context for the human story should guide humans beyond the simplistic notion that, because they understand each other's languages but no other creatures', only they communicate. But this reconsideration still leaves the definition of "subject" problematic, and any claims to knowledge of the proper voicing for such subjects highly suspect, as Peter Quigley emphasizes in his critique of Cheney's concept (302–6). According to many ontological theories of environmental ethics, humans must rely on imputed notions of their being "interest-carriers" in order to attribute subject status to rocks, rivers, and other "inanimate" entities. This issue of status remains an intense topic of debate in the pages of *Environmental Ethics*, and one can see that such a notion must necessarily dominate any Marxist ecological analysis, because only an entity capable of agency can be be alienated.

For other creatures and entities who do not speak human languages, we must rely on humans to render their voices and depict their subject positions in opposition to their objectification by others. I do not believe that some universalizing or context-free ontological proof can be given to verify the authenticity of such voices. Rather, the test of whether such depictions seem accurate as renderings of non-human speaking subjects should be the actions that they call on humans to perform in the world. The voicing is directed at us as agents-in-the-world. Unless we believe that the earth is attempting biospheric suicide, we cannot accept arguments based on instrumental reason as accurately rendering nature as a speaking subject, or J. E. Lovelock's assertions that "Gaia" will take care of industrial pollution, or a judge's decision on whether or not trees have legal standing.

Ursula K. Le Guin has been working on this project in both poetry and fiction for many years. In *Buffalo Gals and Other Animal Presences*, she brings together stories and poems, many of which render the natural world as a speaking subject. For example, in "Buffalo Gals, Won't You Come Out Tonight," she does this through a girl's dream vision of the mythical "coyote," who teaches her about the relationship of wild animals in the desert to urbanization. That these stories are part of a project to rethink human/nonhuman and self/other relationships is revealed by Le Guin's remarks about the feminist revisioning of myth in which she is engaged throughout so much of her recent work: "Very often the re-visioning consists in a 'simple' change of point of view. It is possible that the very concept of point-of-view may be changing, may have to change, or to be changed, so that our reality can be narrated" (*Buffalo Gals* 75). It comes as no surprise that nonhuman "people" are well represented in Le Guin's novel, *Always Coming Home*. But is the evaluation of the work by overtly ecofeminist writers the only area of literary studies that can benefit from ecofeminist theory; or, conversely, can only ecofeminist theory benefit from literature that self-consciously embodies such philosophy? In both cases the answer, as you would expect me to say, is no. Much more can and needs to be done.

Ecofeminist Literary Analysis

One approach would be to use ecofeminism as a ground for critiquing all the literature that one reads. For literary critics in particular this would mean reevaluating the canon that constitutes the list of major works and texts, and calling for a dialogue between critical evaluations based on humanistic criteria and those based on de-homocentric criteria. This would require, for instance, reevaluating the poetic tradition of the "pastoral," which tends to be based on an idealization of nature rather than a genuine encounter with it. A brief example here would be that feminist critics have gradually begun pulling Dorothy Wordsworth out of her brother's shadow, looking at her writings and their influence on his poetry. What is needed now is criticism that can evaluate the differences between their writings in terms of ecological criteria, analyzing the implications of Dorothy's willingness to record rather than order nature and to efface the speaker of the text as a dominating, central observer.

Dorothy Wordsworth serves as an example of an author rescued from obscurity whose writing demonstrates characteristics that could be labeled ecological—if not ecofeminist, which would be to a certain extent anachronistic—because of its attention to nature in its diversity as a thing-in-itself. Willa Cather, on the other hand, serves as an example of an author already famous whose works are being reevaluated in terms of relative merit, as a result of both feminist and ecological criticism. Over the past few years, *The Song of the Lark* has received increasing attention primarily because of its feminist thematics and secondarily because of its ecological implications, which are revealed by the protagonist's growth through her relationship with the Nebraska countryside and her aesthetic maturation as a result of immersion in a steep New Mexico ravine, the former habitat of an early indigenous people. The importance of these aspects of the novel has begun to be analyzed only as a result of changing critical criteria.

With Cather, the critic is not looking for an ecofeminist novel per se, but is looking at an author's work in terms of the extent to which it addresses ecological and feminist issues in positive or negative ways. And while we can certainly talk about feminist rather than protofeminist writing in the Anglo-

American tradition as early as the eighteenth century, if not earlier, we need to clarify whether such is the case for ecological writing. Is there a difference between "nature" writing and ecological writing? If the Transcendentalists and Romantics are any indication, the answer is yes. Self-conscious ecological writing must be defined as a phenomenon primarily of the late twentieth century, and that which precedes it as mostly protoecological. From this perspective, ecologists can more easily explain their adoption of writers such as Charlotte Perkins Gilman, Robinson Jeffers, and John Muir for ecological inspiration without having to attempt to justify every aspect of those authors' visions of nature.

Ecofeminist Novels

Perhaps one of the first of the current generation of ecofeminist novels is Margaret Atwood's *Surfacing* (1972). A woman in an unhealthy heterosexual relationship, going home with her lover and another couple to search for her missing father and mourn for her long-dead mother, undergoes a metamorphosis. This transformation involves a clearly dialogical process in which the revelations that the woman initially experiences regarding the environmental destruction of her childhood Canadian locale are gradually translated into revelations regarding her oppression as a woman, and the intrinsic and indissoluble connection between these two unbalanced states of being. Near the end of the novel she experiences a rebirth through submersion in a lake, which causes a spiritual regression to a virtually pre-cultured state. By means of the purification this act involves and her decision to become pregnant, she purges the guilt she has felt for years over having had an abortion, and her complicity in the anti-ecological, techno-industrial state. Her recognitions, of both nature's oppression and her own, provide her not with a vision of an emancipatory future—Atwood seems always unwilling to offer this—but with an understanding that will sustain her when she returns to the city. The final chapter begins: "This above all, to refuse to be a victim" (222). It continues with the protagonist's recognition of relationship with her child, who will be armed with her new understanding of ecological interconnection, which includes human interconnection. At the end, as the protagonist prepares to return to "civilization," she thinks the final words of the novel: "The lake is quiet, the trees surround me, asking and giving nothing" (224).

Atwood has come to be known as a writer of fantastic or speculative rather than realistic prose. And it seems to be the case that the majority of the most daring ecological and feminist novels have been written in some other mode than realism, with almost all of the feminist utopias and dystopias created in the past two decades predicated upon ecological disaster. While such works frequently do not address the question of how to resolve the ecological crisis (for their focus is on resolving the oppression of women), they almost invariably tie the oppression of women to the degradation of the environment. In Atwood's *The Handmaid's Tale*, the rise of a right-wing theocracy in New England results in part from devastation of the environment. Similarly, in Susy McKee Charnas's *Walk to the End of the World* and *Motherlines*, a totalitarian patriarchy that attempts to enforce the utter domination of women follows upon the heels of the apocalyptic efforts of a seemingly less malignant patriarchy to dominate nature. In Marge Piercy's *Woman on the Edge of Time*, the future utopian society of Mattapoisett that contrasts with the hell of contemporary North American society which oppresses Connie Ramos, the novel's protagonist, is predicated upon ecological balance and equalized nurturing of children. In Sally Gearhart's *The Wanderground*, the ecological theme is foregrounded, but the women have abandoned the cities and their men, establishing a completely separate culture and, perhaps, a separate species. These latter two novels, like Sheri Tepper's more recent *The Gate to Women's Country*, remain highly problematic from an ecofeminist perspective because each is predicated upon some version of biological essentialism, a perception of reality adopted by some who consider themselves ecofeminists but severely criticized by others.

Somewhat different from the preceding utopian and dystopian novels, Kate Wilhelm's *Juniper Time* is near-future science fiction, in which humanity is beset by two approaching apocalypses of its own making: worldwide drought with food shortages resulting from environmental pollution, and subsequent global tensions that make nuclear war imminent. While the plot is complicated by an elaborate hoax designed to draw the peoples of earth together, the real story is that of Jean's development into an eco-activist, who suffers through rape, despair, and then revitalization in the desert among a group of people relearning and adapting the old ways of the Native Americans to the changed environmental conditions. Unlike the previously mentioned novels, *Juniper Time* is primarily ecological and only secondarily feminist, yet it does not seem fortuitous that the hero is female or that she is raped, imprisoned, and oppressed during the course of her experiences. But like the other novels, *Juniper Time* assumes that the construction of a new society must be learned through practice, not theories. In this way, the majority of contemporary feminist utopias maintain a dialogical, developmental approach to society building rather than the monological, closed-system approach that dominates much earlier and nonfeminist utopias.

The novel that balances and integrates ecology and feminism more evenly and successfully than any of the others discussed here is Ursula K. Le Guin's *Always Coming Home*. It combines thematic and formal innovation to the point that it does not conform to the notions popularly associated with the idea of novel at all, but very much epitomizes "storied residence." Rather than a linear, realist narrative, it is a novel much more in the Bakhtinian sense of the term, that is, an open, evolving genre predicated upon change rather than stasis, innovation rather than convention. A work of cultural fiction, it provides a main, plotted story that could be extracted and treated as a separate narrative. This inner narrative is a feminist bildungsroman detailing the experiences of a girl who chooses between her father's patriarchal culture and her mother's matrifocal one. But around and throughout this narrative-within-a-text Le Guin weaves a series of additional stories, as well as cultural information. She also includes a series of interchapters about herself, allegorically depicted as Pandora the anthropologist, visiting from the past these people of our far-distant future. Suffice it to say that anyone wishing to gain a comprehensive vision of a possible ecofeminist culture must read *Always Coming Home*. But at the same time Le Guin avoids blueprinting, in part by setting the work so far into the future that no immediate steps from here to there are suggested and by showing that the culture depicted remains in a process of development and change, internal debate, and external relationship with other cultures.

Ecological, Feminist, and Ecofeminist Poetry

Le Guin has developed her ecofeminist themes in poetry as well as in prose, and here she joins company with a host of contemporary women poets. Like many of them, Le Guin's collections contain poems that are feminist but not explicitly ecological, ecological but not specifically feminist, and only very rarely a poem that overtly combines the two. Yet when one reads an entire volume, such as *Hard Words* or *Wild Oats and Fireweed*, recognition of the interrelationship of feminism and ecology becomes unavoidable. "At Three Rivers, April 80" (*Hard Words* 33), for instance, takes a clear stand on nature as a thing-in-itself rather than a thing-for-us. In a seven-line stanza the speaker contends that a blossoming tree is just as wondrous whether blooming within or beyond the gaze of a woman admirer who would weep in its presence. Le Guin then ends the poem with a single-line stanza: "Only the tears were ours." Yet the poem does not stop at making a de-homocentric statement, reminiscent of the last sentence of *Surfacing*. The specific identification of the passionate participant in the wonder of spring as a woman adds a very subtle feminist dimension in terms of her emotive recognition of fecundity. On the other hand, poems such as "Danaë 46" (*Hard Words* 5) critique patriarchy as part of a general revisioning of myth and also establish a series of connections among the women who repeatedly appear throughout the poems in *Hard Words*, including the woman as author, the woman as Native American water carrier, the woman as bearer of emotions (see Murphy, "High and Low").

For many male writers, becoming an environmentalist has not necessarily led to reevaluating gender relationships. And it would seem that a number of women writers have submerged the gender question in their development of, or search for, a balanced relationship with the rest of the natural world. Mary Oliver, winner of the 1984 Pulitzer Prize in Poetry, has been recognized as a preeminent nature poet. Is she also a feminist? In the early collection *Twelve Moons*, the answer would seem to be no, or at least not apparently. *American Primitive* continues in the same vein. Patricia Yaeger argues, however, that the freedom expressed through identification with the honey bear and with the whales sounding off the coast depicted in several poems indicates a feminist sensibility: "As Oliver's speaker goes honey-mad . . . [t]he tree filled with honey becomes the site of vision and of liberation for the woman writer—a bodily liberation that releases the tree energy, the honey energy into the 'rippling bark' of her poem" (7). But it is not really until *Dream Work* that we find an overtly ecofeminist poem, "The River" (20–21). Here sisterhood and human integration in nature, to be understood as "home," are yoked in opposition to "some cold city or other." Yet even so, the ecological awareness remains far more sophisticated than the feminist one, whereas in a poem such as "Resort" by Patricia Hampl, which I will discuss in detail in a later chapter, the opposite is the case. For Hampl's protagonist in this long sequential poem structured as a dialogical engagement of self and analyst, nature remains secondary but vital for the process of psychic healing that occurs. Nature becomes crucial as a means for self-understanding. Yet the ecological dimensions of the speaker's understanding in Hampl's poem remain as unsophisticated as the feminist understanding of Oliver's speakers. Both could learn much from each other in terms of integrating ecological and feminist awareness. Yet the poems of Oliver and Hampl can serve as valuable literature for ecofeminism because of the relationships between consciousness and impulse that they represent.

Getting Underway

If ecofeminists seek only for a literature that meets equally the criteria of ecological and feminist sophistication, they will be frequently disappointed. If, alternatively, they seek works that to some extent embody both dimensions they will find a vast array of writing that can provide inspiration and evidence of a developing consciousness of the imperatives for cultural change that have given rise to ecofeminism. Similarly, as literary theory and criticism are beginning to incorporate ecological criteria and to address not just feminisms but specifically ecofeminism, ecofeminist philosophy needs to attune itself to and help increase the sophistication of practitioners of such critical work. At the same time, if Bakhtinian dialogics is any indication, there exist aspects of literary theory that can be of benefit in the continued growth of ecofeminist thought and practice. For example, Bakhtinian theory provides valuable critical tools for analyzing the dialogical structure of one of the best-known ecofeminist texts, Susan Griffin's *Woman and Nature*, a point I will elaborate in the next chapter. Dialogics is helpful in terms of articulating not only its organization but also the variety of double-voicing throughout that gives it so much power and accounts for the significant tonal shifts which occur as the debate within the text gradually resolves toward the voice of a community of women in nature.

Dialogics reminds ecofeminist practitioners that every position is really a pivot by which to step and dance, to practice and develop, but not to stand or come to rest. Part of this continued motion needs to be greater ecofeminist attention to literature even as literary theory and criticism need to integrate ecofeminist philosophy into their most basic practices. Many authors today demonstrate a significant awareness of current philosophical trends, and their efforts to integrate the insights of philosophical and literary theory into their writing are apparent. Ecofeminism is clearly becoming a part of that awareness, but much more needs to be done in both the philosophy and the literature. Literary critics and philosophers alike must enter into dialogue with ecofeminism in order to continue their own critical praxis and to evaluate the ways in which ecofeminism calls for changes in that praxis, since their work, as Dale Bauer argues, takes place not only within the classroom but also in "all of the other territories of [their] own lived experience" (xvii).

Chapter Three

Voicing Another Nature

I

For some two centuries, nature writing has been one of those "marginalized" genres of modern writing. Much of what has been labelled as such consists of prose essays or meditational volumes, which are neither novel nor poem, neither fiction nor science. Nature writing has been marginalized at least in part because it fails to fit neatly any of the ongoing genre categories that organize criticism. It has also been marginalized because since the Enlightenment nature has been primarily an object of attention or a site for human endeavors rather than an entity in its own right, a speaking subject, a hero in the Bakhtinian sense, or a locus of sacred power. To the extent that a canon of nature writing is forming in the United States today, it remains generally limited to white males who write a particular type of prose, women who imitate them in that endeavor, and something called "romantic poetry," frequently heavily ego-bound and more often than not concerned with the white male poet's sensitivities and intellectuality rather than its ostensible subject. In either case, alienation from the object of attention and alienation within the authorial subject appear requisite conditions.

A new text, *The Norton Book of Nature Writing*, which by its conditions of production within the academic text marketplace will tend to set the terms of the canonical debate for the genre/mode of nature writing, illustrates this orientation. One begins with the table of contents. Of ninety-four authors, only fourteen are women, only two of the authors—as far as I can determine—are nonwhite, and these both Native Americans. Twenty-one of the men have multiple entries, but only one of the women, so that the contribution of the women is reduced even further than their limited number might suggest. In the first paragraph, the editors define "nature writing" as prose and primarily nonfiction: the "naturalist essay." The *father* of all this is Linnaeus, i.e., nature writing is a product of the Enlightenment, of rationalism, categorization, and classification—patriarchal and hierarchical to the core. It is also fundamentally Judeo-Christian in its prolapsarian position on human origins and human essence. In the introduction to the *Norton*, editors Finch and Elder quote Gilbert White: "A constant theme of the nature essayists was the search

31

for a lost pastoral haven, for a home in an inhospitable and threatening world" (20). A return to the Garden and a definition of the present planet as a "howling wilderness," then, are the hallmarks of a mode of writing arising from colonialism, industrialization, and the growth of an urban leisure class, as the editors assert with approbation. Human alienation is the foundational ontotheology for the attempt to define and canonize this mode of writing.

Alienation provides the primary explanation for the near-exclusion of Native American authors—"a certain kind of intense and self-conscious awareness of nature follows from a loss of integration between society and nature" (26), and native peoples did not experience such a loss until it was forced upon them, nor have native authors tended to accept the permanency of such a condition.[1] It also provides a possible explanation for Annie Dillard's being the only woman to receive a double entry—the excerpt the editors have chosen from *Pilgrim at Tinker Creek* ends: "It is ironic that the one thing that all religions recognize as separating us from our creator—our very self-consciousness—is also the one thing that divides us from our fellow creatures" (Finch and Elder 828). (Dillard apparently uses a definition of "religion" exclusive of animistic and primal spritual beliefs.) And it explains Thoreau's receiving the most space in this collection. Thoreau, like Dillard, goes to nature to observe rather than to participate, forever aloof and transcendent, and to escape that part of nature known as human society. Alienation is disguised in both cases as autonomy.

As Max Horkheimer and Theodor Adorno argued nearly fifty years ago, "the Enlightenment has extinguished any trace of its own self-consciousness" (4). And the crucial element of the self-consciousness that has been extinguished is precisely the recognition that this alienation, which has been enthroned as a necessary condition of rational existence and an absolute human state (at least since the articulation of language), is generated and continuously reproduced by Enlightenment beliefs: "Myth turns into enlightenment, and nature into mere objectivity. Men pay for the increase of their power with alienation from that over which they exercise their power. Enlightenment behaves toward things as a dictator toward men. He knows them in so far as he can manipulate them. The man of science knows things in so far as he can make them" (9). In direct contrast to this enlightenment acceptance of absolute alienation and the reduction of everything outside the human subject as objects upon which to cast the alienated, rationalistic gaze, Donna Haraway posits that "in a sociological account of science all sorts of things are actors, only some of which are human language-bearing actors, and that you have to include, as sociological actors, all kinds of heterogeneous entities . . . this imperative helps to break down the notion that only the language-bearing actors have a kind of agency" (Penley and Ross 5).

At a time when feminist praxis and postmodernist critique have ruptured the assumptions of genre, canon, creativity, and inspiration, an effort is underway in this country to render nature writing a "dead," rather than living, genre, so that only imitation can occur, rather than innovation. The applicability of what Bakhtin says about the novel at the opening of "Epic and Novel"—that it is "younger than writing and the book," "receptive to new forms of mute perception," and "has no canon of its own" (*Dialogic Imagination* 5)—should be cause for celebration over the vitality of this marginalized form of written representation of human experience. But too many veteran nature-writing teachers and critics seem to regret its liveliness and flexibility, perhaps precisely because nature writing has the potential to realize the "ability of the novel to criticize itself," which "is a remarkable feature of this ever-developing genre" (6). And, as a result, new developments in the field might reveal their established knowledge to be inaccurate or render their assurances dubious assumptions. At least in part for self-protection, the proponents of canonical delimitation of nature writing as "the naturalist essay" prefer that we come to know nature writing, as Bakhtin notes, as "we know other genres, as genres, in their completed aspect, that is, as more or less fixed pre-existing forms into which one may then pour artistic experience" (3). The emphases on: one) nonfiction—fact rather than fancy in determining detail; two) the essay—informational rather than artistic style; and three) prose—referential rather than self-reflexive language; all point in this direction of deadening.

As such, then, nature writing will reproduce the absolutes of Enlightenment belief in the power of science over art, observation over imagination, and human systematization and ordering over any indeterminable structures of natural process.[2] In particular, such codification will guarantee the reproduction of existing hierarchies of value, because it will preclude nature writing's engagement with the present, depriving it of the novel's and the novelization of other genres' "zone of maximal contact with the present (with contemporary reality) in all its openendedness" (*Dialogic Imagination* 11), which would necessarily include the possibility of the subversion and transformation of existing hierarchies, paradigms, and ideologies. Dillard's *Pilgrim* is an example of this movement toward "pre-existing forms." It imitates Thoreau's *Walden*, even in its structure, consisting of a year's visit to a body of water by an apparently autonomous single individual. Criticism of existing social institutions and human behaviors toward the environment will be wrapped in nostalgia and the fatalistic regret that accompanies permanent exile from the Garden. The monological conceptualization of nonfictional prose furthers the precluding of subversion of contemporary institutions. The author is imaged as an individual speaking without anticipation of audience response, not conversing but only lecturing about individual perceptions, as John Muir so frequently does. It is a highly romantic, author/self-centered conception of the didactic text, with a concomitant definition of the audience as passive recipient, very much in the encoder-code-decoder mode of communication models, the very antithesis of a Bakhtinian utterance-based conception of participatory discourse.

This prescriptive closing down of the genre is structured in such a way that it excludes the insights and challenges of feminism to the ways in which knowledge and narratives are constructed. As Rachel Blau DuPlessis has noted, discussing Virginia Woolf's depiction of the fictitious Mary Carmichael, for a woman to write her own voice, her own consciousness, to present in effect her own perceptions of nature and human relationship within it, she must break the sentence: "To break the sentence rejects not grammar especially, but rhythm, pace, flow, expression: the structuring of the female voice by the male voice, female tone and manner by male expectations, female writing by male emphasis, female writing by existing conventions of gender—in short, any way in which dominant structures shape muted ones" ("Breaking" 474). If such is the case, then a feminist nature writing will not be able to express the experiences and perceptions of women unless it breaks with the very genre structures, based initially on a certain period style, that Finch, Elder, and others, are attempting to codify at this time.

That women are attempting just such expression can be seen across the entire range of genre categories, including nature essays. And they are doing so in far more dialogical ways than the dominant nature writing tradition would allow, both as a result of self-conscious intent and out of the necessity of their subject positions within contemporary society, since "woman . . . negotiates differences and sameness, marginality and inclusion in a constant dialogue, which takes shape variously in the various authors, but with one end—a rewriting of gender in the dominant fiction" (DuPlessis, "Breaking" 487); that is, the dominant fiction of male universality in every genre of writing. Women writers in the field of nature writing, then, are key figures in the degree of novelness to be found there, which is necessarily dialogical, since "novelness is a means for charting changes that have come about as a result of increasing sensitivity to the problem of non-identity. Greater or lesser degrees of novelness can serve as an index of greater or lesser awareness of otherness" (Holquist, *Dialogism* 72–73). Having posited human alienation from the rest of nature as the fundamental non-identity (in the form of a loss), the nature writing codifiers appear bent on denying any other forms of otherness. They deny also the relation between such otherness and determining ways of negotiating the interanimating non-identity of humanity/nature and the potential for *transgredience* that such interanimation provides,[2] preferring lamentations of the loss of identity or paeans to moments of transcendence.

DuPlessis's notion of dialogue, like that of Dale Bauer in *Feminist Dialogics*, contradicts the male naturalist's imperious assertion of total human alienation from the rest of nature. Many writers, women and Native Americans in particular, are countering with the question: is alienation really the way of the world for human beings who have self-consciousness? Perhaps it is only an invention of those white males who are either trying to return to the mother and her womb, or trying to make the mother return and be once more obedient to them? What if instead of alienation we posited *relation* as the primary mode of human-human and human-nature interaction without conflating difference, particularity and other specificities? What if we worked from a concept of relational difference and *anotherness* rather than Otherness?

Dialogics reinforces the ecofeminist recognitions of interdependence and the natural necessity of diversity; that is, dialogue at the most basic levels of energy/information exchange, as in gene pools and cross-fertilization (*conversari*, the root for conversation, according to my desk dictionary meant "to live with," and was the medial form of *conversare*, "to turn around"). Anotherness proceeds from a heterarchical, that is, a non-hierarchical, sense of difference. If the recognition of otherness and the status of Other is applied only to women and/or the unconscious, for example, and the corollary notion of anotherness, being another for others, is not recognized, then the ecological processes of interanimation—the ways in which humans and other entities develop, change, and learn through mutually influencing each other day to day, age by age—will go unacknowledged. The degree to which patriarchy throughout its historical manifestations (including the Enlightenment, during which the antiseptic and opaque veil of science was placed over patriarchy's machinations and rationalizations) has placed both women and nature in the category of the absolute and alienated other attests to a continuing refusal to recognize reciprocity as a ubiquitous natural/cultural process. Much of the ecofeminist critique in philosophy and the sciences has been devoted to exposing the bankruptcy of such categorization.[3] Bakhtin makes explicit the difference between relational and alienational otherness by the different Russian words he employs for "another" in "Toward a Reworking of the Dostoevsky Book" (Appendix II of *Problems of Dostoevsky's Poetics*). There he points out that "in actuality a person exists in the forms *I* and *another*."[4] He also addresses, according to Gary Saul Morson and Caryl Emerson, the connections among "'I for myself, the other for me,' and 'I for another,'" in the newly translated "Toward a Philosophy of the Act" (Morson and Emerson, Introduction 23).

What all of the foregoing is meant to suggest is that in order to have a women's nature writing, there must be a breaking of genre conventions established by men, and accepted by women, working within patriarchal structures. Such efforts have always been imperiled by the dominant culture's variegated ideological strategems for silencing women's voices, or straining them through male normative discourses to conflate and deny difference. Today, this imperilment takes the form of codifying a patriarchal definition of nature writing. But, unlike previous pivotal moments, women today have the benefit of an increasingly sophisticated conception of dialogic methods of discourse and critique, and a voice from within the realm of nature philosophy itself, ecofeminism. A few examples will help to clarify how women writers have been and continue to be breaking the traditional bounds of nature writing, what we have to gain from their efforts, and the ways in which both feminism and dialogics inform not only our understanding of these texts but the texts themselves.

II

Let me begin my examples of women who break the traditional bounds of nature writing with a recently rediscovered feminist environmental writer from the early twentieth century, Mary Austin. In 1903 she published *The Land of Little Rain*, which has been reprinted only within the past six years. (In 1988 it appeared in paperback as part of the Penguin Nature Library series.) In one sense, Austin's work should be analyzed as a turn-of-the-century text and placed in the context of its production. In another sense, though, due to its recent rediscovery and republication, it ought to be placed in the context of its current reception. Both Ed Hoagland's series introduction and Edward Abbey's book introduction, which precede Austin's text, attempt to confine the author and her writing within their ideological bounds, by defining the genre and the book's contents for the reader, rather than engaging Austin on her own ground. Listen to Hoagland: "Until quite recently indeed (as such things go), the whole world was a wilderness in which mankind lived as cannily as deer, overmastering with spears or snares even their woodmanship and that of other creatures, finding a path wherever wildlife could go. . . . Aristotle was a naturalist, and . . . Darwin and Thoreau. . . . Yet nature writing, despite its basis in science, usually rings with rhapsody as well—a belief that nature is an expression of God" (v). Here wilderness seems to mean here a place in which people do not yet dominate their habitat. I say "not yet" because the rest of Hoagland's description is based on a competition rather than cohabitation model of human and other animal relationships. This competitive model is based on a myth of hunter-gatherer societies that ignores that gathering was the stable, reliable, mainstay method of obtaining sustenance and falsely establishes a patriarchal hierarchy of gender relationships in primal societies. Hunter-gatherer here is one of the patriarchal dichotomies of man/woman, hunter/gatherer, culture/nature, and heroic/menial. Note, too, the curious word choice, in which even the deer are treated as having craft ("woodmanship") and a will to power ("*over*mastering" rather than mastering; they too must be seeking mastery of nature?). There is also reference to the lineage of male thinkers who determine the genre, as well as the an exclusionary definition of theism that posits a transcendent God outside of and separate from nature, in contradistinction to animism, Native American beliefs, and contemporary ecofeminist spirituality, represented by such people as Starhawk and Alice Walker, as embodied in *The Temple of My Familiar.*

I assume that Hoagland commissioned Abbey to write the introduction, which begins with Abbey's dismissing Austin's thirty other books out of hand without having read them—a common response to works by women, especially feminist ones: I know they must be second rate, so I haven't bothered with them. After pointing out that Austin "crusaded for the rights of American Indians and Mexican-Americans" and "was an active feminist at a time when that particular cause entailed risk and trouble"—as if it entails neither today and is merely one cause among many—Abbey then trashes Austin's style, which is "too fussy, even prissy." So what makes this a "living book": "the accuracy of her observational power. . . . The subject matter looms above and burns through the lacy veil of words, as a worthy subject will, and soon takes precedence over the author's efforts to show herself an author" (x and xii). In other words, the value of this book has nothing to do with the woman who wrote it, but results only from the degree to which she aligns herself with normative male thinking and writing on a traditionally male subject. Everything that marks Austin off from her male peers, everything that might suggest another sensibility and another worldview than the dominant one, is denigrated by Abbey and reduced to the problem of a purported effeminate style practiced by all nature writers at the turn of the century. In effect, Abbey has established in his own mind a contemporary equivalent of an "epic discourse" against which Austin and all others will be measured and found wanting. Abbey's contention is not really over authorial style four score and twenty-odd years ago, but over the dictation of an official style for nature writing today, with "its reliance on impersonal and sacrosanct tradition, on a commonly held evaluation and point of view—which excludes any possibility of another approach—and therefore displays a profound piety toward the subject described and toward the language used to describe it" (Bakhtin, *Dialogic Imagination* 16–17).

Both editor and introducer conveniently omit that feminist researchers, recovering the neglected works of women writers, first revived public interest in Austin's work, not naturalists and not male editors. The structure of this book, then, reveals itself as a heated dialogue between masculinist and feminist viewpoints about the nature of writing, the nature of nature, and the tradition and future of nature writing, with two living (at the time) men ganging up on one dead woman.

The gendered character of this polemic is heightened by the fact that another version of Austin's work was reprinted the year before the Penguin edition was published. In 1987 the Rutgers American Women Writers series published *Stories from the Country of Lost Borders,* which contains the stories from *The Land of Little Rain*, the 1909 *Lost Borders*, and a lengthy introduction by Marjorie Pryse. What a different introduction we find here! Austin, who had had a desire to tell stories since the age of four, suffered a nervous collapse while in college, and her male doctor suspected that it "might have something to do with the natural incapacity of the female mind for intellectual achievement" (xi). No doubt he supposed this to be an "accurate" observation of nature. Further, Pryse reveals the importance of the relationships among women writers both for Austin's own development and for her assistance to others, and places Austin in a literary tradition that Abbey utterly ignores, that of the "late nineteenth-century women writers who worked in the genre of literary regionalism" (xv). Further, Abbey omits mention of Austin's involvement in the suffrage and women's labor movements. Perhaps this is because both Hoagland and Abbey are more concerned with universalizing their perceptions of proper experience than recognizing its particularities, including the experiencer's gender. But as Michael Holquist notes in *Dialogism: Bakhtin and His World*: "Existence, like language, is a shared event. It is always a border incident on the gradient both joining and separating the immediate reality of my own living particularity (a uniqueness that presents itself as only for me) with the reality of the system that precedes me in existence (that is always-already-there) and which is intertwined with everyone and everything else" (28; see 47). For Austin the land is the shaping precedent; and, in the desert of which she writes, if individuals do not adjust their particularities of behavior and belief to that shape, their existence will quickly cease.

In the opening and title story of *The Land of Little Rain*, Austin begins by defining the territory through its ancient Indian name, "the Country of Lost Borders," not the name imposed by recent white invaders, because it "is the better word." The power of naming is invoked here and that power remains with the inhabitants who live along its frontiers, "Ute, Paiute, Mojave, and Shoshone," while white men are defined as visitors. White society and its states, rules, and structures are not allowed prominence, but placed in perspective: "Not the law, but the land sets the limit." And while people may not live in the desert heart of this country, "Void of life it never is" (*Land* 1). Austin recognizes that the land may have an ecosystem that neither requires nor facilitates human participation. "This is the nature of that country" to be a thing-in-itself and for-itself, rather than a thing-for-us, a crucial ecological recognition. As Pryse notes, "In Mary Austin's work, the land solely determines the nature of the region"; in addition, it enters the story, as Austin herself claims, "as another character, as the instigator of plot" (*Stories* xv and xix). Thus it becomes a hero in the Bakhtinian sense, with Austin unfolding its narrative both in terms of its presenting "a particular point of view on the world" and through continuously depicting the land's own ecosystem behavior as a viewpoint "on oneself."[5] Although not a speaking subject, the land does function as a signifying agent, with its significations interpreted and represented by Austin.

Throughout this story, in which the desert is the hero and the white man the antagonist, Austin repeatedly gives primacy to nature as a dynamic interactive system in which people may participate if they follow the lead of the land: "Most species have well-defined areas of growth, the best index the voiceless land can give the traveler of his whereabouts" (*Land* 4). This line may be read as both informational and polemical, returning to the issue of who is the inhabitant and who the invader, suggesting that the white settlers of California coming into conflict with the Indian inhabitants already identified might learn to limit their "areas of growth."[6] Interestingly enough, Austin's publishers wanted her books to be coffeetable editions of exotic stories for urban Easterners, but Austin saw herself as writing for the locals who were in contact and confrontation with the land, and attempting to educate them about the world they could not see because they were monologically focused on "overmastering" it. That my doubled reading of "The Land of Little Rain" is motivated rather than capricious can be seen from the final lines in which she directly addresses her audience, placing its members in specific relationship to the rest of nature: "It is hard to escape the sense of mastery as the stars move in the wide clear heavens to risings and settings unobscured. They look large and near and palpitant; as if they moved on some stately service not needful to declare. Wheeling to their stations in the sky, they make the poor world-fret of no account. Of no account you who lie out there watching, nor the lean coyote that stands off in the scrub from you and howls and howls" (*Land* 8). The relationship here of one species of animal to another, and both to the larger natural systems, seems quite clear.

Much of Austin's work has been neglected or buried, and only in recent years have her contributions to an American women's literary tradition, to nature writing, and to critical analysis of Native American literature been reexamined and reprinted. Yet this recovery clearly has not been a simply informational project. Women's writing and feminist perspectives on ecology and human history remain heavily contested terrain. Critical synthesis of ecology, feminism, and dialogics is needed, to recognize and appreciate not only what Austin writes about, but also how she writes, and why. And Austin's case indicates that the recovery of women's nature writing, and the encouragement of its break from with male normative traditions and discourses, remains a significant and polemical task.

III

In many ways, conditions have not improved all that much since Mary Austin's day for writers who attempt to combine women's issues with nature writing.

Susan Griffin's *Woman and Nature: The Roaring Inside Her* proves a case in point. For many feminists and virtually all ecofeminists this has been a touchstone text, yet it is almost never taught in a nature writing course or defined as nature writing by male teachers or critics. It does not fit this definition of the genre because its dialogical novelty explodes the monological, restrictive conceptions they impose as a prescriptive definition. Griffin employs a postmodernist meta-narrative structure, polemically critiques what she observes, posits a utopian conclusion, and includes humans as part of the nature they study—none of which may be appreciated from a monological worldview, but may and will be celebrated from a dialogical feminist worldview. Dialogics enables the critic to articulate not only *Woman and Nature*'s organization but also the variety of double-voicing throughout that gives it so much power and that accounts for the significant tonal shifts as the debate of the text gradually resolves toward the voice of a community of women in nature. A discussion of Griffin's text can illuminate some of the many ways in which feminist thought can novelize, in the Bakhtinian sense, the nature writing genre to maintain and develop it as a tool of cultural critique.

In the 1982 anthology, *Made from this Earth*, Griffin provides an introduction for the extracts from *Woman and Nature* reprinted there, which includes a few remarks about its structure: "It moves by the force of echoes and choruses, counterpoints and harmonies. In one way, the book is an extended dialogue between two voices (each set in different type face), one the chorus of women and nature, an emotional, animal, embodied voice, and the other a solo part, cool, professorial, pretending to objectivity, carrying the weight of cultural authority" (82). Note that she does not say a "male voice," a biologically essential one, but rather an ideologically constructed one, which, historically, has predominantly issued from men. The book also consists of a meta-dialogue about the ways in which nature has been and might continue to be perceived and in which the degree of listening, learning and self-revaluation on the part of the gendered participants is both depicted and evaluated. The relationship of ideology to constraints on dialogue about nature is revealed in that, for Griffin, "a speculation about dialogue is also a speculation about ideology" (*Made* 161). Further, in "The Way of All Ideology," Griffin suggests an explanation for the emphasis on nonfictional prose in the codification of nature writing:

> Audre Lorde has made an illuminating connection between this civilization's fear of the associative and musical language of poetry (a language which comes from the depths of reason beneath rational consciousness, from dark, unknown regions of the mind) and the same civilization's fear of black skin, of the female, of darkness, the dark other, Africa, signifying an older, secret knowledge.

For, of course, it is not simply inventiveness which is feared. The new machine, the new gadget is worshipped. What is really feared is an open door into a consciousness which leads us back to the old, ancient, infant and mother knowledge of the body, in whose depths lies another form of culture not opposed to nature but instead expressing the full power of nature and of our natures. (*Made* 164–65)

Griffin seems to be utilizing a conception of the unconscious similar to that employed by Jacques Lacan in positing that "the unconscious is the discourse of the Other," but with a crucial difference ("Agency" 754). For Lacan this Other is absolutely alienated, a lack incapable of being remedied until death, but for Griffin this Other is *Another*, another part of ourselves just as we are another part of nature.

In the Preface to *Woman and Nature*, Griffin observes that simply to recognize false dichotomies does not make them disappear. The two sides must rather be brought into dialogue and relation in the process of dissolving the polarization. Griffin will use parodic double voicing as one technique for exposing the illusion of objectivity and separation that philosophical and scientific discourses have attempted to perpetuate: "Since patriarchal thought does, however, represent itself as emotionless (objective, detached, and bodiless), the dicta of Western civilization and science on the subjects of woman and nature in this book are written in a parody of a voice with such presumptions" (xv).

The Prologue sets out, through voice and countervoice, the point-counterpoint thesis of *Woman and Nature*: the patriarchal structures of Western civilization alienate man from both woman and nature, which are seen as related and in that relation are established as proper subjects for domination; and, women and nature are interrelated and in that interrelation is to be discovered women's strengths and a way past patriarchy's destructive limitations. "Book One," then, is a study of the development of Western civilization's definitions of "Matter," particularly as they arise from the prevalent mind/body dualism of Western philosophy and religion. The voicing here consists almost entirely of the ideas of "great" Western male thinkers rendered as anonymous indirect discourse. The value of this form of narration lies in the ability of indirect discourse to strip away the emotive, affective, and stylistic subterfuges that the original quotations so often display. This is due, as Bakhtin/Vološinov argues, to "the analytical tendency of indirect discourse," which "is manifested by the fact that all the emotive-affective features of speech, in so far as they are expressed not in the content but in the form of a message, do not pass intact into indirect discourse. They are translated from form into content, and only in that shape do they enter into the construction of indirect discourse" (*Marx-*

ism 128). Thus, Griffin is able to enter into critical dialogue with these historical thinkers through narrative structure, and to place her readers in a more critical posture than they would otherwise assume if reading the originals. This results both from their anonymity and from the situatedness of the utterance: "Indirect discourse 'hears' a message differently; it actively receives and brings to bear in transmission different factors, different aspects of the message than do the other patterns. . . . Analysis is the heart and soul of indirect discourse" (*Marxism* 129).

Not until six pages into the first chapter of "Book One" is the feminist counterchorus allowed voice, and then only to emphasize the lesson already well established primarily by the "Church Fathers," that sin is a product of the earth, that women are closer to the earth, and that woman sinned first: "*And we are reminded,*" announces the counterchorus, "*that we have brought death into the world*" (11). Crucially, Griffin renders this as active voice direct discourse, and does not have the counterchorus speak again until after having presented a chronology of the four centuries of European witchcraft trials and executions and the attendant development of Renaissance Philosophy. Griffin faithfully represents the near total exclusion of women from theology, philosophy, and science except as objects by devoting almost forty pages to patriarchal thought. When the feminist counterchorus does appear it records the interpellation of women as inferior beings, ignorant and fearful of their own nature (on "interpellation" see Althusser).

In the following seven chapters of "Book One," the reader begins to hear more frequently from the counterchorus, as the dialogue relies more and more heavily on the patriarchal ideas and practices of the past few centuries. The final chapter is perhaps the most devastating for readers to engage. Following the chapter titled "Cows," Griffin juxtaposes "Her Body," which emphasizes the ways in which men have attempted to deny women scientific knowledge of their own bodies and to make them over in some ideal physical image. To indicate the extent to which both of these behaviors are based in the misogyny endemic to patriarchal thought, Griffin begins each subsection of "Her Body" with an epigraph on the tortures imposed on "witches," beginning with Henri Boguet's venomous cry: "I wish they all had but one body, so that we could burn them all at once, in one fire!" (83). Not suprisingly, Griffin ends with a parenthetical description of the surgical procedures for a hysterectomy.

"Book Two: Separation" continues with the same kind of discourse structures as the first book, covering such topics as "His Power," "His Control," "His Certainty," and ending with "Terror." Then "Book Three: Passage," consisting of only two chapters, initiates the modern feminist response to the two preceding books. The first chapter, "The Labyrinth," uses a narrative voice that mimics the dominant discourse, reporting a kind of experience that cannot be understood from within the parameters of patriarchal paradigms. The other chapter, "The Cave," is written entirely in the counterchorus voice except when directly quoting specific women. And both the labyrinth and the cave are refigured by Griffin in a dialogical inversion that lays bare the patriarchal ideology behind their classical mythological structuration and the matrifocal prehistory it was meant to suppress. This matrifocal prehistory is then restored, by inverting the original inversion to acknowledge the symbols of the labyrinth and the cave as vaginal, uterine symbols of power and understanding, not distorted by dreams of domination and the divorce of rationalistic logic from the other emotive and affective processes of the mind.

"Book Four: Vision" is divided into two long sections with subchapters: "The Separate Rejoined" and "Matter Revisited," in which all that has been torn asunder and all that has been separated, calculated, classified, and ossified is brought back into relation, connection, and correction (in the sense of healing, not intellectualizing). Even here Griffin maintains the dialogical structure of narration, but now the polemical indirect discourse has been dropped. Instead, the dialogue is between "Herstory" and women's understanding, with some sections composed entirely of the latter, as the counterchorus becomes a chorus bursting into lyricism and dithyramb. The final chapter of the book is titled "Matter: How We Know." Even here, in the most utopian moment of Griffin's analysis, the dialogue continues, as her visionary remarks on possibility are counterposed to her own mother's actual experiences. And Griffin calls for continuing dialogue in her final, but not finalizing, words:

> because I know I am made from this earth, as my mother's hands were made from this earth, as her dreams came from this earth and all that I know, I know in this earth, the body of the bird, this pen, this paper, these hands, this tongue speaking, all that I know speaks to me through this earth and I long to tell you, you who are earth too, and listen *as we speak to each other of what we know: the light is in us.* (227)

Like Mary Austin, Susan Griffin ends not only with direct rather than indirect discourse but also with direct address, challenging her audience to participate in the dialogue established by the text.

Griffin's work demonstrates the ability of nature writers to engage postmodernity, specifically through the blurring of genres and meta-narrative reflexivity. More importantly, her work demonstrates the ability of ecofeminists to write polemically *and* dialogically, which simultaneously exposes the monological character of masculinist normative discourses in science, philosophy, and naturalist nonfiction. Further, while Austin is recognizable as a nature writer, although with a gendered difference, Griffin, in *Woman and Nature*, clearly is not. Yet Griffin's text is a type of environmental writing and can serve as a limit text to critique existing genre definitions.

Meta-narratives and meta-critiques add a powerful and highly self-conscious dimension to the conception of nature writing. And it may very well be precisely this element of self-consciousness, the interrogation of foundational assumptions, that will prove to be postmodernism's greatest contribution to nature writing. It may also be the reason that the proponents of a nature writing canon studiously avoid inclusion of postmodernist texts, because their arguments cannot stand the scrutiny such texts would initiate.

IV

Native American texts prove an impossible stumbling block to the efforts to codify nature writing, as demonstrated by Elder and Finch's and other anthologizers' difficulties in coming to terms with them.[7] For one thing, their teaching-storytelling does not admit a separation between facts and fictions; and for another, these texts, including ones by contemporary writers, do not easily admit a clearcut division between prose and poetry. Many poetry volumes could be used here, such as those by Linda Hogan, Paula Gunn Allen, Luci Tapahonso, Wendy Rose, and Joy Harjo. Let me cite just one Native American collection of poems, to suggest the ways in which poetry can present a dialogical and, in this case, feminist nature writing. *Not Vanishing*, by Chrystos, initiates a dialogue in its title similar to that practiced by Gloria Anzaldúa. "Not Vanishing" refers both to the individual speaking through these poems and to the Native peoples to whom she feels deep responsibility. The poems themselves oscillate between terror and love, between the possibilities for survival and triumph that emerge from a Native heritage and the genocidal threat that the dominant U.S. culture continues to be, and between the experiences of one individual and the relationship of those experiences to all oppressed peoples and groups—natives and other peoples of color, women and lesbians, working-class and street people.

The opening poem, "Crazy Grandpa Whispers," establishes the inversion of sanity and insanity with regard to the speaker's native heritage and contemporary American culture. The ancestral voice tells her to take back the cities and "live as your ancestors," but the speaker counters that if she listens to this voice of ecological sanity, she will be declared insane and institutionalized. But she does not reject the voice. Her conclusion suggests that, at the moment, the emphasis must be on survival, which is in itself subversive because it allows Crazy Grandpa's voice to continue speaking to the present and suggesting the ways out of this contemporary madness. The next poem, "You Can't Get Good Help These Daze," draws on the author's experience as a maid to warn the dominant culture that the underclass is preparing for just the kind of revolt that Crazy Grandpa recommends. In contrast, "Foolish" enacts a lunar celebration, introducing the love that can counter the terror of the two preceding poems. Like the other poems in *Not Vanishing* that focus on Native heritage and experiences, this one is set off by the use of a turtle symbol, which refers to the concept of North America as Turtle Island. In the introduction, Chrystos warns the reader: "While I am deeply spiritual, to share this with strangers would be a violation. . . . you will find no creation myths here." Indeed, she retells no such traditional stories. Yet, for those readers who already know it, the Turtle Island symbol does invoke an extremely popular creation myth. Through this iconography, then, Chrystos is able to suggest another level of meaning for poems such as "Foolish," although for only a segment of her reading audience. For them, "Foolish" can be read as a ritual poem announcing not just the survival of a people, but the beginning of a triumph, for in mid-poem the speaker chants, "*Here we come   Here we come,*" and calls on readers to throw down the doors of their houses (3). "Foolish" connects this celebration with the Spring renewal of plants, implying a certain inevitability to the envisioned return of native values.

Similar arrangements of poems appear throughout *Not Vanishing*. "Today Was a Bad Day Like TB" enunciates a terror felt of "whites" who turn Native spiritual practices and artifacts into tourist attractions and trinkets. The association of this experience with tuberculosis links cultural and physical disease, in much the same way that Gloria Anzaldúa depicts their interpenetration. "Poem for Lettuce," however, humorously presents the road of revenge in terms of the speaker's striking an alliance with "lettuce" by promoting carnivorous behavior. Chrystos pokes fun at people who make rigid distinctions between the human and the animal, animal life and plant life, and rely on dichotomies rather than relationships and continuities to structure their world. "My Baby Brother" and "Vision: Bundle" emphasize the destruction wrought by American culture first on an individual Indian and then on Indian cultures in general. Baby brother is depicted as a heroin addict who rides horses only in his drug-induced dreams, utterly separated from his heritage and his place. "Vision: Bundle" decries the destruction of Native spiritual practices by imperialistic anthropology, museum displays, and unauthorized ethnographic recordings of religious rituals. These violations are linked to a reliance on technology and the resulting evisceration of the human spirit. Yet, despite the record of terror presented in both poems, Chrystos ends the second one with the survivor's recognition that the only thing that cannot be stolen "is what we know" (21).

V

Donna Haraway has posited that the nature-human dialogic is the most pressing issue to work through at this moment in time. Susan Griffin has argued that this dialogic is also inextricably intertwined with the male-female dialogic. Only in the past few years have literary critics even begun to concern themselves with such matters as "ecological criticism," "environmental literature," and the "genre of nature writing." Debate over such concepts is vital, if not for the future of literary studies then certainly for their social relevance. Yet, at a point when such discussion has barely overcome inertia, there are those who would seek to bring it to rest through a codification of prescriptive genre criteria that would render nature writing a dead genre, closed off, conventionalized, and, increasingly, of merely historical interest. Too much is at stake to allow this to occur. Feminists need to encourage this debate, to help introduce a set of criteria for literary evaluation largely ignored by ecological critics. At the same time, they need to listen to those women who are calling for a reintegration of woman and nature, of humanity and nature, so that they can learn how to expand feminist theory to encompass the ecological dimensions of women's lives. This dimension can only adequately be incorporated into feminist thought through a dialogical process that recognizes that human-nature relationships and contradictions will remain throughout all social permutations.

Through a feminist dialogical intervention, we can not only blur the genre of nature writing by dissolving the absolute dichotomies being posited in order to codify it into a monological, centripetal mode of writing. We can also redefine the very terms of human-nature interaction and their literary representations. By encouraging the voicing of another nature, and learning the means by which to generate criticism and analysis of such voicing, we can help to perpetuate the feminist project of developing another mode of human behavior, one founded on relational anotherness rather than alienational otherness, an affirmative praxis necessary in this time of negative critique.[8]

Chapter Four

Reconceiving the Relations of Woman and Nature, Nature and Culture: Contemporary Environmental Literature by Women

The question was asked some years ago by Sherry Ortner, "Is Female to Male as Nature Is to Culture?", as part of a feminist process of reconceptualizing women's relationship to nature as these terms have been defined by Western patriarchy in its scientific, philosophical, and religious modes of thought. Susan Griffin, in her landmark ecofeminist text, *Woman and Nature: The Roaring Inside Her*, interrogated the ways in which patriarchy since the Greeks has used all three of these modes of discourse to render women the objects of male attention, domination, and conquest. At the same time, Griffin's text reveals the close connection between women's subjugation and the ways in which men have defined nature, to render all that is defined as nonhuman as discrete objects also only for attention, domination, and conquest.

The seventies was very much the decade of feminist critique of existing ideologies throughout academia, and, within literary studies, a questioning of the verities of canon and curriculum. This critique occurred in tandem with the rapid establishment of Women's Studies centers, programs, majors and minors, and aggressive efforts nationwide to require the hiring and promotion of women faculty in representative numbers.

The eighties witnessed the continuation and intensification of the foregoing, along with greater attention to gynocritics, as evidenced by the accelerated recovery and reprinting of works by women. As the debate over canon formation heated up, fueled by the sudden availability of an amazing range of women's writing (certainly more amazing for its having been so successfully suppressed than for its quality or quantity), courses in women's literature were not only developed but required to be integrated into existing curricula. In connection with these courses, efforts were made to introduce gender balance as an issue for the content of every classroom, and, by expanding feminist pedagogy, to preclude token approaches to the inclusion of women in the curriculum. But while feminists in literature departments were engaging patriarchy on these fronts, they tended, with rare exceptions, to overlook the interpenetration of ecology and feminism as it was developing throughout the seventies and eighties, mainly outside of academia, and when inside usually in the environmental sciences, philosophy, and religious studies, as in the writings of Carolyn Merchant, Mary Daly, Elizabeth Dodson Gray, Carol Christ, Rosemary Radford Reuther, and others. In the nineties, ecofeminism is finally making its presence felt in literary studies, and as critics begin to develop the insights of ecofeminism as a component of literary criticism, they are discovering as well a wide array of environmental literature by women that is being written contemporaneously with the development of ecofeminist philosophy and criticism, some of which I have discussed in the previous chapter.

While much feminist theory is either heavily enamored of psychoanalytic methods of analyzing women's subject construction or committed to socioeconomic models of interpretation, many theorists ignore the "places" in which women find themselves and the relation of environment to selfhood. Nevertheless, feminists are committed to exposing, critiquing, and ending the oppression of women, overthrowing patriarchy and phallocentrism. And as a necessary moment in such a process, they demand male recognition of the other; yet there are nonhuman as well as human others that need to be recognized. Irene Diamond and Gloria Feman Orenstein explain that

> Ecofeminism is a term that some use to describe both the diverse range of women's efforts to save the Earth and the transformations of feminism in the West that have resulted from the new view of women and nature. . . . as the [seventies] advanced and as women began to revalue women's cultures and practices, especially in the face of the twin threats of nuclear annihilation and ecocide, many women began to understand how the larger culture's devaluation of natural processes was a product of masculine consciousness. (ix)

That is to say, the specifics that both environmentalism and feminism separately oppose stem from the same source: the patriarchal construction of modern Western civilization. Thus, to be a feminist one must also be an ecologist, because the domination and oppression of women and nature are inextricably intertwined. To be an ecologist, one must also be a feminist, since without addressing gender oppression and the patriarchal ideology that generates the sexual metaphors of masculine domination of nature, one cannot effectively challenge the world views that threaten the stable evolution of the biosphere, in which human beings participate or perish.

And so, the recognition and positive identification of otherness—not just among people but also among people and other natural entities—as non-alien, healthy diversity becomes a fundamental recognition of ecofeminism. Recognizing the other as self-existent entity encourages the perceiving and conceptualizing of interanimation, the mutual co-creation of selves and others. As Paula Gunn Allen has noted, "your body is also a planet, replete with creatures that live in and on it" ("The Woman" 52). Static categories that define nature or individuals can only be distortions and illusions, failing even to recognize the circadian rhythms that render our bodies constantly fluctuating, finite biological systems.

The early phases of the contemporary environmental movement in the U.S. have demonstrated that recognizing the exploitation and oppression of nature does not automatically result in extending such recognition to women. The belief that integrating ecology and feminism does not simply enlarge feminism but substantially alters each field's orientation is espoused by Diamond and Orenstein, who claim that feminist environmental activists "reinvigorated both feminism and social change movements more generally" because "the languages they created reached across and beyond the boundaries of previously defined categories." And further, these women "embraced not only women and men of different races, but all forms of life—other animals, plants, and the living Earth itself" (xi). And Ariel Salleh claims:

> In highlighting the ecological dimension and drawing on the grass roots experience of women in both developed and so-called developing countries, ecofeminism opens up the feminist movement itself to a new cluster of problems and it challenges the urban based theoretical paradigms—liberal, Marxist, radical, post-structuralist—which have dominated feminist politics over the last two decades. By pitting new empirical concerns against established feminist analyses, ecofeminism is encouraging a new synthesis in feminist political thought. ("Eco-Feminism/Deep" 197)

At the same time that it can be claimed that ecofeminism is irrevocably altering both environmentalism and feminism, it cannot be claimed that ecofeminism represents a stable, clearly defined theory adhered to or acknowledged by all practitioners of a feminist ecology or an ecological feminism. There are some who define themselves as socialist ecofeminists, and others as spiritual ecofeminists, and still others as radical or cultural ecofeminists. What these people all share is an agreement on what they oppose, what they are seeking to change, and the masculinist linkage of women and nature that denigrates and threatens both. And, according to Donna Haraway,

> Ecofeminists have perhaps been most insistent on some version of the world as active subject, not as resource to be mapped and appropriated in bourgeois, Marxist, or masculinist projects. Acknowledging the agency of the world in knowledge makes room for some

unsettling possibilities. . . . Feminist objectivity makes room for
surprises and ironies at the heart of all knowledge production; we are
not in charge of the world. (*Simians* 199)

Diamond and Orenstein in their Preface to *Reweaving the World* inform
their readers that their volume "with its chorus of voices reflecting the variety
of concerns flowing into ecofeminism, challenges the boundaries dividing
such genres as the scholarly paper and the impassioned poetic essay. In so
doing, it acknowledges poetic vision as a form of knowledge and as one of the
important steps in the process of global transformation" (vii). Wouldn't the
flip side of this be to claim that literary criticism, particularly feminist criticism, acknowledges ecofeminism as a thematics in contemporary literature
worthy of study and representative of the cultural transformations being
wrought by feminist theory and practice?

Environmental literature by women not only cuts across genres, but also
creates new categories and redefines boundaries on the basis of thematics and
sympathies rather than formal properties and prescriptive definitions. And it
may be useful to distinguish between self-consciously feminist writing and
works that are affectively feminist in the themes developed and the conclusions readers may draw. There is, then, to be found a nature writing by
women, consisting of a traditional kind of nonfictional prose, primarily essays
and autobiographical narratives, and some of it promotes an ecofeminist sensibility, but not all of it does. Annie Dillard is one of the best known of such
writers at the moment, perhaps not coincidentally because she writes within
the Thoreauvian tradition, one of the main forms of the dominant tradition of
nature writing, and perhaps also because she tends to emphasize human separateness from the rest of nature. Another main mode of this tradition is the
naturalist essay, practiced by such writers as Rachel Carson and Ann Zwinger.

But then, one comes to a work such as Gretel Erlich's *The Solace of Open
Spaces* and the nature writing genre gets blurred, as does the question of feminist or not. For one thing, Erlich is not attempting to escape people the way
Thoreau and Dillard seem intent on doing; nor does she ignore them, the way
John Muir manages to omit his wife and children from his writing. Rather,
Erlich admits that people are a part of nature as they shape and are shaped by
it. For another thing, Erlich relies neither on the narrative role of nonpartici-
pating observer, nor on that of the meditating intelletual. *Solace* is an emotional autobiography organized by nodes of significant association instead of
by classification, chronology, or plot. Erlich, while not appearing to be self-
consciously a feminist, presents a strong sense of mutual co-creation in her
depiction of the way people, sheep, and the Wyoming landscape interact and
change. She shows an appreciation for diversity, as well as a sense of agency
arising out of interrelationships. For me, agency is based on *volitional interde-*

pendence; we make choices about how to respond to necessities and subject constructions. Our every action is neither wholly determined nor is it wholly free. Erlich's people often act out of a recognition of interdependence, and it is this that earns them her respect. Erlich also writes of settling in, of becoming a part of a specific, geographically, historically, and culturally situated place. Fundamentally, Erlich tries to share with the reader her experience of learning how to function productively and healthily in a living ecosystem.

Postmodernist texts disrupt the dominant tradition of nature writing far more radically than does Ehrlich's *Solace*. A case in point is Donna Haraway's *Simians, Cyborgs, and Women: The Reinvention of Nature*. Haraway introduces this book as one that "treats constructions of nature as a crucial cultural process for people who need and hope to live in a world less riddled by the dominations of race, colonialism, class, gender, and sexuality" (2). She reveals the interaction of ideologies and "objectivity" in scientific discourse in terms of the ways that patriarchal science, like genre definitions, limits what can be perceived, studied, and discussed. In other words, Haraway's historical analyses of the ideologies that have structured scientific discourse and the paradigms that have guided scientific research reveal the naivete underlying such a claim as Thomas J. Lyon's in *This Incomperable Lande*: "I have limited this book to essays on natural history and experiences in nature, believing that in fiction and poetry, though there are often beautiful descriptions of nature, other themes and intentions tend to predominate" (xv). Apparently, Lyon believes that the essays he has selected contain few or no ideological determinants, and no themes that guide the selection of observations to be recorded, rewritten and packaged for reading consumption. Yet any summation of an individual's experiences must be culturally and ideologically constructed, as Hayden White has so compellingly demonstrated in the case of history (see *Tropics*), not to mention the decision to undergo and to reflect on such experiences in the first place. Through her meta-critiques of scientific discourse Haraway is able to reveal the interaction of ideologies and objectivity. Lyon seems to sugggest that observation is a theme in itself. But the answer to "whose science and which guiding paradigms" will reveal in whose service any given nature text has been written.

Susan Griffin ends *Woman and Nature*, discussed in the previous chapter, with a utopian ecofeminist vision of the potential for female community in line with Rosemary Radford Ruether's desire for the realization of "the full range of human psychic potential" (210) and what this might mean for life on the planet. Haraway, seeing her own work as demonstrating what Hazel Henderson defines as the reality of "heterarchy" in the world, contends that

> Nature emerges . . . as 'coyote.' This potent trickster can show us
> that historically specific human relations with 'nature' must some-

how—linguistically, ethically, scientifically, politically, technologically, and epistemologically—be imagined as genuinely social and actively relational; and yet the partners remain utterly inhomogeneous. . . . Curiously, as for people before us in Western discourses, efforts to come to linguistic terms with the non-representability, historical contingency, artefactuality, and yet spontaneity, necessity, fragility, and stunning profusions of 'nature' can help us refigure the kind of persons we might be. These persons can no longer be, if they ever were, master subjects, nor alienated subjects, but—just possibly—multiply heterogeneous, inhomogeneous, accountable, and connected human agents. (3)

A dialogic construction of human/nature interactions, one that does not attempt to posit static absolutes and hierarchical dichotomies, poses the possibility of developing a new human self-consciousness that would render most nature writing, as it is currently practiced and generically prescribed, superfluous. In particular, Haraway recognizes the illusory character of so much of the monological observations that pass themselves off as naturalist essays, solitary observations, and the individual "fronting nature." Additionally, Haraway warns us against the monological maneuvers that conflate human and nonhuman interests through anthropomorphic depictions of the rest of nature, as well as the foundationalist arguments that dominate the debates over environmental ethics.

Such metacritical texts as Griffin's and Haraway's add a self-conscious dimension to the conception of nature writing, empowering the reader who can join in the authors' critiques of ideology as well as learn how to critique the ideologies in which the authors operate while they undertake those critiques. This function of interrogating foundational assumptions, which has been recognized as the primary shared territory of feminism and postmodernism, threatens any program of canon formation that is not self-avowedly provisional and self-critical.

Gloria Anzaldúa's *Borderlands/La Frontera* may serve as a case in point. This is not nature writing as we have known it. It does, however, very much address the issues raised in the lengthy quotation above from Haraway. Anzaldúa begins her Preface with the premise that geography and psychology are engaged in mapping mutually interpenetrating territories:

The actual physical borderland that I'm dealing with in this book is the Texas-U.S. Southwest/Mexican border. The psychological borderlands, the sexual borderlands and the spiritual borderlands are not particular to the Southwest. In fact, the Borderlands are physically present wherever two or more cultures edge each other, where people of different races occupy the same territory, where under, lower, middle and upper classes touch, where the space between two individuals shrinks with intimacy. (n.p.)

And in these borderlands are occurring "the further evolution of humankind" in intimate relationship with the lands and places of their inhabitation. Ecology and feminism are requisite conditions for such intimacy.

Throughout *Borderlands*, culture and territory are developed as mutually defining structures even as both structure and are structured by human consciousness: "Indigenous like corn, like corn, the *mestiza* is a product of crossbreeding, designed for preservation under a variety of conditions. . . . she will survive the crossroads" (81). The ground of these crossroads is literal and metonymic, not figurative and metaphorical. Anzaldúa's allegiance to the Southwest displays a sense of bioregionalism, which, allied to her political stance, crosses over and crosses out the cultural and national borders of the state. As Anzaldúa declares, "I am cultured because I am participating in the creation of yet another culture, a new story to explain the world and our participation in it, a new value system with images and symbols that connect us to each other and to the planet" (81). This claim could be as easily applied to Griffin's text as to Anzaldúa's. Both clearly share a belief in the principle of mutual co-creation as an ongoing process of human-nature interaction and as a responsibility of human agency.

The Southwest borderlands from which Anzaldúa hails also serve as the inspirational locus for Pat Mora's *Chants*. The opening poem of *Chants*, "Bribe," establishes Mora's view that poems are chants in sacred rituals that celebrate human dependence on the natural environment and reflecting the earth's "music." This chanting is part of the heritage the mestiza inherits from Indian women. In "Unrefined" and "Mi Madre," Mora personifies the desert as female and as mother, but "The desert is no lady" ("Unrefined"); rather, she is a "strong mother" ("Mi Madre"). Interestingly enough, Mora uses Spanish in the title to differentiate her own cultural identity from the Indian women already introduced, but at the same time through reference again to turquoise identifies a connection between them. Perhaps she wants to tap the matrilineal and matrifocal structures of southwestern Indian tribes, not just historically but as they continue into the present day, and to ally that with her perception of the earth as mother. Such a move would enable her to call upon this cultural and environmental heritage, as a counterpoint to the patriarchal dimensions of Chicana life that she laments in other poems, such as "Discovered" and "Plot."

The desert as female mother is treated by Mora as whole and self-sustaining, like the earth-initiating Pueblo Thought Woman. And, as a natural source of strength, nature defined as female counters the reliance on culture as determinant of gendered values. Mora's ecofeminism, then, contains a specific type of cultural politics that refutes not just patriarchy in general, but Chicano patriarchy in particular. For, as W.D. Neate notes, "while the Chicano tradition proposed the grandfather, Chicana writing looks to the mother and the grand-mother as keepers of the tradition" (15), who are often identified as both Indian and as wild nature.

An example of the cultural restrictions on women is presented in "Aztec Princess," where the mother tells the girl her umbilical cord is buried under the house to keep her tied to domesticity. At night the girl digs it up and finds only "rich earth," which she takes out into the moonlight "whispering, 'Breathe.'" While Native American women writers tend to identify tribe and family as means of regaining a relation to nature that has been impaired or destroyed by colonization and urbanization, Mora sees custom and family as part of the schism between woman and nature. As a result, in "Aztec Princess," the girl chooses the outdoors and moonlight *against* family and domesticity. In "Bruja: Witch" and "Curandera," Mora suggests that women gain freedom by becom-ing widows and witches, freeing themselves from negative cultural restraints and freeing themselves into a relationship with wild nature otherwise denied them. "Curandera" closes with the healer listening to the messages of, and breathing with, "the owl, "the *coyote*," "the mice," "snakes," and "wind."

Luci Tapahonso, Paula Gunn Allen, Leslie Marmon Silko, and other Native American writers, speak of the southwestern tribal cultures, based on matrifocal values to which Anzaldúa, Mora, and other Chicanas turn, as an example of an alternative heritage on which to draw for bulding a new mestiza culture in North America, one embodying both feminist and environmental values. Tapahonso does not identify herself as a feminist, but points out that perhaps she does not need to, since being a Navajo means for her that she does not live in a patriarchal culture, although she has experienced the dominant culture's oppression: "I grew up in a matriarchal culture and it's not necessar-ily that women are more important, but it's just that women have a better sta-tus in the Navajo society and in the Navajo family. . . . The status that the woman has in the Navajo culture has always been there" (Moulin 15). The title poem of *A Breeze Swept Through* focuses on birth, with an intertwining of the mythic and the mundane that emphasizes the co-creation and interrelatedness of all life. Human birth is an interdependent process and part of the rest of nature into which the infant enters, so that the baby's "first earth breath" and her kicking and crying are on the same plane of activity as the mist's lifting that morning.

The nuclear family, that is, the Euro-American bourgeois structure for approved human generation and the appropriation of women and children as male property, is not what Tapahonso celebrates, but she does celebrate family, which is also tribe and community. Throughout Tapahonso's work, as well as that of many other Native American women, the extended multi-generational family, with its various uncles and aunts and grandmothers and grandfathers, includes virtually the entire community in its recognition of blood ties. As Allen explains her own Keres Pueblo beliefs, "every individual has a place within the universe—human and nonhuman—and that place is defined by clan membership. In turn, clan membership is dependent on matrilineal descent. Of course, your mother is not only that woman whose womb formed and released you—the term refers in every individual case to an entire generation of women whose psychic, and consequently physical, 'shape' made the psychic existence of the following generation possible" (*Sacred* 209).

The defense and nurture of this type of family, for Tapahonso and other Native Americans, constitutes one of the first lines of resistance to Western patriarchy. As Allen unequivocally states, "the central issue that confronts American Indian women through the hemisphere is survival, *literal survival,* both on a cultural and biological level" (*Sacred* 189). As a result, defense of the tribal family becomes an ecofeminist issue. Linda Hogan devotes a chapbook of poems, *Daughters, I Love You,* to her adopted daughters and ties their survival into opposition to nuclear weapons. In Louise Erdrich's *Tracks,* the heroic figures are Nanapush and Fleur, who attempt to defend tribal ways against the effects of the Dawes Act, which demands that land be individually owned and tribes broken up. Unable to prevent the clearcutting of her land, which she has lost to government taxes, Fleur brings the trees around her cabin down on the heads of the lumbermen and then leaves with dignity and power. And in Leslie Marmon Silko's *Ceremony* the necessity to maintain environmental integrity is intimately bound up with the individual's own physical and psychic health. For Tayo to regain such balanced health, he must reintegrate himself with the gynocratic values of his Pueblo people: "We are the land, and the land is mother to us all. There is not a symbol in the tale [*Ceremony*] that is not in some way connected with womanness, that does not in some way relate back to Ts'eh and through her to the universal feminine principle of creation" (Allen, *Sacred* 119).

One of ecofeminism's contributions to the rethinking of feminism in general may prove to be a sophisticated reconsideration of the concept of family and the structures of interpersonal relationships in which the criteria for evaluating healthy ecosystems are applied. Clearly, family is not only a concern for Chicanas and Native Americans, but for other people of color as well. Alice Walker's *The Temple of My Familiar* focuses on familial relationships, a vast array of them. The thematic structure of this multi-plotted novel is based largely on the spiritualist wing of ecological feminism, with many of the ideas of Anzaldúa's *Borderlands* realized through plot rather than discursive prose. The relationships that are plotted out, racial and interracial, marital and extramarital, and multigenerational, cannot be understood outside of an ecological framework, one that is based on feminist recognitions of multiplicity, heterogeneity, and heterarchy.

The "familiar" of the title may be interpreted to be a symbol of the thread that connects every individual to the ecological web. The first page of the novel compares two people who pluck feathers from living birds to make costumes with an old woman who works only with "found feathers" (3); of the three, she is the only one who appears to be at peace with herself. Later in the novel, Walker explicitly calls for a return to animistic spirituality (145; 287–89). While Allen speaks of generations of mothers and grandmothers giving birth to a person, Walker presents a single woman in this text who has experienced memories of reincarnations all the way back to before the evolutionary split of human from hominid. If we accept Walker's depiction of Lissie's reincarnations as an expression of spiritual belief, rather than merely a literary metaphor, then we can conclude that all people are interconnected back through time to the "mother of us all," which genetic researchers claim to have discovered recently. In like manner, then, all exploitation, oppression, and violence are interconnected, so that racism is as much an ecofeminist issue as is environmental exploitation and the oppression of women, inasmuch as each feeds into the other through the debasement of difference and the logic of domination.

Walker, however, does not suggest that everyone need to combat everything. Rather, like the other authors discussed here, Walker seems to prefer to promote addressing the global through attention to the local. Walker's collection of essays, *Living By the Word*, prepares the reader for such a stance. In the Preface to that volume, Walker states: "I set out on a journey to find my old planet. . . . I saw, however, that it cannot tolerate much longer the old ways of humans that batter it so unmercifully, and I spent many hours and days considering how it must be possible to exist, for the good of all, in what I believe is a new age of heightened global consciousness" (xx). Perhaps that is what *The Temple of My Familiar* is all about, consciousness, but an environmentally integrated consciousness rather than the dualistic anti-natural one perpetuated by patriarchy. Like Ursula K. Le Guin in *Always Coming Home* and Marge Piercy in *Woman on the Edge of Time*, Walker avoids providing the reader with a totalizing blueprint. As with the conception of Mattapoisett in Piercy's novel and Sinshan valley in Le Guin's, the new world consciousness Walker depicts is still developing, filled with contradictions, dead ends and errors, and therefore fully alive. Through their panoramic novels, Walker, Le Guin, and Piercy provide readers with ways of thinking about human possibility more than they project human probability. And in all three cases, ecology and feminism are already integrated and mutually reinforcing, with Walker, like Piercy, adding the dimension of race to those of environment and gender.

In the works of Walker, Le Guin, and Piercy, as well as those of Griffin, Haraway and Anzaldúa, the real story for the reader is that of the necessity for, and difficulty of, building healthy new cultures. Such cultures would be able to retrieve lessons from past and current peoples, such as the gynocratic clans of Native American tribes, in order to build contemporary societies capable of regaining ecological balance without forsaking the vision of future ways of living in place and at home. They would also be able to generate multicultural social interactions that recognize the inevitability of difference and conflict without domination or forced assimilation.

There exists a significant body of environmental literature by women, and such writing is being committed by women across the color spectrum as well as genre categories (a convenient multicultural starting point is *Sisters of the Earth* edited by Lorraine Anderson). This literature must be studied, critiqued, and taught, far more widely than has so far occurred. And it might do some good to ask some people: can you really be an environmentalist without being a feminist; and others: can you really be a feminist without being an environmentalist?

So far, the nineties have shaped up as a period of reaction against women and nature. The winding down of the Cold War may very well reflect not a breakthrough into an era of goodwill and peace for all men, but goodwill and peace among men so that they can better exploit and oppress all that they define as not-man, women and nature for example. At the same time, the changes in consciousness and behavior that feminism has brought about in the past few decades will be stifled and suppressed no more easily than the consciousness and behavior that environmentalism has shaped since Earth Day 1970. For both, two decades of advance are currently threatened; integrated they will surely prove more resilient than divided. And to aid in this decade of ecofeminist integration is a growing body of environmental literature by women to facilitate a reconceiving of the relations of both woman and nature and nature and culture, in the process of evolving beyond patriarchy.

Chapter Five

Sex-Typing the Planet: Gaia Imagery and the Problem of Subverting Patriarchy

In recent years, bioregionalists, scientists, ecologists, and poets have reinvigorated the image of this planet as Gaia, Earth-Mother and originating nurturer. Does this re-personification of the planet as a female nurturer truly oppose the patriarchal ideology of domination that destroys the very environment that sustains human life, or does it, through its metaphoric implications, inadvertently reinforce elements of that ideology and thereby limit its own effectiveness in subverting the system it opposes? Can Gaia imagery actually serve to subvert patriarchy when it continues the tendency to sex-type the planet Earth as female? Or do we need to abandon the patriarchal mythologies altogether and develop a culture-building mythopoeic imagery that can progress beyond sex-typing and its inherent ideological limitations?

The Gaia imagery of contemporary ecological consciousness represents part of a broader movement to resacralize nature; it also is the most recent manifestation of the Western tendency to render the planet in female gender terms. Yet, what are the dimensions of such rendering? Although the conception of Earth as Mother/Goddess predates patriarchal cultures, the imagery perceived throughout Western culture derives mainly from patriarchal Greek and Roman mythology.[1] In that mythology, Gaia begins as a parthenogenetic initiator, but quickly becomes subservient to her son-husband, Uranos. As soon as the male arrives, the female loses her independence. Hesiod states that Earth arose first and created Heaven-Uranos "equal to herself," and yet he is immediately deemed "Father Heaven" and gains control of his mother. That the Greeks' respect for Earth was crippled by patriarchal misconceptions, however, does not mean that current users of the myth must necessarily fall prey to sexism; nor does it mean they must only refer to patriarchal perceptions of the Earth goddess. The issue, rather, is whether or not they can use Gaia imagery *without* evoking patriarchal perceptions. It seems highly unlikely that Gaia imagery can be used without invoking any of the Greek patriarchal baggage attached to the symbol. Donald Davis, whom I shall take to task later, argues "for the impossibility of a 'neutral' philosophic position" in relation to perceptions of the "natural world" (152), and supports this position by noting that

The sociology of knowledge position (the Frankfurt School) maintains that our visions of nature reinforce our own prejudices toward each other. And since man's relationship to nature is replicated in man's relation with women, a truly self-consistent biological egalitarianism cannot become socially manifest until the deep ecologists radically accept this view. (152n6)

The ecological rebirth of Gaia imagery was initiated specifically by James Lovelock, Sidney Epton, Lynn Margulis, and others.[2] In 1975, Lovelock and Epton published this statement:

It appeared to us that the Earth's biosphere was able to control at least the temperature of the Earth's surface and the composition of the atmosphere. . . . This led us to the formulation of the proposition that living matter, the air, the oceans, the land surface were parts of a giant system which was able to control temperature, the composition of the air and sea, the pH of the soil and so on as to be optimum for survival of the biosphere. The system seemed to exhibit the behaviour of a single organism, even a living creature. One having such formidable powers deserved a name to match it; William Golding, the novelist, suggested Gaia—the name given by the ancient Greeks to their Earth goddess. (304)

As soon as Lovelock and Epton state this, which seems to have no gender implications given the complexity of the "organism," they refer to Earth as "she." And while the essay is largely free of sexist stereotyping, one may be troubled by these concluding sentences: "In man, Gaia has the equivalent of a central nervous system and an awareness of herself and the rest of the Universe. . . . Can it then be that in the course of man's evolution within Gaia he has been acquiring the knowledge and skills necessary to ensure her survival?" (306). "Man" functions as the intellect and protecter of his mother and mate; *he* ensures *her* survival. Clearly, Lovelock and Epton's purpose in providing such an analogy is to explain the relation of humanity and biosphere and thereby, in part, to counter anthropocentrism. In so doing, however, they unwittingly reinforce androcentrism by rendering the female side of the duality passive. It would appear that the name Gaia is an unfortunate choice as it immediately encouraged stereotypes that reinforce the patriarchal thinking that has produced the very anthropocentrism they oppose.

That this charge is not critical hairsplitting can be seen from Lovelock's later book, *Gaia: A New Look at Life on Earth.* In his opening sentence, Lovelock states that "the concept of Mother Earth or, as the Greeks called her long ago, Gaia, has been widely held throughout history and has been the basis of a belief which still coexists with the great religions" (vii). Lovelock states that he adopted William Golding's suggestion of calling the entity he hypothesized Gaia because "it was a real four-letter word and would thus forestall the creation of barbarous acronyms" (10). The pun hints at a problem that Lovelock failed to realize fully at the time: Gaia designates a female entity; designating an entity female in a patriarchal culture guarantees its subservient status, because, as Karen Warren observes, "a patriarchal conceptual framework is characterized by *value-hierarchical thinking*" that "gives rise to *a logic of domination*" ("Feminism" 6; emphasis in original).

Lovelock seems somewhat aware of this danger when he remarks that "there seems no need inevitably to attribute the pleasure we feel on a country walk, as our gaze wanders over the downs, to our instinctive comparison of the smooth rounded hills with the contours of a woman's breasts. The thought may indeed occur to us, but we could also explain our pleasure in Gaian terms" (142). Lovelock questions the notion that the pleasure stems from sexual identification, but his very example indicates the problem with continued sex-typing: it occurs primarily in female terms that subordinate the planet to the male because the sex-typing occurs within the parameters of a patriarchal culture. Lovelock's comparison may be "instinctive" for heterosexual males, but it is not universal for the "we" that constitutes his audience. Rather, it reflects the dominance of patriarchy in linguistic patterns and authorial habits. He does not, for example, also speak of an "instinctive comparison" for some of the "we" in viewing a glacier-created megalith thrusting toward the heavens.[3] (In *The Greening of Mars*, Lovelock makes significant efforts to avoid such pitfalls; it is *Gaia* and its analogies, however, that have had widespread popularity and influence.)

Let us turn from Lovelock to Bill Devall and George Sessions, authors of *Deep Ecology*, a text that remains one of the most popular introductions to Deep Ecology in the United States. This key ecological document uses Gaia as a consensually recognized term requiring little or no explanation for the book's audience (a number of women writers use the term in the same way, such as Hazel Henderson[205]). Gaia has become an immediately recognized, acceptable ecological term for Earth. And this entity remains unconditionally female in the conception of the men, as well as a number of the women, who dominate the ecological discussions. Even as Devall and Sessions oppose the dominance of "masculine over feminine," they reproduce patriarchal patterns. In their discussion of the "Women's Movement," they are concerned with traits and values they say have been "labeled 'feminine,'" thereby recognizing the problem of sexual stereotyping. And yet, by placing these traits, such as "receptivity . . . listening, patience, nurturing, deep feeling, affirmation, quiet statement," in the section titled "Women's Movement" they reinforce the sex-typing of these concepts and the subordination of women by equating them with "feminine" (335). They do this without distinguishing between socio-gender and bio-gender differences, thus downplaying the reality that "masculine" and "feminine" characteristics exist within each individual and that neither gender holds genetic patent on a particular characteristic. They also, through their choice of terms, reinforce the same kind of stereotype Lovelock and Epton echo when they consider Earth the body and humanity the intelligence of the planet: women are the intuitive, receptive, engendering body; men are the intellectual, initiating, disseminating mind.

In response to such a dichotomy, Michael Zimmerman, in discussing Ariel Salleh's critique of Deep Ecology, raises some significant questions:

> Is the term *woman* meant to refer to the feelings, emotions, and relational sensibility with which many men are out of touch? Yet to conceive of such traits as "feminine" seems to suggest an essentialist and/or genetic doctrine of the differences between men and women: that man is thinker, woman is feeler. Is such a doctrine consistent with the conviction of many feminists that men and women alike are distorted products of the psychological, social and cultural practices of patriarchy? If we humans are essentially or naturally dichotomized by sex-linked traits (reason vs. feeling), then there is no real point in trying to change human cultural practices. (40)

Zimmerman outlines here precisely the kind of problem that arises when a matriarchist conception of women inverts the hierarchical valuation of gender and depicts women as superior to men.[4] Warren criticizes the claims made by some feminists that women are intrinsically closer to nature than men and remarks that "other radical feminists . . . criticize nature feminists for regressing to harmful patriarchal sex-role stereotyping which feeds the prejudice that women have specifically female or womanly interests in preventing pollution, nurturing animals, or saving the planet" ("Feminism" 14). And Ynestra King points out that "this position also does not necessarily question nature/culture dualism itself or recognize that women's ecological sensitivity and life orientation is a socialized perspective which could be socialized right out of us depending on our day-to-day lives" ("Toward" 122).

One sees that Devall and Sessions cannot avoid, anymore than Lovelock or I can, reflecting some of the values of the dominant patriarchal culture in which they live, despite their desire to "see through these erroneous and dangerous illusions" (66). Their adoption of Gaia imagery, as they profess, in its mythic rather than scientific-model role, unfortunately perpetuates some of the very domination patterns they seek to overcome (see 151). In their desire to resacralize nature, they have opted for a feminine stereotyping of the planet that reinscribes, through inverting traditional gender valuation, the patriarchal sex-typing that they seek to subvert. They ask "how can we rediscover the enchantment of Gaia, the sacredness of Gaia, and thus heal ourselves" (152); but the conception of the fertile female as enchanting, sacred, and mysterious is a perception that hinders the healing they seek and emphasizes, inadvertently, the very otherness and alienation they are trying to overcome.

Donald Davis runs into the same problem when, in criticizing Deep Ecology for its rationalistic patriarchal thinking that fails to provide "liberating spiritual wisdom," he names the transforming union of "masculine *and* feminine" knowledge "Sophia, which transcends rationality and intuition to become a *whole* life" (153). He renders reason the province of men and intuition the province of women, and implies that women are *naturally* closer to wisdom through their intuition. This dualistic presentation of intellectual capabilities regresses dangerously close to the male as mind and female as body stereotype of humanity and nature; and, it grievously fails to embody the androgynous perception Davis is trying to conceptualize.[5]

One should also consider the issue of Gaia imagery in larger mythic terms than just those of classical Greece and their contemporary applications. In particular, one needs to view such imagery in the framework of feminist revisionings of a key component of modern patriarchy, the Judeo-Christian "God." For example, Ingrid Shafer in *Eros and the Womanliness of God* presents a conception of the Christian God as female, as well as male:

> Buried deeply near the root of institutional Christianity and threatening the soundness of its foundation there lurks a fatal flaw, the ever-recurring and never-resolved challenge of metaphysical and ethical dualism which not only severs spirit and nature, male and female, autocracy and egalitarianism, *agape* and *eros*, God and the world, but also insists on pronouncing one-half of each pair good and the other evil. (xxv; see also LaChapelle 304-5)

Shafer argues further that "the central insight contained in the mythic formulations of the creation reveals God, that is, the divine original, shaping humanity in 'Its' image, female as well as male, thus demonstrating that the creative source itself is not an 'It' at all . . . but rather the dynamic interplay of primal femininity and masculinity" (xxviii). Gaia was parthenogenetic, and, thus, could not be female until she bore Uranos and created something that could be male, at which point the male could be designated "masculine" and Gaia "feminine." The Greeks had Gaia give birth to a male, rather than another parthenogenetic god, because they could only conceptualize a living being in terms of their culture's dualistic paradigm.[6] Shafer observes that the same dualism entered the Judeo-Christian world and that even though "the Incarnation implies a vision of the Christ (to be distinguished from the historical

Jesus) as male/female," the savior has always been identified as exclusively male (xxviii).

Without entering into great detail, I believe it can be said that god imagery has been, since the morning hours of Western culture, caught up in a dualism that denigrates one half of the mutually constitutive opposites it creates. And although Earth goddess imagery began before patriarchal cultures and outside as well as inside the Western tradition, Greek Gaia imagery specifically began amidst this dualism and has remained largely subject to it. Shafer speaks positively of Gaia imagery because it betokens subculture efforts to maintain the sacred associations of the female along with those of the male. Such is the primary emphasis of the contemporary reintroduction of Gaia imagery. But is this effort to revive a sacred sensibility being bought at the expense of perpetuating the cultural subordination of women, and along with it value hierarchical, dualistic thinking?

The earlier brief treatment of *Deep Ecology* suggests just such an expense on the theoretical and programmatic levels. But what of the literature of ecological consciousness? Perhaps it demonstrates a deeper anti-patriarchal insight, given literature's function as the "antennae" of a culture's intellectual growth. Devall and Sessions heavily promote the poetry of Robinson Jeffers and Gary Snyder, while others in the ecological movement also praise Wendell Berry's writing. And it is in poetry that one should expect to find the most significant, and frequent, use of imagery to present perception. While only Snyder employs the term "Gaia" directly, all three of these ecological poets use what could be considered Gaia, or Earth Mother, imagery.

Jeffers develops a variety of images of nature in his poetry, some of which remain gender free, others of which employ both female and male sex-typing. In the early poem, "Continent's End," he defines the ocean as female and the planet as something preceding both ocean and humanity. In evolutionary terms and in the amniotic metaphor, when Jeffers writes that "we crawled out of the womb," one sees the viability of the "mother" imaging of the ocean. But more importantly, Jeffers concludes, "Before there was any water there were tides of fire, both our tones flow from the older fountain" (1:17). Jeffers avoids limiting this earlier entity's existence by means of a false poetic sex-typing, which helps emphasize the godhead he wishes to imply through an animism that attempts to avoid anthropomorphic deification.

But we see the pull of anthropomorphism running strong as Jeffers sex-types the sea; and in "Night" he defines the sun as male and mortal and the darkness of deep space female and immortal, being caught up in the image of the female as "mystery" (1:114–16). Yet he constantly pulls against this very tendency, always struggling to render nature in nonanthropomorphic terms because of his quest to end humanity's false egotism fed by anthropocentrism and notions of "man" as the image and likeness of God. Interestingly enough, he intuits the Gaia hypothesis in "De Rerum Virtute" when he claims that the "globed earth" does not bring into being entities purely by chance "But feels and chooses" (3:401–403). He then extends such agency to the entire galaxy, a step that many who invoke the Gaia hypothesis do not take. Jeffers spontaneously defines the earth as female in this poem, yet he maintains a gender-free conception of the rest of the universe. As with "Continent's End," a strong tendency exists to define a natural mother, to render the planet the men inhabit female. That this female imaging carries with it a sense of the patriarchal implications of the original Gaia myth may be suggested by this line from another Jeffers poem, "The Beaks of Eagles": "The she-eagle is old, her mate was shot long ago, she is now mated with a son of hers" (2:537). The female is mated to the male, just as Gaia was mated to her son; in him she finds her completion. Sex-typing the planet, even within the parameters of Jeffers's efforts to express the "transhuman glory," leads to a dualistic conception of humanity and planet that too often leaves the Earth in the mother/wife, passive/subordinate position. Such dualism maintains the dichotomies that Deep Ecology seeks to dissolve in its conception of the Earth as an entity of which humanity forms a part. Jeffers's own examples suggest that patriarchal stereotypes form one of the cultural conditions that continuously pulls the individual back from inhumanist transcendence.

Like Jeffers, Berry never speaks explicitly of Gaia. Although in earlier years he emphasized a more animistic and "primitive" conception of the religious, as in "A Secular Pilgrimage," by the time of "The Gift of Good Land," he expressed a clearcut Judeo-Christian conception of God as Father, Earth as Promised Land, and man as steward, in both prose and poetry. But all through his writings, Berry's concern has been primarily with agriculture. This orientation has led to a presentation of the land as not only female but also feminine in a stereotypic sense of being passive, of waiting to be seeded and shaped. Concomitantly, his poetry tends to present the woman in traditional roles in relation to farming. His agricultural division of labor for women and men and his sex-typing of the planet go hand in hand. His male steward is a protective nurturer of the land, the intellect who will "ensure her survival." His "feminine" conception of the land, with all of his reverence, awe, and concern for regeneration, demonstrates the shortcomings of any form of sex-typing. The image of the land as female stereotypes and subordinates both the planet and women, as well as stereotyping men. (It should be noted, however, that Berry has recognized this problem to some extent, as indicated by his excising several of his more problematic pieces from the *Collected Poems*.) Deep ecologists have already attacked the notion of stewardship, with Devall and Sessions criticizing Berry specifically for the limitations of such a concept; as Judith Todd warns, we should be wary of self-proclaimed "stewards" precisely because that term implies another: "stewarded" (433).

With his emphasis on wilderness and the wild as sacred, Snyder has been spared the influence of the agricultural perception of the Earth as recipient of seed (see "Good, Wild, Sacred" in *Practice*). Yet, much of the indigenous and aboriginal cultural heritages he draws on, the "old ways" of which he so frequently speaks, are riddled with chauvinistic conceptions of women, some of which, while reverencing the female/feminine, simultaneously silence and disenfranchise actual women. Snyder has been the male poet who has most pervasively used explicit Gaia imagery. And, as indicated by his references to it in *The Old Ways*, derives the image from both Lovelock and Epton's Gaia hypothesis and the long history of goddess worship (38-40). But while utilizing the image of Gaia in order to promote a reverence for the Earth, Snyder has also recognized its limitations. In "To Hell With Your Fertility Cult," in *The Back Country* (73), he first tried to express a woman's perception of male efforts to revitalize ancient goddess worship and the sexual stereotyping and male dominance implicit in such practice.

But if his use of Gaia in *The Old Ways* and in the Foreword to *Songs of Gods, Songs of Humans* is any indication, Snyder's use has much more to do with the scientific model, the Gaia Hypothesis, than the myth that Devall and Sessions hold up in contradistinction to it. For example, in that Foreword, Snyder states: "This view clearly has relevance, after a lapse of many millenia, to us again: the planet Earth::Gaia must now be seen as *one system*" (viii). Here, as in the hypothesis, Gaia names an entity, a unified biological system; it does not serve as simply a metaphor to emphasize the need to reimage the Earth as sacred (see Martin, "Pattern" 114–16). Similarly, in "Little Songs for Gaia" in *Axe Handles* (47–58), the female dimension of Gaia receives very secondary attention with more of an emphasis on planetary engendering. In a letter to Sherman Paul printed in Paul's *In Search of the Primitive*, Snyder has expressed his recognition of the problem of sex-typing the planet, cultural values, and religious paths. In responding to a remark by Paul calling the solitary quest for enlightenment a "patriarchal" undertaking, Snyder states:

> I'd rephrase it slightly: "To serve the matrifocal values by (not patriarchal but) solitary transcendence." Remove the question of gender. . . .
>
> "Patriarchal values" are values of hierarchy, domination, and centralization—definitely not transcendence. True transcendence *completes* one, with the return to the preciousness of mice and weeds. (299)

This tension between the solitary act and community values is the root of the strength and magic of the Old Ways for Snyder. "Patriarchal" societies become one-dimensional, neither transcendent nor communal—just materialistic and violent (Paul 300).

The use of Gaia imagery is designed to encourage this "return to the preciousness of mice and weeds" that Snyder depicts, yet to the degree to which it carries with it gender stereotypes the imagery interdicts this return by postponing the necessary reorientation of individual perception.[7] As Snyder himself has recognized, as he remarked in an interview with Julia Martin published in 1990, "too many of these people want to jump over the details of biology right back into mythology before they've got themselves grounded in it. So I backed off from the use of the term *Gaia* except as an interesting metaphor. . . . But talking about the plant as Gaia per se will not do the planet a lot of good though" (Martin, "Coyote-Mind 154–55).

I would say it does the planet no good. Sex-typing a gender-free entity invokes and reinscribes not a natural, heterarchical duality of bio-gender whose identity through integration "*completes* one" but a cultural dualism that hierarchically divides. An understanding and elaboration of the distinction between *hierarchical* and *heterarchical* differentiation is a crucial one to make for the development of ecofeminist consciousness, as I argued in Chapter One, particularly in terms of Hazel Henderson's definition of heterarchy. A heterarchical viewpoint can recognize bio-gender differences between women and men as well as "feminine" traits in men and "masculine" traits in women without falling prey to the socio-gender, hierarchical sex-typing rampant in our contemporary culture.[8] It also fulfills that basic ecological principle that diversity is a key component of systemic health (King, "Toward" 119).

Sex-typing a gender-free entity also reinscribes an anthropomorphism that *alien*ates Earth by trying to render it in our image. To say that we must describe it in human terms in order to understand it claims that we and it are separate and *other*. A division that alienates male and female can hardly serve to unite Earth and humanity (see Ruether 203–4). To end the division on both planes we must "remove the question of gender," as Snyder suggests, as a valuating determinant. The difficulty in such a removal can be seen by the tendencies within ecological and feminist theorizing to reinscribe hierarchical gender valuation in some of the very critiques intended to erase it. Davis, for example, repeatedly renders women *spontaneously* superior in the areas of wisdom, knowledge, and ethics: "Wisdom, as a metaphysical category or as a highly intuitive symbolic metaphor, does seem to be an intrinsic characteristic of the feminine psyche"; "Knowledge for the female has been participatory, empathetic, and often 'unconscious'" (156 and 157). Such concepts ignore the social conditioning that all men and women have experienced in patriarchal cultures, deny the need for women to become as actively involved in psychic reintegration and intellectual development, and unconsciously reinforce a patriarchal Judaic idealization of the woman as intuitively knowledgable and, hence, in no need of education. Such a sex-typing conception of wisdom, knowledge, and empathy encourages an idealization and anthropomorphism of the Earth that leads to viewing it as benign and benevolent. As critics of the Gaia hypothesis note, such a view suggests that we need not worry about pollution because Gaia will adapt to compensate for it.

The scientific hypothesis of Earth as a single symbiotic entity works well for changing consciousness. Naming it Gaia, however, fails to encourage the same change through its inadvertent reinforcing of current hierarchical socio-gender stereotypes (Davis's naming wisdom "Sophia" has the same failing).[9] Any sex-typing that occurs within a society heavily laden with patriarchal values cannot expect to avoid reinforcing the gender biases that constitute part of the dominant ideological paradigm. Everett Gendler argues that "to reclaim the matriarchal spirit and our bond with the Earth Mother strikes me as necessary if we are to address at all successfully the ecological crisis confronting us" (143). And Bruce Allsopp observes that "it was much better to conceive the earth as a mother goddess than to treat our environment the way we do" (30). The use of Gaia imagery and the envisioning of the Earth as a sacred female may have been and may remain a necessary step to get people moving toward a higher consciousness, but it cannot serve as the right stride for the path of planet-human harmony.

In a parallel vein, Davis states that "to embrace Sophia as an epistemological equal is to rekindle the dying embers of the feminine fire within each of us. If the use of feminine metaphors can accomplish this, so much the better. To become spiritually whole, the masculine must embrace the feminine in an androgyne act of empathy and love" (162). What is the basis for thinking that such "embers" are dying? Why is the male still the initiator here, the embracer, while the feminine remains passively the embracee? "Dying" implies that in some past golden age an androgynous culture and psyche existed (Sandra Harding argues that the very strength of contemporary epistemology is "the refusal of the delusion of a return to an 'original unity'" [193]); "embrace" implies that men must remain initiators even in the age of androgyny, stereotypically presenting masculine as active and feminine as passive. Domna Stanton, in analyzing the "philosophy of difference" pervading contemporary critical theory, suggests that "it is possible, then, that the feminization of difference and its articulations involve a replaying of that age-old scene in which . . . the male discloses, the female disposes" (158). The description seems particularly applicable to Davis's imagery, as well as to that of humanity as intellect and Earth as body.

Rather than yearning for a nonexistent androgynous golden age in which male and female and humanity and planet harmoniously coexisted, we must look toward creating a new culture and evolving a new paradigm. Charlene Spretnak contends that "every person contains the entire range of options for thinking and behaving; s/he may be predisposed to some more than others, and cultural values will encourage or discourage the development of various options" (Introduction xix). We need a mythos and verbal imagery that can emphasize and promote such cultural equality between women and men, planet and people, and that recognize differences without hierarchically valuating them. Ruether argues that "without sex-role stereotyping, sex-personality stereotyping would disappear, allowing for genuine individuation of personality. Instead of being forced into a mold of masculine or feminine 'types,' each individual could shape a complex whole from the full range of human psychic potential for intellect and feeling, activity and receptivity" (210).

We are moving toward a new paradigm of decentering multiparticipant co-evolution. But to achieve this paradigm shift, we must deconstruct the intellectual edifice of the old paradigm: "This means transforming that worldview which underlies domination and replacing it with an alternative value system" (Ruether 204). We need, in Annette Kolodny's words, to "place our biologically- *and* psychologically-based 'yearnings for paradise' at the disposal of potentially healthier (that is, survival-oriented) and alternate symbolizing or image systems" (159). Deep Ecology needs to recast or cast aside entirely its Gaia imagery, which is trapped in the old paradigm, in order to create a new imagery that can promote rather than hinder the birth of a radically new consciousness:

> What we need is a radically new symbolic mode for relating to "the fairest, frutefullest, and pleasauntest [land] of all the worlde"; we can no longer afford to keep turning "America the Beautiful" into *America the Raped*. The tantalizing possibility that metaphor, or symbolizing in general, both helps to give coherence to the otherwise inchoate succession of discrete sense data, and, also, helps us explore the *possibilities* of experience, suggests that we might, on a highly conscious level, call into play once more our evolutionary adaptive ability to create and re-create our own images of reality. (Kolodny 148)

We must continue the search and discussion for other avenues of conceptualizing our relationship to the rest of the world, and we must do so both through the ways in which we live and the debates we hold over the thoughts and feelings that guide such living.

II

Chapter Six

Somagrams in An/Other Tongue: Patricia Hampl's "Resort"

In *The Flesh Made Word*, Helena Michie claims that "feminist poetry has carved out a special place for the female body and takes a special place in the writing that struggles to represent it" (129); and, further, "at this point in history, feminist poetry seems most nearly to embody feminist theory" (130). Michie is referring to American poetry and theory primarily; but it would have been at least as accurate to claim that American feminist poetry embodies French feminist theory. A case in point is Patricia Hampl's nine-part, thirty-nine page sequence, "Resort," which received positive reviews when it appeared in 1983, but no critical attention. On the back cover the claim is made that "Resort" is "in essence a poem about healing oneself through paying attention to the world outside." Such a description can be interpreted in very different ways. For example, Catharine Stimpson, building on the work of Ellen Moers, has observed that the use of landscape as a means of presenting female sexuality is a "female literary tradition" (191). But Hampl's poem does more than recapitulate a subversive tradition; it also adapts and critiques contemporary feminist ideas about the body, sexuality, and identity. Hampl's somagram can be read as an interrogation of the terrain of French feminist theories that finds them both liberating and limiting, and takes a step beyond the synecdoches that often render them essentialist.

Further, the poem reveals that "the world outside" is much more than landscape, and, if considered closely may even suggest that there is no inside/outside dichotomy, but rather a shifting attention to perceptions of separation and relation. Feminist recognitions of sexuality and embodiment in literature contain tremendous potential for nature-culture revelations, but too rarely are such revelations brought to consciousness by their authors and critics who are ecologically illiterate. As I suggested in Chapter Two, the speaker in "Resort" seems unsophisticated in terms of environmental relatedness, but this is not necessarily a weakness in the poem. Failing to recognize and elaborate the relatedness would, however, be a weakness in the critical interpretation.

Each section of "Resort" is broken into two stylistically different parts, a meditation and a dialogue. Spatializations of scenery occur in the meditations, as seen in descriptions of postcards, letters, and allegorical landscape images. All of these constitute anti-sexual, anti-dynamic forms of denial and repression, expressing stasis, disinterest, and death, and contain traditional male figurations of female identity, as flower, lover, daughter, and embodied fertility: "Though girlish, these roses, flounces of a new dress," for example (41). Nature is landscape, scenery, set piece in these parts, and explicitly gendered. The second, dialogue portion of the text, however, breaks with the monologue's meditational appearance of control; there intrudes a patriarchal, rational, querying voice that establishes a scene of analysis. The purpose of such analysis is to fix the identity of the female protagonist, both in terms of a therapeutic adjustment to society and in terms of a permanent, culturally defined concept of self, like a butterfly pinned to a specimen board. This analytical voice remains constant throughout, defining, limiting, containing: "But—forgive me—we can count on you not to go on and on" (47). But as the sequence proceeds, the female speaker increasingly challenges and disrupts the adjustment to the world that traditional analysis presumes signifies mental health. How can a woman have a healthy adjustment to patriarchy? The arational answers of each analytical dialogue challenge the presumed rationality that the questioner represents and that much of the thoughts in the meditation sections presume. In Part IX, the questioning voice disappears altogether and both the meditations and dialogues are replaced by a section that combines meditation, internal monologue, and direct address.

As the process of constructing an identity is increasingly wrested away from the analyst and his society, through the poem's progression, spatialization gives way to tension; the "rose," for example, becomes an activity rather than an object (79); it is a condition of being and a rupturing by an arational female pleasure of the repressive analytical attempt at patriarchal fixing of identity. This process of identity construction in opposition to the analyst's "rational" questions that emphasize fixity and naming takes the form of a feminist "somagram," the writing of the female body and psyche through language into the male text of reality, which should not be confused with the world. Such a rejection of the analyst must occur in order for development to occur without the individual's subjugation to the patriarchal imperatives of traditional psychoanalysis. Teresa de Lauretis has cogently warned:

> But even when it diverges from the Lacanian version that is predominant in literary criticism and film theory, and when it does pose the question of how one becomes a woman (as does, for instance, object-relations theory, which has appealed to feminists as much as if not more than Lacan or Freud), psychoanalysis defines woman *in relation to* man, from within the same frame of reference and with the analytical categories elaborated to account for the psychosocial develop-

ment of the male. That is why psychoanalysis does not address, cannot address, the complex and contradictory relation of women to Woman, which it instead defines as a simple equation: women = Woman = Mother. And that, as I have suggested, is one of the most deeply rooted effects of the ideology of gender. (20)

Marianne DeKoven argues, in the course of applying Derrida and Kristeva to the somagrams of Gertrude Stein, that repression of the nonlinear, i.e., an alternative consciousness and perception of the world, is the result of the ascendancy of patriarchy and logocentrism that privileges male rationality, which is epitomized by Hampl's stylized analytical voice. Repression of arationality suppresses both the female and the human unconscious (176–81). It also creates the illusion of the world as object, as landscape or place for human action, and as androcentrically manageable. The feminist countermove, as exemplified by "Resort," to express arationality and nonlinear cognition is an attempt through language to render the unconscious consciously recognizable as such. In Lacanian terms, the acquisition of symbolic language following the acquisition of the more basic presymbolic language demonstrates the assimilation of the individual into culture, which is the resolution of the Oedipal crisis by means of a capitulation to the father, and to the Rules of the Father. The move to a presymbolic language, which we find running throughout "Resort," is a move toward a pre-Oedipal stage of being, which if recovered can lead to a passage beyond the post-Oedipal stage of capitulation to patriarchy. Stimpson, adapting Kristeva, refers to this as a post-post-Oedipal stage in which the pre-Oedipal is self-consciously recovered (194).[1]

At the same time, we can interpret the move toward a presymbolic language and toward somagrams as an effort to achieve psychic health in opposition to an acculturated mental illness through embodiment in the world. It is a way to challenge the domination of the androcentric construction of the mind as rational ego by demonstrating the relatedness of mind as part of the body, and consciousness as part, rather than determinant, of mind. And, therefore, it also challenges dualistic and androcentric constructions of human/nature and nature/culture by positing mind as embodied, and the human as *innatured*.

The struggle to *wri(gh)te* the female body through an "other" tongue—the inscribing of the somagram by means, and disruption, of the patriarchal *parole*—is foregrounded through the sequence's concern with language, its self-reflexive dimension in which language explores language, in particular the inability to express anything more than absence. This begins with the simile in which "pink fact" is "like a rumor," and in which, later in the poem, the flowers become allegories for the speaker as child under patriarchal guidance. "Wild roses" are contrasted with the later appearing "cultivated roses" that her father tended, just as the "tender green necks" of the "wild roses," which are broken and maimed, become an allegory for the child's neck later in the recollection, in Part VII, of father and daughter standing in the rain. In particular, the experience with the father is tied into the girl's use of language, of questioning; with the problematics of that questioning having been posited in the first lines of the poem.

Similarly, in Part VIII, the relation between external nature and the construction of self, or internal nature, through *parole*, by others and by the society from which such utterances arise, is made explicit with the role of language privileged. But here the process of interpellation rather than the stasis of absence is emphasized. The first part of VIII's meditation focuses on conversations overheard in a cafe and how they define the other and therefore the self, and then switches to a walk "home through the abandoned resort," during which the protagonist remarks that it is a day not only of rain but also of its promise, which may mean that the speaker not only recognizes the event of this particular weather but also the relationship of rain to other environmental conditions, viewing it as a related process. Hampl intertwines hearing and seeing, language and vision, in Part VIII, to prepare for the self-reflexive transformation in Part IX, where vision, like language leads to identity, but an identity based on difference: "not rose, but rapture" (79). This is not the static naming of domination but the interanimation of self and world.

Throughout the sequence, the actual subject, the cause of the resort to the resort, remains absent. The writing of the body reveals absence and silence, an emptiness at the center from which the speaker must recover, but which cannot be overcome, undone, or refilled. The nine parts of the sequence, and numerous implications, suggest that the woman has either lost an infant in childbirth, had an abortion, experienced a hysterectomy, or some combination of the three—all forms of absence, but the last perhaps most problematic, given the patriarchal conception of woman as essentially mother/childbearer.[2] Hence, the inscribing of the somagram is a struggle against not only patriarchal language, but also patriarchal objectification that intensifies the sense of loss the speaker feels because that loss renders her a woman "which is not one," by virtue of her inability to bear. The refusal to name announces that the specific loss/lack does not matter.[3] Rather, only the oppressive attempts to define woman psychoanalytically as a lack and socioeconomically as an empty vessel for reproduction matter, insofar as the protagonist's recovery as discovery of self-identity repudiates such oppression. Hampl refuses to undertake what Julia Kristeva calls the "thetic function of naming, establishing meaning and signification, which the paternal function represents within reproductive relation" (*Desire* 138). The speaker will not be defined by a single biological attribute, but neither will she deny her body as part of her identity. Her nature is relationship as well as the rupturing or absence of certain relationships.

At the same time, this struggle against patriarchal objectification not only poetically employs significant elements appearing in French feminist thought but also challenges some of the key concepts employed there. In particular, by leaving the absence unnamed, and refusing to allow that which is absent, or absence itself, to serve finally as the defining characteristic of identity, Hampl's protagonist overcomes the tendencies toward essentialism that appear at times in the work of such thinkers as Irigaray, Cixous, Leclerc, and others. Hampl refuses to resort to the standard synecdoches of self-identity, such as lover, uterus, fertility, mother, labia, or clitoris that French feminists and others have tended to employ in reaction against, and as substitution for, the traditional male images of female sexuality and power. As Michie has noted, "full representation of the body is necessarily impossible in a language that depends for meaning on absence and difference." As a result, "the battle against synecdoche has reproduced and replicated synecdoches" (149), and while the imagery employed by French feminists has been valuable in foregrounding the significance of the somagram, and in helping to understand and analyze the burgeoning of somatic writing by women in poetry and prose, it does not suffice to overcome, to vanquish that which it opposes. It subverts, but remains more negative critique than affirmation, since it limits female self-identification to terms that remain vulnerable to patriarchal assimilation and reversion. As Luce Irigaray has recognized, "[woman] finds herself defined as a thing. Moreover, the mother woman is also used as a kind of envelope by man in order to help him set limits to things" ("Sexual" 122). And even anatomical specificity can be made to serve as another type of limit.

For example, Drucilla Cornell and Adam Thurschwell argue that when Kristeva attempts to move toward some type of affirmation through an analysis of motherhood, she theorizes that "woman can overcome the destructive dualities created in the separation from the mother by relating as mothers themselves. This mode of relating, [Kristeva] suggests, gives women an advantaged position in the struggle to overturn existing modes of discourse and social relations" (149). It also, however, would limit the ranks of those capable of such overcoming.[4] That Kristeva's discussion of motherhood should be the main site of her contribution to feminist theory remains doubtful, however, given the attention in her early work to language and analysis.

One could make just such a case for the work of Annie Leclerc. The shortcomings of her work and the inherent conservatism of biological determinism have already been critiqued by Christine Delphy, who observes that "while Leclerc's book [*Parole de femme*] strives to revalue women's procreative functions, it also strives to imprison us in them. . . . In short, she continues to define women in the same way as men (and the general ideology) do: by their relationship to men, and more particularly by their usefulness to men. Our use lies in our ability to bring into the world the only thing men cannot make" (91-92; see also Gallop 322). Like Delphy, Hampl's "Resort" rejects the biology-as-destiny line of French feminist thought exemplified by Leclerc, and promoted by some other American feminist somatic poems, such as ones by Ann Sexton, Robin Morgan, and Erica Jong (see Michie, chap. 5).

But unlike Delphy, who emphasizes political economy and the social relations of reproduction, Hampl focuses in her poem on a line of thought more emphasized by Kristeva and expressed in "Women's Time": "to break the code, to shatter language, to find a specific discourse closer to the body and emotions, to the unnameable repressed by the social contract" (478). Here, language is the focus of attention, not biology or economy. It is, however, language-in-action as a social contributor to the ideological constructions of identity—"the interpellation of individuals as subjects" (see Weedon 30–31)—that are requisite for the continued deployment of patriarchal relations of reproduction and production, and these apply not only to women but also, of course, to the rest of nature, and are founded upon the scientific validation in our culture of objectification as truth finding.

As Kristeva further claims, "the new generation of women is showing that its major social concern has become the sociosymbolic contract as a sacrificial contract" (478); and what greater symbol of sacrifice can there be than the Madonna, the sacrificing mother, an image of woman that remains open to patriarchal recuperation as long as the essence of Woman is sited as that of reproduction. The Madonna, the suffering mother, is also invariably a passive figure, one subject to the destiny of biological sexual difference. The protagonist of "Resort" rejects just such an imposition of a social concept of destiny through a radical practice of feminist self-analysis. In so doing she breaks with the active/passive dualism as well as the instrumental reason that Man employs to define all other entities in terms of their use-value.

Kristeva argues in *Revolution in Poetic Language* that "practice is determined by the pulverization of the unity of consciousness by a nonsymbolic outside, on the basis of objective contradictions and, as such, it is the place where the signifying process is carried out" (203). At such a site stands the protagonist of "Resort" at poem's beginning, but by poem's end a radical transformation has occurred. To quote Kristeva again, "in this moment of heterogeneous contradiction, the subject breaks through h[er] unifying enclosure and, through a leap (laughter? fiction?), passes into the process of social change that moves through h[er]" (205). In "Resort" one finds a self radically reconstited by breaking out of an illusory self-conception imposed by patriarchal ideological apparatuses. And while Irigaray breaks from either the social concepts of woman either as lack or as empty vessel, her own synecdoche of "two lips in continuous contact" suffers from a similar tendency toward biological determinism and an attendant passivity.

Paul Smith notes that "women's efforts to speak and to change patriarchy must first be subverted by a sense of their own specific identity and Irigaray suggests that this identity can itself be funded by reference to a somatic specificity" (144). But if, as a result of the synecdochic character of most—if not all—somatic specificity, the treasury remains impoverished, then such funding will impose a limit on the very liberation that is being attempted (see Stanton 162). While "woman 'touches herself' all the time, and moreover no one can forbid her to do so" (Irigaray, "This Sex" 24), neither does she choose such contact nor does it function as the kind of self-conscious practice that Hampl's protagonist experiences. Rather, as the sequence proceeds, the speaker more and more relearns to touch her body with the rest of the world, although it is the touch of the wild rose, with its thorns, rather than the manipulation of the cultivated rose.

While Hélène Cixous, with her focus on writing and language, tends to avoid this problem of biological essentialism in theory, she often displays it in her imagery, as in her fixation on the maternal, milk-giving breast in "The Laugh of the Medusa." As the *Questions Feministes* editorial collective has noted, "it is worthwhile to expose the oppression, the mutilation, the functionalization and the objectification of women's bodies . . . it is also dangerous to put the body at the center of a search for female identity" (quoted in Smith 145). Identity is never singularly self-determined, but it need not be exclusively culturally determined either, as long as the individual seeks to test such determinations against immersion in the world. I would not conceptualize such immersion in terms of seeking after unmediated experience, but rather of seeking after experience in/with the nonhuman rest of nature as a mediating of cultural determinations of identity. To imagine that mediation only goes from the human to the nonhuman or the culture to the individual is to fail to recognize the necessary reciprocity and "dependent origination" operating in any process or system.

Hampl's "Resort," in its appreciation of the ways in which the protagonist's identity is constrictively constructed by others, including her mother, implicitly critiques any theory that defines woman in terms of a single physiological feature. In its movement toward a "rapture" based on the body as part of the self, but not dependent on any specific anatomical feature, it repudiates any strategy or theory that posits the uterus, the labia, the clitoris, or for that matter physical sexuality per se, as the site of female identity and power. Hampl's sequence succeeds in avoiding the double bind that Domna Stanton posits:

> Clearly, then, the problematic of the unrepresented is not peculiar to the maternal metaphor. It is endemic to any practice that tries to name the unnamed; it is embedded in the bind that all affirmation of difference creates. For either we name and become entrapped in the structures of the already named; or else we do not name and remain

trapped in passivity, powerlessness, and a perpetuation of the same. Either way, to paraphrase Cixous, "we still flounder in the ancience order." (164)

"Resort" refuses to name at the same time that it affirms the power to heal oneself from the patriarchal wound of objectification and functionalization. In so doing, it both enters into dialogue with other feminist somatic poetry, such as the work of Sexton, Plath, Morgan, Grahn, and Jong, as well as somatic criticism, such as the work of Cixous, Irigaray, Leclerc, and others.

Biology as destiny will not lead to the disassembling of patriarchy but to more dissembling, just as the undercurrent anatomical essentialism of much French feminist theory is used to controvert the radicalizing power of its critique. Jane Gallop pointedly notes that "the early mother may appear to be outside patriarchy, but that very idea of the mother (and the woman) as outside of culture, society, and politics is an essential ideological component of patriarchy" (322). I would add that the very idea that culture is outside of nature, or the psyche is inside the mind and not part of the body that is part of nature, is also an essential ideological component of patriarchy. Nature may provide mediating mechanisms for critiquing androcentric truth claims about male-female relationships and objectifying male constructions of female identity, as it is represented as doing in "Resort," but only to the degree that the individual seeking such mediation gains ecological literacy and undertakes ecosystemic thinking.

In addition to its role of repudiation, "Resort" also demonstrates a direction for feminist praxis by means of the text as a practice that demands from the reader not imitation but new and different practice. Kristeva sets up the appropriate analogy:

> The text turns out to be the analyst and every reader the analysand. But since the *structure and function of language take the place of transference* in the text, this opens the way for all linguistic, symbolic, and social structures to be put in process/on trial. The text thereby attains its essential dimension: it is a *practice* calling into question (symbolic and social) *finitudes* by proposing *new signifying devices*. (*Revolution* 210)

"Resort" is to be read not as confession, not as model, but as an illustration of practice, and just as the analyst must disappear from the poem at that point in which the protagonist achieves re-definition, so too the reader must set aside the poem in order to engage in her own re-definition and re-engagement with the world, a step encouraged by the refusal to name the specific loss or to identify the content of "rapture." As Chris Weedon has posited, "at any particular historical moment . . . there is a finite number of discourses in circulation, discourses which are in competition for meaning. It is the conflict between these discourses which creates the possibility of new ways of thinking and new forms of subjectivity" (139). Not only does "Resort" display the victory of one type of such competing discourse over another in the progress of the poem but it also provides an illustration of a new form of subjectivity, a feminist counter to patriarchal interpellations and androcentrism.

Chapter Seven

Ecology and Love: The Spiderwebs of Joy Harjo

I

From the opening poem, "Early Morning Woman," in *What Moon Drove Me To This?*, through "Eagle Poem," which closes *In Mad Love and War*, Native American poet Joy Harjo has combined an abiding ecological awareness of human/world interdependence with an intense love for others, human and nonhuman. Together, these qualities evoke a sense of connection, continuity, and promise best imaged as spiderwebs wet with rain shining and moving in the sun like "early morning woman," who is literally and figuratively pregnant with/in the circle of life. As Harjo remarked to John Crawford and Patricia Clark Smith in an interview a few years ago, "the world is much more fluid and alive and that's how it really works; it doesn't end, you know, just because one carrier dies" (175).

This sense of interconnection and fluidity, with its attendant emphasis on the flow rather than the individual whorl in that flow, is not unique to Harjo, but arises out of her Creek tribal heritage, as well as her storied residence in the Native lands of the Southwest, where she has been living since leaving Oklahoma to attend high school at the Institute of American Indian Arts in New Mexico. In praising her poetic/musical performances as a demonstration of "intertribal oral traditions," Meg Aerol remarked that Harjo "can take you into a future where the red earth reawakens or carry you back to a past forgotten by all but the elders" (19). That storied residence is most vividly imaged in *Secrets from the Center of the World*. Harjo knows well what Patricia Clark Smith, with Paula Gunn Allen, states in "Earthly Relations, Carnal Knowledge": "Long before *context* became an academic buzz word, it was a Spider Woman word. It speaks of things woven together, and of understanding the meaning of a thread in terms of the whole piece of goods. For southwestern American Indians, that whole is the land in its largest sense" (176). As Harjo wrote for Cynthia Farah's *Literature and Landscape*, "the compelling spirit, or at least a powerful and recognizable force behind what I write, is certainly the Southwestern landscape" (32).

It is important to note that both terms, "ecology" and "love," have to be understood in multifaceted senses in order to address the interanimating characteristics of Harjo's poetic cosmos. For Harjo, ecology is not only a viewpoint on the "natural world" but a viewpoint on humanity's participation in that world as one of its natural elements as well, whether a person is under the stars or the neon on any given night. In "To a Black-haired Daughter Sleeping" (*What Moon* 4), Harjo expresses this elemental sense through an interpretation of her nine-month old daughter's dreams, in which Rainy Dawn remembers our most ancient evolutionary aerobic ancestor, "the first fish that walked" (*What Moon* 4). Ecology is also a viewpoint on the spiritual realm in which all of the aspects of nature, human and nonhuman, participate, as seen in her conception of *Secrets from the Center of the World*: "In a misty dawn at the center of the world is the morning star, tending cattle at the other side of this fence. Several years away you can see smoke from a hogan where an old man is cooking breakfast. He has already been outside to pray, recognized the morning star and his relationship to it, as he stands at the center of miracles" (14); and, again, later in that book: "This earth has dreamed me to stand on the rise of this highway, to admire who she has become" (50). In these last two lines abides a wondrous dehomocentric, heterarchical stance, well known by animistic, indigenous cultures, and claimed by many contemporary Native American writers.

Love is human, certainly physical as sensual pleasure and procreative power, for Harjo. In "Round Dance Somewhere Around Oklahoma City/November Night" (*What Moon* 5), she recalls not only sexual pleasure but also the powerful fecundity from which it arises. And in "Kansas City," from the "Survivors" section of *She Had Some Horses* (33–34), Harjo tells once more of her poetic character Noni Daylight, now at a point of recollecting the many different fathers of her children, and affirming the multiplicity of her loving. Yet this love is not simply anthropocentric, for as Patricia Clark Smith notes, "Her children of different colors are comparable, in their beautiful singularity, to the each-ness of stars and horses. Noni's children, Noni's men, and Noni herself are singular and vitally connected with that natural universe of stars and horses" ("Earthly" 195). I think it important to note that Patricia Clark Smith uses the word "singularity" rather than "individuality," and thereby maintains the sense of interrelationship, a volitional interdependence, that a contemporary ecological sense of personhood would recognize, whereas individuality carries with it notions of autonomy and separateness that arise only within an alienated culture, such as the dominant one in the United States. As Harjo remarked in an interview just before the publication of *She Had Some Horses,* "The world is not disconnected or separate but whole. All persons are still their own entity but not separate from everything else—something that I don't think is necessarily just Native American. . . . All people are originally tribal, but Europeans seem to feel separated from that, or they've forgotten it" (Bruchac 92).

Harjo's poems also celebrate love as more than human and as spiritually powerful, as in "Song for the Deer and Myself to Return On" from *In Mad Love and War* (30). This may not at first seem a love poem because it does not record a sexual romance between lovers, as many of Harjo's poems do. Rather, it records two other kinds of love, that between friends bonded by heritage and shared wisdom, as indicated by its dedication to Creek elder Louis Oliver, and between humans and deer, who are bonded by ecosystemic connections and mutual respect. The spiritual power arises from the success of the song and the speaker's faith that an even more powerful song of love can be discovered "to get them back, to get all of us back"—"them" being the deer recalled from memory and the spirit world to revitalize the speaker. Harjo's use of "back" plays on its multiple meanings, of both a return to a previous state and a regaining of something lost from the past. To reclaim the deer requires reclaiming the heritage in which the deer and the people played out their lives together, *and* realizing that heritage as cultural practice in the present-day world of Kansas cities, white ranchers, telephone lines, airplane trips, and far-away poetry readings to earn a living to raise two children.

Love in Harjo's poetry also widens out beyond one-to-one relationships, to become tribal, ecosystemic, and materially universal. Love becomes a crucial thread in the web that can heal family, tribe, and earth, as in "The Blanket Around Her," from *What Moon* (10). There Harjo calls on a woman to remember who she is: "it is the whole earth." It is the search for such love and the faith in its existence expressed in the poem "Grace" (1), which sets the tone for Harjo's *In Mad Love and War*, her most recent collection. At poem's end, the speaker declares that she knows that there is something greater than just "the memory / of a dispossessed people. We have seen it." Here "it" refers back to the finding of "grace," which the speaker defines as "a promise of balance." This promise hearkens back to Harjo's previous collection, *Secrets from the Center of the World*, the place from which balance arises. At that book's end she guarantees that "It is more than beautiful at the center of the world" (60).

II

While I might claim that it is more than beautiful to read Harjo's poetry, I will not claim that ecology and love are at the center of her poetic world. Rather, let me contend that ecology and love are intertwined, if not in a particular poem then throughout a volume, in such a way that to ignore one is to fail to appreciate the other. Likewise, I will not claim that my readings here are adequate to the Native contexts in which they are written and to which they turn repeatedly, but only that ecology and love are already part and parcel of one another in inhabitory cultures, and that the ecology and love that Harjo expresses are crucial lessons that all readers of her poetry need to learn. More modestly, let me argue that my appropriation of Harjo's poems to elaborate the spiderweb of ecological consciousness and belief, particularly in an ecofeminist sense, is justified by the themes and imagery apparent in these poems, both when their indigenous contexts are recognized and even when they go undetected as a result of critical ignorance.

Lynda Koolish, in her essay "The Bones of This Body Say, Dance: Self-Empowerment in Contemporary Poetry by Women of Color," claims that "the journey to transcendence, to self-celebration, begins with anger at cultural, economic, physical, and psychic violence. Resistance to violence, the determination—even in the face of death—to not be a victim empowers the poetry of Third World women writers" (1–2).[1] All but the beginning of this quotation rings true for me, with the focus on "transcendence" and "self-celebration" troubling in relation to published contemporary Native American women poets as a group. Much better, I believe, than "transcendence" is the term "transformation," which appears in the first sentence of "The Bones of this Body." The effort to recuperate a term popularized by a nineteenth-century New England Romantic movement, derived from eighteenth-century German idealist philosophy emphasizing the process of thought over the objects of sensory experience, seems particularly inappropriate for application to this continent's first human inhabitants (see Momaday 15).[2] Gerald Vizenor, speaking of "traditional tribal people," has remarked that "to imagine the world is to be in the world; to invent the world with academic predications is to separate human experience from the world, a secular transcendence and denial of chance and mortalities" (qtd. in Ruoff 24).

It is toward transformation that I think Harjo is headed, and she draws such a goal from the tribal traditions she invokes particularly and perhaps most spiritually in *Secrets*. Koolish's intentions in attempting to recuperate "transcendence" for women poets of color are praiseworthy, but the term is so imbricated in Western tradition, especially mind-body dualism, that I do not see how it can be accurately applied to other types of spirituality and philosophy.[3]

In contrast, Jim Ruppert claims of Harjo that "her poems recognize the problems of covering that distance [between the mundane world and mythic space], while presenting the perceptions of fusion or connectedness which are necessary to *transform* mundane reality" (31; my emphasis). Similarly, I would argue that Harjo's "Grace," as well as many other *In Mad Love and War* poems, remains steadfastly hopeful and *non-transcendent*. The speaker is too rooted in history and survival to opt for an idealistic overriding of the reality that Native American peoples must work through in order to survive and eventually thrive: "But reaching a state of internal grace does not necessarily solve external problems of murder, genocide, and ongoing history, and thus 'Grace' introduces Harjo's ongoing search for what lies beyond grace itself" (Lang, "Through Landscape" 158). The speaker anticipates and deflates any reader's tendency toward an idealized conclusion about the finding of grace. Commenting that she would like to be able to tell the reader that the characters, having gained grace, "picked themselves up" and went forward into a "spring thaw," the speaker admits instead that "We didn't; the next season was worse." Spring here is clearly not a single season, but an age. Yet even as there is no transcendence, there is also no despair because the speaker retains the vision of Spring: "We have seen it," and will continue to work, and love, and be crazy in the service of that vision, that "promise of balance." To claim transcendence or to seek it even at this point in the poem would deny the necessity and the benefit of the work of author James Welch, identified in the dedication and addressed directly in the poem. "Grace" enables Welch, Wind, and the speaker, to continue the struggle believing in the possibility of walking in balance, which is to walk in beauty; but in either case it is to continue "walking." The revolution requires transformation, and transformation requires not only the survival but also the rebuilding of community.[4]

Transcendence remains at root in Western tradition anti-material, a denial of humanity's position as part of a larger nature, rather than its alienated other, its conqueror or victim, and I will have more to say about transcendence in the next chapter. Even Harjo's poetic "otherself," the individualistic Noni Daylight (Lang, "Twin Gods" 42–43; see also Wiget), ends up being held, by the trains shuttling through Kansas City bound in a web of love and interdependence with her many lovers and children. Harjo expresses all the anger and resistance of which Koolish speaks, although in a poetry far less direct than a Chrystos or a Sonia Sanchez, but she has larger worlds to celebrate than herself as individual. She will celebrate herself as poet, which means a carrier of messages among worlds. As for her role as teacher, she told Crawford and Smith that "I figure I'm there to educate people to the diversity within themselves and the diversity in America" (174). And Harjo recognizes clearly that such diversity cannot be explained by running a riff solely of transcendental notes: "It frightens me to think that while we're moving among this incredible beauty we have to recognize the other side, and how do you do that without being sucked in? I've noticed that the last few years of my life I'll get to places or plateaus where one day I can understand this amazing creation, the amazing beauty and the intricacies and so on, and the next day it seems like I'm just at the other end of it, and everything is so blank and not clear. And *then* I see it all, then I understand" (Crawford and Smith 178). Such a moment of vision, I would argue, is the apprehension of the spiderweb, the ecological matrix.

III

Patricia Clark Smith contends that "American Indian people—even urban dwellers—live in the context of the land. Their literature thus must be understood in the context of both the land and the rituals through which they affirm their relationship to it. Women and female sexuality are at the center of many of these rituals" (176). And so begins *What Moon Drove Me To This?*, with "Early Morning Woman," in which the sun, the child, and the woman are part of one circle (3). Such interconnectedness may be easy to feel as a pregnant woman near term, or as the nine-months-old "girlchild" of "To a Black-haired Daughter Sleeping" (4). But it is not easy, it is nearly impossible, for a hunter "who is all these years emptyhanded," in "Chicago or Albuquerque" (*What Moon* 6), and the poet feels deeply for this externally imposed disenfranchisement from the land and attendant loss of dignity (cf. Ruppert 29). This same loss of dignity accounts for the uncertainty in the next poem of *What Moon Drove Me To This?*, "Answer to Your Letter / Dated: The Long Winter" (7). The instability of marriage and the waywardness of the man are the result of this long, "unusual winter" resulting from Anglo-European domination of North America and its indigenous cultures. This does not mean that Harjo has Indian women assume the position of uncomplaining, ever-forgiving victim. For her the definition of "stand by your man" is very different from Country-Western tradition.

In "Conversations Between Here and Home" and "I Am A Dangerous Woman," Harjo presumes the continuity of the gynocratic, women's leadership heritage of many tribes (*What Moon* 18–19). "Early Morning Woman" is also "Dangerous Woman" because oppression has damaged tribal, clan, and familial links and the respect and authority of women within those cultural forms of human relationship. But the "angry women," let there be no doubt, will reclaim their position and, those who still want them, their husbands, because they "are building / houses of stones" (18). But, most of the poems of distress and dysfunction appear in the "Winter" section of the book, with an increasing emphasis on trickster behavior, passion, and success in the "Summer" section, as when in "3AM" the speaker concludes that even at this hour one can "find the way back" (43); and the last poem is "Morning Once More" (68).

Throughout her first full-length book, Harjo weaves poems of promise, plenitude and salubrious rituals, such as the appeal to the four directions in "Four Horse Songs," and mythic magic, such as the thirty-year dancing crow or the "Kansas City Coyote," among poems that expose the depradation experienced by Native peoples. Repeatedly she returns to the land and to love, in order to offer the promise of survival and celebration, as in the facing poems "The Blanket Around Her" and "San Juan Pueblo and South Dakota Are 800 Miles Away on a Map" (10–11). In the former, as I have mentioned, the poet admonishes a woman to remember that she is "the whole earth." In "San Juan Pueblo," the love of the one Southwestern woman for a Pine Ridge Sioux and the other's sharing in her pleasure bridge tribal and regional differences, even as Harjo posits the respective strengths of the characters as residing in their rootedness in place.

Rootedness in land and love can only result from respect, ritual, and reclamation. Both land and love must be accepted on their own terms, whether as trickster coyote or Grandmother Spider. As Patricia Clark Smith notes, "what does pulse throughout Harjo's work is a sense that all landscape she encounters is endowed with an identity, vitality, and intelligence of its own" ("Earthly" 195). And all lovers are in some way connected with the land, or else their failings/departures/disasters result from disconnection with the land. Speaking of "September Moon" in *She Had Some Horses* (60), Patricia Clark Smith concludes that "the land and the person acknowledging each other as living beings, sensate and sensual, their lives inextricably woven together in Spider Woman's Web—this is what lies at the heart of American Indian ritual and southwestern American Indian women's writing" ("Earthly" 196).

Certain singularities have a special role to play in voicing this mutually constitutive acknowledgment of the relational *anotherness* of humans and other actors in the natural world. Harjo in interviews speaks of being a carrier of the message and bearing a special responsibility here and now. In *She Had Some Horses*, the poem "For Alva Benson, And For Those Who Have Learned To Speak," addresses this responsibility as being that of all mothers who have learned to speak to the earth in answer to its speaking to/through them. Alva Benson, who has grown up bilingual in Navajo and English, has also learned, in contradistinction to the recent settlers who are deaf and dumb to it, to speak not only for herself but also for the ground, "its voice coming through her" (18). Harjo's poem encapsulates Patricia Clark Smith's claim that "ritual is the means by which people, spirits, rocks, animals, and other beings enter into conversation with each other. One major part of people's ritual responsibility is to speak with these nonhuman entities and to report the conversation" (177). Such reporting is fundamentally a dehomocentric ecological orientation toward the heterarchical character of biological diversity. Harjo in "For Alva Benson" emphasizes the importance of matrifocal ritual by imaging this responsiblity specifically in terms of birth and rebirth. "One Cedar Tree," later in the volume (24), echoes these relationships again, as the speaker recounts her practice of praying to a cedar tree outside her window. And the connections between the singularity with such responsibility and all those who have gone before her in maintaining this human-nonhuman dialogue are invoked in the conclusion of "Skeleton of Winter" where Harjo declares: "I am memory alive" (31).

IV

Secrets from the Center of the World, being a combination of Harjo's prose poems with the photographs of Stephen Strom, represents a departure from her other volumes of poetry, but reflects her multi-talent artistic interests.

Harjo began her artistry not as a wordsmith but as a painter and even after being adopted by the poetic voice studied filmmaking and has undertaken screenwriting; she also plays the saxophone (Crawford and Smith 173). The marriage of voice and visual images, of picture and text, then, should come as no surprise. But what may surprise readers is the apparent lack of tension, and ecstatic celebration of human-environment interanimation, running throughout, in stark contrast to so much of the recording and bemoaning of alienation to be found in other writing about human-nature interaction. Clearly, the land framed by the photos evoked these emotions, and Harjo declares in the Preface that the land speaks, and she has attempted to lend that voice words by which outsiders might, if not understand, at least appreciate the life of this Native-peopled place. "Strom's photographs," according to Harjo, "emphasize the 'not-separate' that is within and that moves harmoniously upon the landscape. . . . The land in these photographs is a beautiful force, in the way the Navajo mean the word 'beautiful,' an all-encompassing word, like those for land and sky, that has to do with living well, dreaming well, in a way that is complementary to all life" (n.p.).

The prose poems of *Secrets* are written after the photographs and, as a result, a text such as this chapter cannot do them interpretive justice. As Nancy Lang observes, "both text and picture working together also develop an interlocking double statement of story (or poem) and landscape (or photograph) that fuses into a powerful statement of physical and spiritual place" ("Through Landscape" 154). For example, in the first poem-photograph pairing, Harjo writes of the "fool crow" near the corral, and ends with his laughing over the "centuries of heartbreak and laughter" (2). But to appreciate this emphasis on the crow rather than the "house" or the people implied by the opening word "my," one has to notice the way that the unplotted land fills the photograph, and the corral and house with its pickup truck are off-centered, barely within the frame—as if they were late arrivals at the celebration presided over by this clown/trickster figure. The second pairing again addresses the trickster, but now it is three crows, who "at the edge of the highway, laughing, become three crows at the edge of the world, laughing" (4). In the photograph, however, there is neither any highway or any crows; just the "red earth" offering the viewer another perspective. For Harjo, this perspective is one of identification of human and land in the force that she has defined as "beautiful." The subjunctive clause of this second pairing, "if you look with the mind," becomes crucial for entry into the pairings that follow.

When Harjo writes in the third pairing of "two red stars" and universal energy flow, while the reader is viewing a photograph with two telephone poles framing a depression in the desert, it is the mind that must link with "galactic memory" (6). And it must do so at a level beneath the dominant culture's mania for the illusory rationality of Enlightenment beliefs (what Gerald

Vizenor names "terminal creeds" in *Bearheart*), the Cartesian dualistic legacy that separates mind and body, human and earth. Harjo's attention to the transiency of particular manifestations of energy as humans, as deserts, as stars, evokes what she claims elsewhere: "the world is not disconnected or separate, but whole"; with that wholeness understood as process, not stasis. This attention is, in effect, her response to the complaint she makes of the English language: "I have felt bound by the strictness imposed by its male-centeredness, its emphasis on nouns." But she will not remain bound: "So, it's also challenging, as a poet, to use it to express tribal, spiritual language, being." And when pressed on this issue of language by Laura Coltelli in the interview from which these words are taken, Harjo said that she saw herself contributing to that language: "a certain lyricism, a land-based language" and "the spirit of place" (Coltelli 62–63).

This "spirit of place" remains participatory throughout the volume, sometimes for the observer and at other times for other kinds of "people": crows, humans, horses, bears, and even "a skinny black dog" (12). And that participation stretches across the eons of time. In the piece I quoted at the beginning, Harjo writes of the old man praying outside his hogan as being "several years away" from "a misty dawn at the center of the world" (14). And on Moencopi Rise the "I" participates in the moment not only with that skinny, hungry dog she feeds and "the frozen memory of stones," but also with those who have gone before and, like her, have just been passing through this place: "Nearby are the footprints of dinosaurs, climbing toward the next century" (12). The play on words here calls into question conventional notions of temporal linearity. Were the dinosaurs climbing toward the next century of their period on the earth, as the narrator of the poem is also climbing toward the fast-approaching twenty-first? Or could it be the case that all physical beings are dinosaurs, no greater and no less diminished than those vari-sized reptiles, and neither any more enduring? Have we as "Americans," rather than inhabitory people, become locked into certain mindsets and practices that may prove the equivalent of the great meteor cataclysm of the reptile kings? And, if so, have we already become obsolete in an evolutionary sense, while some among us are "climbing" toward a transformation to *homo eco-ludens* (humans-playing-in-place)?

Perhaps the horses "Near Shiprock," who shake their heads at human behavior, have a better sense of the situation than the federal government and the power companies responsible for "the smoking destruction from the Four Corners plant" (16). The horses are the ones who run toward "the vortex of circling sands where a pattern for survival is fiercely stated" (16). And that vortex may be read in many ways, particularly as a symbol of female power, of the circle of life, of the processes of "galactic memory" identified earlier, and of the survival of Native Americans in the face of attempted genocide. As Harjo told

Joseph Bruchac, "it's like a big joke that any of us are here because they tried so hard to make sure we weren't, you know, either kill our spirits, move us from one place to another, try to take our minds and to take our hearts" (91). Lang correctly notes that beneath the ecstasy and the wonder of *Secrets* "also quietly develops a subtext that comments and explains Harjo's indirectly stated anger at Anglo past and continuing domination and exploitation of Native American lands and peoples" ("Through Landscape" 157).

Throughout *Secrets* it is the larger patterns identified that provide the cause of celebration, of ecstasy, of "faith," which Harjo invokes. It is not humanity as entity that is the focus of her pleasure, but humanity's participation in larger relationships, specifically of community in place in time. But all of this larger patterning does not lead Harjo to determinism, fatalism, or an escapist sense of survival. Process remains filled with possibility, random and chosen behaviors. Near the end of *Secrets* she claims: "I am witness to flexible eternity, the evolving past, and I know we will live forever, as dust or breath in the face of stars, in the shifting pattern of winds" (56). I believe that the word "flexible" proves crucial here. There is a cosmic destiny that will not be denied, but there is flexibility between now and then. And the ability to realize in that flexibility a healthy humanity depends on walking in beauty, remaining grounded by realizing the spirit of place, the earth-house-hold of this biosphere. Harjo ends *Secrets*: "It is an honor to walk where all around me stands an earth house made of scarlet, of jet, of ochre, of white shell. It is more than beautiful at the center of the world" (60).

V

Indeed, it is more than beautiful there, but it is difficult for the descendants of the peoples of pre-contact inhabitation to remain there, or even to feel that center at times in modern day "America." With *In Mad Love and War*, "Harjo returns more directly," according to Lang, "to her ongoing socio-political concerns with memory, history, anger, and contemporary life" ("Through Landscape" 157). Harjo said to Coltelli that these new poems "are not so personal. . . . they aren't so personally revealing, and the space has grown larger. . . . there is even more traveling into the inner landscape" (65). "Grace," the opening poem of this volume, already discussed, serves as a preface or foreword to the rest of the poems, which are divided unevenly into two sections, the smaller "The Wars" and the larger "Mad Love."

"The Wars" opens with "Deer Dancer," its title signalling the entry of "myth" into the subject matter. But here, as in *Secrets*, the mythic and the mundane, two manifestations of the real world, intermingle in an ecology encompassing mysteries as well as microbes. The emphasis of the poem is on the debilitated conditions of the speaker and her peers, "Indian ruins" (5). But as debilitated is the woman who functions as the deer dancer, at least in her initial rundown manifestation. It is her other manifestation, however, that the poem's speaker and her fellow "ruins" must see: "She was the myth slipped down through dreamtime" (6). As the speaker imagines her as the mythic figure of the dancing deer woman, she also feels the presence of her ancestors, and is beginning to learn how to survive that next worse season named in "Grace"; which is to say, she is recalling the richness of a people in place connected to a web comprising a community through time that can be recovered and reborn.

The possibility of such recovery is reiterated in the second poem in its title, as well as its text, "For Anna Mae Pictou Aquash, Whose Spirit Is Present Here and in the Dappled Stars (for we remember the story and must tell it again so we may all live)" (7–8). Harjo begins with images of Spring and the parallel of the speaker waking from the dream world each morning. In this poem about a young AIM activist (the facts provided in a footnote) and the speaker's spiritual affinity for her, Harjo links the two worlds by identifying Aquash's activism with the previous poem's deer dancer, and both of them with the people's surviving Winter. This linkage suggests that whatever form restored tribal community may take, that form must be based on the inclusion of the mythic and the mundane, and a rejection of the dominant culture's secular and nature-alienated world.

One could say that much of the rest of this first section of *In Mad Love and War* reflects the speaker's working through her anger and her identification with other struggles of self-determination and liberation in North America and elsewhere. For example, "Strange Fruit" speaks of an NAACP activist lynched in California in 1985, while "Resurrection" is addressed to a mountain town in Nicaragua. "The Wars" ends, however, with "The Real Revolution Is Love," which conflates times and places and critiques the rationalistic language of "politics" that speaks only in terms of ideologies in the abstract. The speaker's identification, in the end, with the Nicaraguans is not on the basis of the rhetoric of revolution espoused by the chauvinistic males seeking sex with their exotic visitors. Rather, it is on the basis of a shared history of restoring their relationships with the land that has shaped them as a people: "This is not a foreign country, but the land of our dreams" (25). Yet it is not the dreams that will realize the land, but the land with the people reworking their relationship to it that will realize the dreams—and, concurrently, end the nightmares depicted in previous poems.

"Many of the poems," claims Lang, "making up the second section, 'Mad Love,' begin to provide answers for her earlier nightmares and terrors" ("Through Landscape" 161). The land and its history of relationship with inhabitory peoples are imaged in the first two poems of this section, "Deer Ghost" and "Song for the Deer and Myself to Return On." I have already discussed the latter of these. The former sets the deer wandering through a cityscape locating the speaker and calling on her to reclaim her heritage. The deer metonymically represents that heritage, in that "it has never forgotten the songs" (29). And the choice of the deer for this role evokes the ecological relationships of past cultural practice.

Frequently, the poems that follow these "deer songs" focus on human relationships and struggles, addressing death, wild youthfulness, and the "Indian" lost in the cityscapes of the new America (see Lang, "Twin Gods"). But "Transformations" suggests that even the darkest pictures that have been painted do not lead to a perpetual night. Here, in a prose poem set in the city, Harjo argues that hatred, pain, bitterness can be transformed within an individual's spirit (59). But the promise of the reknitting of the cultural web and the ecological web is only foreshadowed by the invocation of the image of animals in the heart; it is announced in the following depiction of reciprocity: "Down the street an ambulance has come to rescue an old man who is slowly losing his life. Not many can see that he is already becoming the backyard tree he has tended for years" (59). The final "Eagle Poem" is set off from the preceding section and serves as the coda to the volume in the way that "Grace" serves as its prologue. It reiterates reciprocity by commenting on the process of prayer: "To pray you open your whole self" to the rest of the world and know that there is more to it than what is apparent (65); the spiritual and the material are all one world. The blessing received by an eagle's returning visit requires of the speaker an enunciation of the responsibility reciprocity entails. And this process of bringing into being the balanced practice of humanity in the ecological web needs to be done "in beauty."

"Transformations" reminds us that balance is not a place or an achievement but an ongoing process, a flow of energy that each person engages in, like the old man of that poem before he leaves this existence. Thus, in response to the images and dreams of death, as well as the experiences of violent and senseless deaths that Harjo has depicted, she can write in "Eagle Poem," proudly and joyfully, that people are genuinely blessed as a result of knowing that they live and die in a "True Circle of Motion" (65).

VI

Although the emphases change and Harjo's concerns expand across a range of cultural and multicultural issues, connections between ecology and love are to be found in all of her books, stronger and more ecstatic in some and more subtle and troubled in others. Harjo is not a "nature poet" in the narrow sense that some critics use; few Native American writers are. But she is a visionary poet, and her vision includes an adaptive perception of the ecological web in which Native American peoples must establish a balanced position to survive, as well as a recognition that all peoples must adapt themselves in their own specificities to the larger circles of life through which balance, and beauty, may be conceptualized, reinstated, and maintained. These are the spiderwebs of joy that each of us needs to embody in our daily lives, and their embodiment begins with memory: "Remember that you are this universe and this universe is you" ("Remember," *She Had Some Horses* 40).

Chapter Eight

"A Mountain Always Practices in Every Place": Climbing over Transcendence

Partly because so much of the nature writing in the United States is heavily indebted to Thoreau and Emerson, and partly because so much of it either reflects a Romantic, nostalgic idealism or at least opens itself to such a reading by critics so oriented, "transcendence" proves to be a seemingly ubiquitous term in ecocriticism. It is used in a variety of ways, some mutually contradictory, ranging from purely secular notions of maturing beyond a certain phase of cultural norm or personal practice, to purely religious escatological visions of rising above all that is physical, finite, and mortal. To my mind, it is fundamentally anti-feminist, non-dialogical, and contrary to the inhabitation that we need to learn for an environmentally ethical life practice.

In this chapter, I want to consider a single author whose work has often been the object, or the excuse, for discussions of—and longings for—transcendence, and suggest some of the ways by which this term needs to be problematized from the perspective of a sophisticated ecocriticism, and from the perspective of a multicultural perception and conceptualization of being in the world. Whereas other cultures and religious traditions have been described and analyzed as being "transcendental" or seeking "transcendence," I believe that this concept remains an exclusively western product based on the idealism of mind-body dualistic thinking, particularly as it was refined in the eighteenth and nineteenth centuries. Just as with sex-typing the planet, I would like to see a moratorium on the use of "transcendence" in ecocritical articles, and an attendant search for more exact, detailed, and non-Romantic terms to define the perceptions and configurations of being in the world that are to be found in contemporary environmental writing.

I

"A Mountain always practices in every place" (98), according to Zen Master Dōgen in the "Mountains and Waters Sutra" (*Sansui-kyo*, presented as a lecture in 1240). While Gary Snyder considers this sutra and Dōgen's other writings extremely significant for his own understanding, this single statement displays the focal point for analyzing Snyder's spirituality and the relationship of his literature to the notion of transcendence. The word transcendence has been applied many times to Snyder,[1] and not surprisingly so, whether defining him in relation to a Western Romantic tradition of poetry and nature writing, such as a Thoreau-Whitman-Snyder genealogy, or in relation to an Eastern religious metaphysics, such as Hindu kalpa cycles, the Zen Void, and *samsara*.[2] I would like to suggest that such a term has been far more problematic than the critics who have applied it seem to realize. Snyder himself suggested over twenty years ago in "Poetry and the Primitive" that the concept was insuffi- cient for defining his practice:

> The goal of Revolution is Transformation. Mystical traditions within the great religions of civilized times have taught a doctrine of Great Effort for the achievement of Transcendence. This must have been their necessary compromise with civilization, which needed for its period to turn man's vision away from nature, to nourish the growth of the social energy. The archaic, the esoteric, and the primitive tradi- tions alike all teach that beyond transcendence is Great Play, and Transformation. . . . After the mind-breaking Void . . . is a loving, simple awareness of the absolute beauty and preciousness of mice and weeds. (*Earth House Hold* 128)

Before detailing the hows and whys, then, of mountains practicing in every place, we need to rethink the word transcendence.

The verb "transcend" in English derives from the Latin *transcendere*, liter- ally "to climb over" (*trans* = "over" and *scandere* = "to climb"). But we also know that *trans* means "across," so that *trans* translated as *over/across* has to do more with a relationship, a contact with that which is being "climbed," rather than a separation or a value-laden distance, such as that implied by "above" or "beyond." Thus, when one turns to a dictionary for the usages of the words "transcend" and "transcendent," a problem immediately arises, particularly in the fields of philosophy and theology, because the definitions are peppered with such words as "beyond," "superior," "separate," and "apart." For example, Kant uses it to mean "beyond human knowledge" and others use it to mean "existing apart from the physical universe." Thus, definitions in currency today derive from and perpetuate a dualism that relies on a singular interpretation of the bound prefix of the word rather than its root morpheme: "over" displaces "to climb" in significance for most of those who wield the word.

Masao Abe argues, however, that in Dōgen's understanding of Buddhism, a reversal or returning to the root occurs: "Dōgen carries the dehomocentric nature of Buddhism to its ultimate end by transcending the dimension of gen- eration-extinction," and "transcending" here means precisely "moving to and then breaking through" (41). A detached engagement is the basis of Dōgen's understanding of Buddha-nature and is also the orientation that Snyder assumes by saying that his practice is Zen.[3] As Charles Molesworth notes, in discussing the theme of the "Burning" section of *Myths & Texts*, "put simply, this theme would argue that the physical world might be treated as an illusion, but it is an illusion that must be worked with and worked through" (39). Despite the old Chinese saying that "without stepping outside his gate the scholar knows all the wide world's affairs," such is not the case, even in the age of Fax technology. Snyder knows this very well, and the rest of us would benefit from learning it better: "If I don't have a ground of actual physical experience," says Snyder, "I don't make reference to it, if I can help it, in almost any area" (Flaherty 20), including that of spirituality.

If one, then, is to apply the word transcendence to Snyder's poetry, the only way to unmuddy the waters is to redefine it in terms of its root emphasis: "to climb across/over." One sees this definition at work in Snyder's usage of the word when he says to Paul Geneson: "there is a body of paths which do come to the same goal—some with a more earthly stress, some with a more spiritual stress. But what they have in common is the exploration of consciousness itself: self-understanding, transcendence of self" (Geneson 68). Here one sees a linkage between transcendence and "exploration." In this application, one should bear in mind that the word "scan" also comes from the same root, and means: 1) "to analyze (verse) into its rhythmic components"; 2) "to look at closely or in a broad searching way; scrutinize"; 3) "to glance at quickly; consider hastily." Many critics have applied only the first and third of these definitions to Snyder's work. To scan his poetry in terms of the relationships between literature and religion, poetry and the transcendent, requires that we transcend it by climbing over it, poem by poem, cobble by cobble, as he instructs us to do in the title poem of his first book, *Riprap*.

In order to follow this poetic directive, readers need to understand not only that the statement "a mountain always practices in every place" applies to Snyder's life and poetry, but also that his own statement applies as well: "the fact is that all the entities of nature themselves are undergoing constant change, including mountains, steady dribbling of rocks down cliffs. The mountains are not that solid" (Krauss 203). Snyder's transcendent behavior has undergone change and so has his perception of that behavior. In a certain sense, as others have argued, Snyder's poetry can be interpreted as emphasizing different aspects of Dōgen's statements at different periods in his life. The first is developing the understanding of "always practices," and the second is developing the understanding of "in every place." These can also be related to the distinction between the practice of meditation and the practice of involvement. But while the emphasis may shift to some degree between the earlier volumes of *Riprap, Myths & Texts*, and *The Back Country*, and the later volumes of *Regarding Wave, Turtle Island,* and *Axe Handles,* with *Earth House Hold* as the transitional prose pivot, they have always interpenetrated, since practice and place cannot be artificially separated without a descent into abstraction.[4] And the penchant for such abstraction is nowhere better exemplified than in the Western tendency to describe the transcendent aspect of the Zen perception of enlightenment only in terms of its first two phases rather than its three-fold movement, since the last phase returns us to the world that so many individuals want to escape after having been largely responsible for decreating it. Zen master Ch'ing-yüan Wei-hsin has encapsulated the triad of enlightenment:

> Thirty years ago, before I began the study of Zen, I said, "Mountains are mountains, waters are waters."
> After I got an insight into the truth of Zen through the instruction of a good master, I said, "Mountains are not mountains, waters are not waters."
> But now, having attained the abode of final rest, I say, "Mountains are really mountains, waters are really waters." (Abe 4)

To speak, then, of Gary Snyder's poetry and the transcendent, one first has to perform a transvaluation of the word transcendent, loosening the Western philosophical hardpan that obscures its roots. Then one has to transplant it, not from one place to another, but across several places, the West of the various Native American peoples, the East of the Asian Buddhists, and the world of the contemporary environmental bioregionalists. As Snyder explains, "by the time I came back to the United States, my sense of membership in place had expanded so much that there was a much huger territory in which I could feel at home" (O'Connell 316; see Dean 75–77).

II

With the preceding explanation in mind, one can begin to see the ways in which the truly "climbing-over" requires that "a mountain always practices in every place." Snyder's implementation of such practice began very early. As Dantika, one of the original Buddhist nuns and a contemporary of Buddha (Murcott 11–23), expressed it: "Seeing what was wild before / gone tame under human hands, / I went into the forest / and concentrated my mind" (qtd. in Murcott 17). Snyder did precisely that, beginning with sojourns and overnight camping into the Cascade mountains near his Depression-period subsistence family farm. What must have begun as an intuition began to become a conscious way of life as he searched for a spiritual path that would unite "the solitary eye and the nourishing kitchen" (Paul 299–300). The link to

Native Americans came with locals he met in his area, and, later, formal anthropological study; the link with the East came first with the Chinese scroll paintings in the Seattle museum that he saw as a child, and with which he identified his own mountainous home (Chowka 93–94). One could argue, adopting the Buddhist perception of the development of understanding, that Snyder experienced his first *kensho*, the experience of seeing into one's own nature (Hopkinson and Murcott 32), at that moment of identification of the Pacific Northwest mountains with the Chinese mountains—a recognition of interrelationship, based primarily not on ego identification but on recognition of immersion in *anotherness*.

Not suprisingly, Snyder sought the nearest representatives of anotherness, local Native Americans, to seek guidance, "and got close to some American Indian elders" while in college, but soon found that their way was not open to non-Indians (Chowka 94). Rather quickly, Snyder moved toward Buddhism as a way open to people of other nationalities and origins, beginning his own *zazen* practice while an undergraduate, and then by the age of 22 determining to go to Asia to study Buddhism (Chowka 95). Again, Snyder experienced a moment of sudden realization: "I had this flash, you know, it happened to be during this summer [before starting graduate school], that everything was alive—you know, really had a gut level animistic perception which was shamanistic and animistic and maybe now when I look at it, ecological, but I didn't have those words for it then" (McKenzie 8).

The ground upon which to practice, then, was very clear to Snyder even as a youth. It would expand to encompass far more than the Cascades: "it's western North America, the North Pacific, and the eastern coast of Asia," but would remain focused on the North American Pacific rim (McKenzie 20; Wyatt 203–4). Yet the practice itself was not at all clear until after Snyder had completed his B.A. and undertaken graduate study. He had passed through the phase when "mountains are mountains," and was beginning to feel that "mountains are not mountains," a sense that would be deepened through formal study. After abandoning academia as a path, he set his sights on Japan and Zen training (Chowka 95). Once begun, this exploration would not allow him to return permanently to his home ground to practice inhabitation until nearly thirteen years had passed. But we should also distinguish here a difference between religious practice, that is, Buddhism in this case, and cultural practice, that is, poetry, readings, writing, and teaching. The poems gathered in *Riprap & Cold Mountain Poems* depict Snyder's gaining of focus regarding his ground and the direction of both his religious and cultural practices. While to Jack Kerouac and others Snyder may have seemed very calm and focused even before journeying to Japan, the *Riprap* poems suggest that the early fifties involved far more conflict than his exterior may have expressed (see, e.g., "T-2 Tanker Blues," and Molesworth 20). Such conflict, rather than revealing a shortcoming, provides a crucial lesson for all who read him: discovering the path is often one of the most difficult steps; this becomes even more obvious when reading the poems written in the 1950s but not collected until *The Back Country*. The commitment to study Buddhism had been made by 1952, but the commitment to poetry proved another matter. As David Robertson notes, in the year before the famous Six Gallery reading of 1955 at which Ginsberg read "Howl" and Snyder and others made "Beat" poetry a matter of public record, "Snyder had given up his ambition to be a poet" (52).

Taking the summer off from his language studies at Berkeley—part of his Japan preparation—Snyder went to work in Yosemite Valley in the California Sierra Nevada, instead of returning to the Cascades. Without conscious intent he began writing verse again after a few years' gap (see Robertson 53–54).[5] "Riprap," and other poems, came from this. Snyder had once again climbed over to a new awareness of the connection between his life and cultural change, developing beyond a past understanding and experience of the relationship between art and life. As a child, Chinese landscape paintings had produced a sudden moment of enlightenment; as an adult, the actual mountains of the Sierra Nevada produced another one. First, art informed him about his affiliations with the world and a certain perception of it; and, second, a new perception of that world informed him about his affiliations with art and the responsibilites attendant to such a vocation (In a craft interview, Snyder stated that "poetry is not a social life. Nor is it a career. It's a vocation" [*Real Work* 40]). The study of Buddhism in Japan, then, was recognized as not an alternative vocation but part of the practice of a developing vocation as poet. When asked years later by Barry Chowka whether or not he knew he would return to the U.S., Snyder answered that "it wasn't just returning—the next step of my own practice was to be here" (Chowka 99).

Rather than a dialectic, one sees here a dialogic process of synthesis, with art and life, ground and being, continuously and mutually interpenetrating. Robertson argues that the *Riprap* poem "Water" is an instance of a recurrent goal in Snyder's trail poetry: "encountering the Other" (55). I would modify this, by suggesting instead that it signifies a recurrent experience arising from his practice at that point in his life: encountering, entering into dialogue, and, in effect, participating in *pratitya-samutpada*, "dependent co-origination" (Abe 153–56; Martin, "Practising" 6–7); and doing so not with the "Other" in an alienated or psychoanalytic sense, but with *another* mutual participant in the interpenetrating jewelled net of the world. Snyder demonstrates some recognition of this distinction when using "an other" and "another" in "Across Lamarck Col" (*Back Country* 120). This is not to say that he self-consciously understood the process at work in the early 1950s, but that he had opened himself to such a process.[6] This openness resulted in part from his novice development of a certain detachment, such as the detachment from the "ambition" to be a poet. This detachment enabled him to write poems without the strong ego investment one finds in those poems in which he feels anxiety about his own, rather than the world's, direction.

The opening poem of *Riprap*, "Mid-August at Sourdough Mountain Lookout," suggests the developing but not yet successful adoption of detachment (1). Such continuing attachment also appears in "Piute Creek" as the speaker becomes overwhelmed by the world in which he finds himself with "This bubble of a heart" in the first stanza. The second stanza resolves his anxiety through the recognition of the reflective quality of "a clear, attentive mind." Yet the conclusion of the poem, with the speaker leaving the location while cougar and coyote watch him from a distance, suggests that the resolution remains more an intellectual synthesis of experience than a psychic integration restructuring the ground of his being (see Molesworth 14). The sense that such a restructuring requires a continuous processing, building on but not submitting to any tradition or undergoing a quick conversion to a new ideologically defined identity, is expressed in "Above Pate Valley," where he distinguishes his own trail from those of the indigenous people who have gone before him.

The trail did not end in Yosemite. As "Nooksack Valley" and "Migration of Birds"—written in February and April of 1956—record, Snyder would have to crisscross an ocean to learn about that part of his practice that neither the North American Pacific mountains nor the Native Americans inhabiting them could teach him. At twenty-five, he found himself at a "Mind-point" requiring formal training in Japan (15). Yet this specific place exerts a stronger pull than even he apparently anticipated and the closing sentence of "Nooksack Valley" suggests both that Snyder envisions the trip to Japan as part of a (re)turning and that he feels ambivalent and unsettled like the dog in the poem. By April, however, "Migration of Birds" suggests that he has worked through his troubled feelings to a tranquility enabled by perceiving his journey as equivalent to a natural cycle, not in an intellectual and abstract way—that is, a rationalziation—but in a concrete and felt way. This distinction is indicated by the contrast Snyder establishes in this poem between reading and experiencing. Two acts of reading are described, Kerouac's reading of *The Diamond Sutra* and Snyder's own reading of *Migration of Birds*. Snyder balances his reading with an experience, but there seems, at first, to be no balance for Kerouac's reading, with the poem apparently closing on a description of the migration of seabirds that will take them to Alaska. Yet the close, while accurate in its description, is not about their migration, but Snyder's. As the "Japan First Time Around" section of *Earth House Hold* reveals, Snyder would be at sea by May 7th, arriving in Kobe on the 21st (31–33). Thus, Kerouac's abstract reading will be balanced by Snyder's concrete experience (see Dean 24).

While Snyder through his various experiences from 1956 through 1968 focused on developing his practice rather than the relationship of that practice to place, it was not a single experience cut from the same cloth. The most continuous period of living in Japan covered the years 1959 to 1964, but even this included a six-month visit to India, which reinforced what he had already recognized in Japan: that Buddhism in and of itself does not guarantee right living; much of its practice has been too focused on individual enlightenment and personal withdrawal from the world. The boddhisattva vow to bring all other beings to enlightenment has been ignored (see, e.g., "Burning 10" of *Myths & Texts*). In "Buddhism and the Coming Revolution," the first version of which was published in 1961, Snyder indicts Buddhism for complicity in the history of human and natural oppression, and, at the same time, salvages the fundamental features still relevant for the "coming revolution" (*Earth House Hold* 90). As Snyder summarized about India after his visit, "the culture that articulated (especially in Jain and buddhist religions) the most thoroughgoing philosophy of carefulness with life (Ahimsa, non-injury) is a land of ecological degradation and human difficulty" (*Passage* ix). And while Snyder could clearly behold Japan's differences from India, he also recognized its failure at compassion for the non-human, its own addiction to "heavy energy use" (*Turtle Island* 103). Thus, still early in his most extended period of Zen study in Japan, Snyder could argue:

> The mercy of the West has been social revolution; the mercy of the East has been individual insight into the basic self/void. We need both. They are both contained in the traditional three aspects of the Dharma path: wisdom (prajna), meditation (dhyana), and morality (sila). Wisdom is intuitive knowledge of the mind of love and clarity that lies beneath one's ego-driven anxieties and aggression. Meditation is going into the mind to see this for yourself—over and over again, until it becomes the mind you live in. Morality is bringing it back out in the way you live, through personal example and responsible action, ultimately toward the true community (sangha) of "all beings." (*Earth House Hold* 92)

One does not find in Snyder's writings an identifiable extended period during which his understanding is strictly limited to the phase that "mountains are not mountains." His firm grounding in place and his unceasing attention to the nonhuman as a significant another seem to have created a situation in which the latter two phases of enlightenment depicted by Ch'ing-yüan Wei-hsin must have alternated and continuously interpenetrated, and probably continue to do so to this day. This is perfectly reasonable, since as Masao Abe points out, "the third and final stage includes both the first and second stages," and, more to the point, "the third stage is not a *static end* to be reached progressively from the lower stages, but the *dynamic whole* which includes both great negation and great affirmation, a dynamic whole in which you and I are embraced and which excludes nothing" (15; emphasis in original). A concern for place remained ever-present during Snyder's years of primary attention to maturing his practice. And by the time of the death in 1966 of his roshi, Oda Sesso, the emphasis had clearly shifted to practice in *place* over *practice* in place. When he finally returned to the United States, to make it the focus of his practice, he was both husband and father looking to build a permanent home, what has become "Kitkidizze," part of the San Juan Ridge near Nevada City, California (see Yamazato, "Kitkitdizze").

III

Fully recognizing that "mountains are mountains," and prepared to practice as a mountain, but in a very specific place, Snyder returned to the United States and published, not a book of triumph, but one revealing the difficulties, the conflicting emotions, and the uncertainty of the physical and spiritual path that he had travelled since first leaving the United States. As Bob Steuding notes of *The Back Country*, "the trials and tribulations, the pain and exaltation of his psychic journey, his quest for sanity and wholeness, are recorded" (122; Molesworth 56). This book collects in four sections poems written in some cases more than twenty years before its 1968 publication, plus, in a fifth section, Snyder's translations of poems by Miyazawa Kenji (1896–1933). The organization of Snyder's own poems for the 1968 edition into four parts, "Far West," "Far East," "Kālī," and "Back," reveals its function: to record the three-fold journey in which place is home, place is not home, and, finally, place again is home.

This conception applies equally to place as nature and place as mind (see Dean 49). Steuding suggests that despite his years in Japan, India revealed the dark side of the back country of the unconscious with which Snyder had not yet come to terms (126). The title of the section, "Kālī," then, is certainly not fortuitous. In the 1983 foreword to *Passage Through India* (originally published in 1972 as "Now, India"), Snyder states: "An anvil the spirit is pounded finer on, India. Skinny, and flashing eyes" (xi). Titling the fourth section "Back," then, suggests a return, both in terms of geography and mind, and, thus, it could be labelled a depiction of transcendence in the sense of crossing over from immersion in the East to immersion in the West, and in the sense of a climbing over the dark side of the unconscious, the final descent in which "mountains are not mountains," before achieving a new perception that "mountains are mountains." I would argue, however, that this new perception is one not yet fully realized in Snyder's book publications until the prose volume *Earth House Hold* in 1969 and the poetry volume *Regarding Wave* in 1970 (see Molewsorth 57).

Earth House Hold: Technical Notes & Queries to Fellow Dharma Revolutionaries is Snyder's first book-length prose publication, although certainly not his last, and "is in a way his reentry into America" (Molesworth 65). The structure of title and subtitle suggest Snyder's new emphasis on place in practice, since ecology is assigned to the title and Buddhism to the subtitle. Like *The Back Country,* its contents cover a broad span of years (1952–1967 to be exact), in part because it contains the bulk of Snyder's prose work up to this time (excluding *Passage Through India* and his undergraduate honors thesis, *He Who Hunted Birds in His Father's Village,* which Snyder was persuaded to publish in 1979). But more to the point, it contains a primer on much of Snyder's own spiritual education (McNeill 45). Many of the entries are, in effect, teaching by example, reinforced by Snyder's "Record of the Life of the Ch'an master Po-chang." Translated without commentary, it provides an argument about the need for discipline, for training, and for a specific practice, in this case Ch'an buddhism, the precursor, as Snyder's opening genealogy presents it, of Rinzai Zen. Most significant here is the final section on "The Regulations of the Ch'an Line," emphasizing discipline, community, and comradeship, three practices necessary to insure the flourishing of the Dharma and the transmission of the "three inheritances" (80). As Snyder remarked in a 1985 interview, "Buddhism is not just a religion or practice of personal, psychological self-knowledge and enlightenment, but is also a practice of actualizing personal insights in the real world" (Hertz 52). And *Earth House Hold* is a part of Snyder's promoting the three inheritances, by actualizing his personal insight that Zen provides a way for revolutionizing life in the United States.

Having established the right to speak through the presentation of his personal practice and the tradition in which that practice takes place, Snyder then focuses on his perceptions of the implementation of that practice in the particular place of North America in the mid-sixties through the essays "Buddhism and the Coming Revolution" (1961; revised 1967), "Passage to More than India," "Why Tribe," "Poetry and the Primitive," and "Dharma Queries," with the last four all apparently written in 1967. Throughout these writings, Snyder intimately connects ecological activisim and Buddhism, for example: "The soil, the forests and all animal life are being consumed by these cancerous collectivities. . . . The joyous and voluntary poverty of Buddhism becomes a positive force. The traditional harmlessness and refusal to take life in any form has nation-shaking implications" (91).

Perhaps most to the point in terms of Snyder's own practice in the coming years are his fairly newfound emphases on "tribe" and "family," both of which specifically elaborate on his more general remarks about community. With a commitment to practicing realization in a specific place, Snyder has to focus on the practical details of community, not simply in terms of negating and critiquing the "doomed" societies that he has condemned for years but also by promoting positive alternatives: "sexual mores and the family are changing. Rather than the 'breakdown of the family' we should see this as the transition to a new form of family" (112). Interestingly enough, Snyder does not end the collection with an essay prescribing practice or theorizing about the future, but rather with a descriptive essay about right practice, "Suwa-No-Se Island and the Banyan Ashram." This entry includes a description of his and Masa Uehara's wedding, and concludes on a note of supreme optimism befitting a newlywed: "It is possible at last . . . to imagine a little of what the ancient—archaic—mind and life of Japan were. And to see what could be restored to the life today. A lot of it is simply in being aware of clouds and wind" (143).

With that conclusion to *Earth House Hold*, it comes as little suprise that so much of Snyder's next volume of poetry, *Regarding Wave*, consists of celebratory poems and songs. Yet the celebration never becomes an escape from reality, although it often serves to widen radically the perception of what should be recognized as real. Such is the case in the collection's second poem, "Seed Pods," an ecstatic meditation that connects Snyder's own sexual intercourse with a variety of other transmissions of lifebuilding matter (4). In "Sand," a stream of consciousness list of various kinds of sand around the world identifies the experience of lovemaking in the "dunes at Bandon / Oregon" with the universality of worldwide sand formation, while the next poem situates Snyder and Masa as lovers within a human community in the larger natural community (7). But not all is celebration. The last two poems of Section One speak of the Vietnam War and its life-destroying effects, both direct and indirect. In contrast with the previous poems celebrating life-affirming sexuality and fecundity, "In the House of the Rising Sun" emphasizes "burned-off jungles," and then "White Devils" depicts American urbanization's rape of nature. Life and death remain interrelated, and one's own celebrations do not eliminate another's suffering. Snyder presents here both the Buddhist recognition that suffering is a given of being in the world and that compassion is the proper response to such suffering.

Much of the rest of *Regarding Wave* is given over to celebrations of erotica, community, marriage, and family, including the birth and infant years of the first Snyder son, Kai. But much of this community consists of the one that Snyder is leaving, that of the Banyan Ashram and Japanese friends, rather than the community he is entering. Family, more than community, is being established here along Buddhist lines and with specific practice of ritual and nurture in place, as exemplified by the poems "Meeting the Mountains" and "Why I Laugh When Kai Cries." *Regarding Wave* ends, though, with a poem titled "Civilization," and here Snyder clearly sets forth his place and practice as one of opposition to the current aberration of human society called civilization, affirming the primitive, archaic values that he has already espoused for years, as well as delineating his work as both poetic and physical. His responsibilities to community, to family, to place require both forms of his "real work" (see Molesworth 85). In fact, one could argue that poetry is his real work for the international community who reads his books and hears his readings, while heaping stones is his real work for the local community (McKenzie 13; see also Wyatt 204).

Snyder's next two books of poetry, widely spaced after the flurry of late sixties and 1970 publications, *Turtle Island* and *Axe Handles*, reflect more strongly than any of his previous works his commitment to practice in a specific place, while always engaging in "planetary thinking," with the local gaining in importance in the second of the two books. To reinforce his alternative vision of a balanced, sane daily life in which an entire community, or tribe, practices in every place, Snyder initiates *Turtle Island* with "Anasazi," a poem depicting the ecologically balanced life of an ancient Native American tribe. Snyder follows this with a poem outlining the dimensions of the circumpolar bear cult, both its ancient origins and its alleged continuations in the present—"elder wilder goddesses reborn" (5). And this, in turn, is followed by the poem "Without." Here Snyder claims that "the path is whatever passes" (6). And these are followed by two other poems relating specific practice in the present.

If readers link these five, rather than treating them separately, the poems establish a pattern in which "Anasazi" depicts a specific path in a particular physiographic province, a historical example of right habitation by an entire community. "The Way West, Underground" then connects Native American experience, through the bear cult archetype, to other peoples around the globe, and their various practices, and includes the possibility of a new "underground" that may transform human relationship to ground worldwide. It embodies Snyder's call at the end of his "Introductory Note" to "hark again to those roots, to see our ancient solidarity, and then to the work of being together on Turtle Island." "Without" links mind and nature with the variety of "energy-pathways that sustain life," the diversity that a healthy ecosystem maintains. A part of one such pathway is the implementation in Northern California of the Buddhist practice of utilizing road-killed animals, both for food and for other purposes. This is the first poem that introduces an observing-participating "I," but the practice still seems somewhat out of time. "I Went into the Maverick Bar," however, brings the speaker into the fullness of time, the immediacy of the present, through a visit to a New Mexico bar. This visit reminds him of the responsibility arising from Buddhist compassion, which in turn tells him that he has a job to do, working to move the world.

The poems of *Turtle Island*, all contributing to the tasks set out in the introduction, display a remarkable variety of styles and foci, from family to planet, from animal to human, from celebration to elegy. They realize a conception of his writing that Snyder had spelled out some ten years before: "My poems, on one level, call the society's attention to its ecological relationships in nature, and to its relationships in the individual consciousness. Some of the poems show how society doesn't see its position in nature" (Fowler 4). And Snyder has continued to hone this conception, writing a few years after the publication of *Turtle Island* about one type of poem that appears in that volume, "healing songs": "Here the poet is voice for the nonhuman, for the natural world, actually a vehicle for another voice, to send it into the human world, saying that there is a larger sphere out there; that the humans are indeed children of, sons and daughters of, and eternally in relationship with, the earth" (Snyder, "Poetry" 98). But despite the diversity, the long-range and far-reaching understanding displayed by Snyder, what stays in the mind of many readers is a note of urgency, a confrontational directness, and a political activism that was never so overt or didactic as it is in *Turtle Island*.

This immediacy is reflected particularly in the fourth part of *Turtle Island*, the prose pieces of "Plain Talk." The first is "Four Changes," revised for this volume from its initial 1969 draft. In the introduction to it, Snyder states unequivocally that "whatever happens, we must not go into a plutonium-based economy" (91). But such an urgency does not lead Snyder to negate the dialogic relationship of immediate action and ongoing practice. Immediately after this pronouncement, he also remarks: "My Teacher once said to me, /— become one with the knot itself, / til it dissolves away. /—sweep the garden. /— any size" (91). Snyder here confirms again that Zen practice guides his way in the world. And later in the essay, he defines the garden and the sweeping: "no transformation without our feet on the ground. Stewardship means, for most of us, find your place on the planet, dig in, and take responsibility from there" (101). How more clearly could one suggest the appropriate way in 1974 on the North American continent for a mountain to practice in that very place?

In *Axe Handles*, published nine years later, one no longer hears the same sound of urgency, but one does hear even more so the emphasis on practice in place, both in the family, the community, and the region. And teaching, as a form of acting, has also taken on a more important function in Snyder's practice as well. One could argue that Sndyer had transcended a perhaps momentary feeling of apocalyptic change on the horizon, and matured to a clearer sense of the long cycles of cultural and ecological change. I would suggest that it is also the case that he has contributed to a widespread and diverse movement, which has caused that horizon to recede. Snyder has entered his fifties by the time of *Axe Handles* and in this collection takes to heart the message he reports coming to him from his dead friend Lew Welch, "teach the children about the cycles" (7).

That message took on new meaning when Snyder accepted a position teaching at the University of California, Davis. The mountain had come to the valley, practicing in both places as part of practicing in every place, since "he who truly attains awakening knows that deliverance is to be found right where he is. . . . He lives his daily life in awakened awareness. His every act from morning to evening is his religion" (Sokei-An qtd. in Nelson 214). What then is there to transcend? Snyder, knowing well his friend Nanao Sakaki's remark, "no need to survive" (Geneson 79), will continue on his way, climbing over whatever his practice requires. For the rest of us, we might recall Dōgen's words that close the "Mountains and Waters Sutra":

> Therefore investigate mountains thoroughly. When you investigate mountains thoroughly, this is the work of the mountains.
>
> Such mountains and waters of themselves become wise persons and sages. (107)

Chapter Nine

Pivots Instead of Centers: Postmodern Spirituality of Gary Snyder & Ursula K. Le Guin

I

In Chapter Eight, I emphasized the relationship between Gary Snyder's ecological awareness and Buddhist beliefs in terms of their expression in his writing about a particular type of practice in place. Here I want to analyze his poetry in terms of a concept of "postmodern spirituality." And I will develop this analysis by considering Snyder's writing in conjunction with that of one of his old friends, Ursula K. Le Guin. While Snyder's daily religious practice is grounded in Zen Buddhism, Snyder's eclectic religious studies and allusions, as well as his focus on praxis rather than eschatology, disengage his spirituality from any single religious system. He himself tends to describe Buddhism as part of a much older tradition, and takes care to distinguish and discuss the various manifestations of Buddhism that inform his practice. In like manner, although she is not as widely recognized for her poetry as for her fiction, Ursula K. Le Guin brings to all of her writing a deep immersion in Daoism, anarchism, utopian thought, and, increasingly, ecology and feminism (see Le Guin, *Dancing*). Her poetry also resonates with a spirituality distinct from any specific orthodoxy.

Both Snyder and Le Guin display a posthumanist and postmodernist self-consciousness of their own teleological impulses in terms of epistemology and ontology, at the same time that they resolutely eschew any totalizing dogma or idealist systematization. Their poetry and attendant spirituality, then, are both postmodern in sensibility. Such a postmodern spirituality—which, although sounding like an oxymoron, is more a paradox in the tradition of Daoism and Zen—can best be interpreted, given their concerns and themes, by means of a dialogic method, in order to analyze the ways in which these two writers develop philosophical pivots rather than idealist centers on which to base a nondualistic, nondichotomizing process of being-in-the-world, which is very much an ecological perspective.

Marjorie Perloff claims that "postmodernism in poetry begins in the urge to return the material so rigidly excluded—political, ethical, historical, philo-

sophical—to the domain of poetry . . . a poetry that can, once again, accom-
modate narrative and didacticism, the serious and the comic, verse *and* prose"
(180–81, emphasis in original). And Tzvetan Todorov argues that "postmodern literary texts. . . . would be those that reintroduce representation and the
history of the world into their framework, yet without reverting to realism"
(34; see Hutcheon 27). Such is clearly the case with poems by both Snyder and
Le Guin in which consensual reality and the fantastic are treated as equally
phenonmenal (see, e.g., Murphy, "Left Hand" and "Mythic"). Ihab Hassan,
however, focusing on a particular aspect of that history of the world, suggests
that "postmodernism may be a response, direct or oblique, to the Unimaginable which Modernism glimpsed only in its most prophetic moments" (*Paracriticisms* 53). But rather than rushing to resolve the "Unimaginable," postmodernist poetry tends to confront it by means of an intensification, rather
than a transcendence, of the problems that have been variously defined as the
features of the historical moment labelled postmodernity. But, as I have
argued in "De/Reconstructing the 'I': postFANTASTICmodernist poetry,"
such intensification need not be the evocation of the Heideggerian "dread"
that William V. Spanos reserves for his allegedly "genuine" postmodernist
poetry, nor the focus on subjectivity in language that Andrew Ross names as
the only true postmodernist perception. I would suggest instead, paraphrasing
Hassan (*Dismemberment* 23), that much of postmodernist poetry moves in
"mystic play [and] skeptical [non]transcendence," with a de-teleological spirituality that is simultaneously serious and playful, although less frequently
ironic.

The near-ubiquity of irony in postmodernism, an irony already largely
present in much of modernism and in the Cleanth Brooks wing of New Criticism, arises as a necessary result of a pervasive lack in much of the literature
and theory. As Linda Hutcheon argues, "the postmodern . . . does work to
turn its inevitable ideological grounding into a site of de-naturalizing critique," and "postmodernism works to 'de-doxify' our cultural representations
and their undeniable political import," but they do all this while having "no
effective theory of agency that enables a move into political *action*" (3; emphasis in original).

Perhaps irony is offset by a seriously playful spirituality in the works of
authors such as Snyder and Le Guin precisely because they do have *effective
theories of agency*. Snyder and Le Guin, in different but increasingly similar
ways, embody what Hutcheon finds the distinction between feminisms and
the rest of postmodernism: "feminisms want to go beyond this work to *change*
those systems, not just to 'de-doxify' them" (153, emphasis in original). The
same can be said of another significant praxis movement, one of which
Hutcheon is apparently unaware: ecology (which is, of course, as ideologically
multiple as feminism[s], and has its own range of spiritual beliefs and prac-

tices). Like many of the authors appearing in *Feminism/Postmodernism,* edited by Linda J. Nicholson, Hutcheon, in *The Politics of Postmodernism,* locates feminisms as being in relationship with but not subsumed by postmodernism, precisely because of the difference in theories of agency. But such a maneuver simply replicates another patriarchal dichotomy: center/margin. The "center" of postmodernism has no effective theory of agency and, therefore, necessarily remains more complicitous with what it critiques than the "margins" that have theories of agency and thereby suffer less complicity. But this grants a greater stability and durability to the in-effective and depicts postmodernist disruption as fundamentally a loyal opposition.

Instead, if we conceptualize a three-dimensional playing field along the lines of plate tectonics, consisting of zones of ideological positions arising from and in turn affecting specific historical conditions (the majority of them manifestations of the dominant culture), with interzonal gaps, fissures, fault lines, and impact points, and perceive this diachronically—adding the fourth dimension—then we can locate chronotopes for agency, shifting pivot points in which disruption can transform into eruption, and negation into affirmation. Being temporal, such chronotopes, at which change can be initiated and achieved, cannot be consolidated into centers or barricaded margins, because the specific conditions that enable a momentary pivot for concerted praxis are just that, momentary, relative, and partial, i.e., decentralized and decentering. As Nancy Hartsock suggests, "the point is to develop an account of the world which treats our perspectives not as subjugated or disruptive knowledge, but as primary and constitutive of a different world" (171), one of process and participation of human and non-human alike in being-in-the-world (see also Probyn). This is very much akin to the Whiteheadian notion of "unique actual occasions" involving, according to process studies, "unpredictability" and "decision" (McDaniel).

With such an orientation, we can visualize a continuum of postmodernist strategies in the face of the chronotopes that arise from the multiplicity of ideological contradictions constituting the Euro-North American cultures of multinational capitalism: at one end would be the static or entropic non-agency negative critique, which has characterized the predominantly white, male, universalizing "literature of exhaustion"; toward the other end would be the dynamic affirmational agency critique, which has characterized the predominantly feminist and nonwhite gender-, race-, and class-specific "oppositional consciousness" literature (see Haraway 155–56, 173–81). Both Snyder and Le Guin have managed to envision an affirmative agency of pivots in their poetry. And not suprisingly, they have done so through a post-humanist, affirmative heterodoxy that is anarchic, multicultural, and ecological. Jay McDaniel notes that "the word *spirit* often connotes the animating principle in the cosmos: the life-like quality of a given being" (317), and argues that such spirit can be found everywhere, from subatomic particles outward. I would like to suggest that Snyder and Le Guin both embrace such a worldly spirituality as part of affirming "the life story" of existence, rather than "the killer story," as Le Guin has termed the traditional, patriarchal heroic quest (*Dancing* 168).

II

Although Snyder has come to learn the lessons of feminism, and to incorporate them into his world view, fairly late in his life and poetic career, his own process of ideological development contains features that parallel some of those which define the difference between male postmodernism and feminism (see Spretnak, "Dinnertime" 361). For example, as Hutcheon notes, "in Catharine Stimpson's terms: 'Experience generated more than art; it was a source of political engagement as well.' If the personal is the political, then the traditional separation between private and public history must be rethought. This feminist rethinking has coincided with a general renegotiation of the separation of high art from the culture of everyday life" (160–61).[1] Both are resoundingly present in Snyder's own development. From early in his life he abjured the public/private dichotomy, both in terms of poetic life and spiritual life. He has also worked diligently at his own mediations of "high art" and "everyday cultural life," as can easily be discerned in the simultaneous appearance of complex poems and sequences obviously heavily indebted to modernist technique, and simple aphoristic and narrative pieces based on the rhythms and experiences of immediate social experience and labor (as with *Myths & Texts* and *Riprap*, the two volumes of the fifties, and poems in such collections as *Regarding Wave*, *Turtle Island*, and *Axe Handles*).

More than twenty years ago, in "Poetry and the Primitive," he indicated that individual salvation was inadequate: "The archaic, the esoteric, and the primitive traditions alike all teach that beyond transcendence is Great Play, and Transformation" (128). This follows a certain line of Zen thinking that emphasizes "involvement, identification, acceptance," with engagement being the basis of Dōgen's understanding of Buddha-nature; this is the orientation that Snyder assumes when he identifies his practice as Zen.[2] By defining Zen as a practice, rather than a religion, Snyder is emphasizing a process and an activity in the world, rather than a belief system or a static state of being. As part of such practice Snyder emphasizes the "interbirth" and dependent co-creation. Such a perception of interconnectedness not only enables one to move from the self/other as dichotomy to viewing both terms as mutually constitutive forms of being another, but also enables one to listen to others, whether human or not, as speaking subjects, sentient and creative (see McDaniel).

As Seyla Benhabib has remarked from a feminist perspective, "you cannot respect the otherness of the other if you deny the other the right to enter into a conversation with you, if you do not discard the objective indifference of the ethnologist and engage with the other as an equal" (19). At which point, I would add, the other ceases to be alien, noninterpretable and unworthy of respect. Snyder's conceptualization of "healing songs," as "actually a vehicle for another voice, to send it into the human world," links contemporary poetry with traditional shamanic ritual ("Poetry" 98; see also O'Connell 320). In line with Donna Haraway's notion of "situated knowledges" as a postmodernist epistemological agency, Snyder's linkage argues for each of us to turn from being "ethnologist" to being "informant," to move from objectifying detachment from the other to subjectivity-sharing engagement with the other as another.

One sees such an orientation in the two poems that Snyder has chosen from the years 1947–48, when he was still a teenager, to serve as the introduction to *Left Out in the Rain*. In "Elk Trails" (5–7), one sees intuitions of Zen and ecological perceptions. The speaker follows "ancient trails," personifying them at the same time that he pays attention to the physical world through which they course. Then Snyder goes beyond the focus of the poem, the Elk trails, to recognize in the last stanza the Elk themselves, implying an understanding that following the trails is not the same as finding or becoming the Elk (cf. Hicks). "'Out of the soil and rock'" (8), in contrast, is set in the city, but evokes the same foreshadowing and intuitions. The illusion of permanence that New York City creates is dismissed after the poet has limned the natural web of life that generates human beings. The emphasis, at poem's end, on the future prepares the speaker and reader for the Buddhist concept of compassion for all beings, and supports Dōgen's belief that "practice is practice in realization." According to Snyder,

> Zen mysticism says, well, wait it's already all a Buddha right now, if you can just see it, so that's ahistorical. It's the eternal moment. I think in those terms, but I also think in terms of organic evolution, and from that standpoint we have a critical time now in which decisions are being made which will have long reaching effects on the survival of many forms of life.[3] (Faas 109–10)

In 1961, even as he was most immersed in his Japanese Buddhist practice, Snyder had begun developing a critique of institutional Buddhism's limitations (which was reinforced by his half-year trip to India the next year): "Institutional Buddhism has been conspicuously ready to accept or ignore the inequalities and tyrannies of whatever political system it found itself under. This can be death to Buddhism, because it is death to any meaningful function of compassion" (*Earth House Hold* 90). After critiquing such complicity in

"Buddhism and the Coming Revolution," Snyder nevertheless recuperates Buddhism for a contemporary life practice, by interconnecting "meditation" and "morality." At that point in time, therefore, when Snyder was immersed in formal Buddhist study at a Rinzai Zen temple, he recognized the importance of not allowing the doctrine to become an immovable, absolute center of belief, and focused instead on the function of Zen meditation as a pivot for elaborating a spiritual practice responsible to all the other beings in the world, who represent various manifestations of one another, "the true community (sangha)" (*Earth House Hold* 92). This emphasis on true community is perhaps most forcefully depicted not in any of Snyder's poems but in the dedication of the central room of Kitkitdizze [Snyder's home] as a zendo, to promote, by his own account, "creative commitments to women-men-babies-houses-soil-and All Beings" (Yamazato 55–56).

Charles Molesworth has claimed that "Snyder's vision largely ignores the . . . mechanisms of daily life and such mundane concerns as urban experience and bureaucratized work schemes—in favor of the political, such as the question of our relation to the environment, the blindness engendered by loyalty to the nation-state, and our allegiance to ideological systems based on domination and waste" (8). But this is precisely the kind of false dichotomy that Snyder's poems reject, by combining and addressing precisely the social and the political. Rather than focusing on urbanization and work schemes, he depicts a vision of an alternative, life-affirming and personally/socially fulfilling daily life based on the goal of "moving the world a millionth of an inch" (McKenzie 12–13). The "Introductory Note" to *Turtle Island* states his position quite precisely: "A name: that we may see ourselves more accurately on this continent of watersheds and life-communities—plant zones, physiographic provinces, culture areas. . . . Each living being is a swirl in the flow, a formal turbulence, a 'song.' The land, the planet itself, is also a living being—at another pace." The animistic recognition of every another as "living" is precisely the notion of spirit that McDaniel defines (317), and that animates all of Snyder's practice. It breaks from the alienation, disjunction and dualism that dominated modernism, yet it does not ascribe to a merely negative postmodernist critique. Through grounding in social and historical—which are primarily ecological—frameworks, Snyder's postmodernist sensibility remains informed by an affirmative spirituality. Molesworth's concern over Snyder's lack of depiction of Americans living within the dominant cultural-economic framework may be a demonstration of a problem typical to much postmodernist cultural analysis: it relies on, and accepts as a totalizing reality, the world as it is imaged by multinational capitalism. "Global consciousness" represents just such an acceptance in its totalizing claim of universal knowledge of/for/about the entire planet. In contrast, Snyder calls for "planetary thinking," which he defined for Barry Chowka as being "decentralist, [it] seeks biological rather than technological solutions, and finds its teachers for its alternative possibilities as much in the transmitted skills of natural peoples of Papua and the headwaters of the Amazon as in the libraries of high Occidental civilization" (Chowka 126). And, as is the case, Snyder's poetry—and his more recent prose—ranges across the experiences of such peoples as he has encountered them, as in the Australian outback, in "Uluru Wild Fig Song" (*Axe Handles* 95–98), or in an Inupiaq school in Alaska (*Practice of the Wild*, Ch.3), or sitting in a sweatlodge on Baranoff Island ("The Sweat," *No Nature* 364-65). But it should also be remembered, in response to Molesworth's concern, that Snyder's poetry is filled with the lives and actions of locals, with the various inhabitants of this continent. These inhabitants are not, however, often the people for whom Molesworth was apparently looking, nor are they necessarily even human. Like us, they are another passing through this place and time, and Snyder treats them with respect.

III

Ursula K. Le Guin, like Snyder, is a deeply rooted writer. For Le Guin, the poem and its world are one with the creation of a better world occurring—coming home to us and us to it—through the active imagination and imaginative action. And spirituality plays a crucial role in all of this, but without being teleological. Le Guin, in *Always Coming Home*, which I briefly discussed in Chapter Two, defines the beliefs of the people who are the text's focus, a definition which also clearly serves to delineate her presentation of spirituality and myth throughout her published works:

> The whole system is profoundly metaphorical. To limit it to any other mode would be, in the judgment of the people of the Valley, superstition. It is for this reason that I do not refer to the system of the Nine Houses as a religion . . . despite the obvious and continuous relation of Valley living and thinking with the sacred. They had no god; they had no gods; they had no faith. What they appear to have had is a working metaphor. (51–52)

And in this sense, poetic creation itself can be understood as a way of placing oneself and one's peoples and relatives, human and non-human alike, in a particular relation to the rest of the world.

This conception of poem as locating place-in-world appears in her first poetry chapbook, and forms, in her own words, the basis for the writing of *Always Coming Home* (Talk and Reading). The untitled opening poem of *Wild Angels* depicts the mythopoeic practice that guides so much of her work: she defines first a people, "wild angels," and then a place, "the open hills. . . . of my childhood" (277).[4] Here Le Guin is laying the foundation for an integration of place, people, and spirit that evokes respect and activity, and which she will come to see as subversive of the dominant culture: "At least the Spirit of Place is a more benign one than the exclusive and aggressive Spirit of Race, the mysticism of blood that has cost so much blood. With all of our self-consciousness, we have very little sense of where we live, where we are right here right now" (*Dancing* 84).

In the poem, "Footnote" (288), the speaker identifies herself as one named "Ostrogotha," who declares her relationship to a variety of animals, such as falcons, crabs, bats, and moths, and to at least one of the elements, rain. This integration of the other into family constitutes a key and recurring feature of Le Guin's Daoist-based action of creating a world balanced by a yin/yang harmony that recognizes the unity of polar complementarity as the completion of self; or, in Bakhtinian terms, "the more other, the more self" (Holquist, "Surd" 148). For Le Guin, self and other, and individual and community, are complementarities that when unified produce a sense of wholeness, although not necessarily completedness. While many other writers try to promote anti-dualistic thinking by attacking the false concepts of other races as alien in science fiction, and female as other in feminist writings, they usually limit their perception to human beings or humanoid creatures. Le Guin takes a further step into ecological decentering, attacking anthropocentrism as well as androcentrism, through the inclusion of other animals as well as natural elements in her conception of family.[5]

Le Guin also initiates her practice of a feminist revisionist mythmaking, re-mythopoeia, in *Wild Angels,* with the poem, "Mount St. Helens/Omphalos" (312).[6] In this poem, she cites Mount St. Helens as the mountain umbilical center of the earth, and describes a seven-stone circle upon it as a new "Henge." This poem participates in a revisionist mythmaking in which the traditional myths are not merely revitalized, but also critiqued (see DuPlessis, "Critique"). In early Le Guin, it is a shamanistic and Daoist-oriented mythopoeia that takes the traditional henge and makes it a figure of life in the service of a decentering faith that places the earth, the mountain, and stone at the center of the world, rather than men. To the degree that Le Guin alludes to the Greek notion of the world's navel through "*omphalos,*" she seems to do so in order to link Mount St. Helens with the oracle at Delphi, and hence a gynocentric tradition of wisdom.

The dimensions of Le Guin's feminist mythopoeia are more fully developed in *Hard Words* than in *Wild Angels,* and her feminist concerns take her more deeply into an ecologically-based spirituality. Speaking in the mid-1980s, Le Guin stated that "we who live at this time are hearing news that has never been heard before. . . . The women are speaking. . . . Those who were identified with nature, which listens, as against Man, who speaks—those people are speaking. They speak for themselves and for the other people, the animals, the trees, the rivers, the rocks. And what they say is : We are sacred" (*Dancing* 162). In the "Wordhoard" section of *Hard Words*, Le Guin suggests that these "other people" are also already speaking for themselves. Several poems present the image of stones as words, which is transformed by Le Guin into a spiritual belief in both the prose and verse of *Always Coming Home*. But here one finds the imagery already partaking of both metaphoric and metonymic associations, in the same way that some Native Americans apprehend symbols—according to Lame Deer: "We Indians live in a world of symbols and images where the spiritual and the commonplace are one. To you symbols are just words, spoken or written in a book. To us they are part of nature, part of ourselves" (quoted in Booth and Jacobs, "Ties" 40).

Le Guin's "The Marrow," in particular, establishes a concrete relationship between sign and referent. It suggests that a contemporary shamanistic poet, a writer of "healing songs," writes to represent in words an apprehension of nature, that if treated as reality, in place of the dominant consensual one, can transform the dualistically divided human world through poetic vision. And the validity of that vision can be determined by whether the poet fights to shape the stone into the image of some false word that she wants, or accepts the true word the stone gives her, which is to say the "voice" of the other as a speaking subject. As Charlotte Spivack notes, "it is only after the deliberate effort has ceased that the long-sought word suddenly appears as if on its own" (138). This appearance results from a Daoist approach to the comprehension of reality. Only by letting-go of the struggle for success that falsely feeds the ego does the speaker gain access to the mystery of nature. The poetic act is not to create the natural world in our image and likeness, but to enunciate an apprehension of the way of the world based on listening for other voices, other subjects, in order to transform our way of life into one more in relationship with, rather than opposition to, such other world inhabitants. The "better world" that Le Guin wishes to create is a human conception of the world that more accurately reflects, and thereby integrates people with, the rest of the natural world, from which we have alienated ourselves just as we have alienated female from male, emotion from reason. For Le Guin, stone best represents the enduring quality of the earth upon which we live and to which we return, and which lives beyond us.[7]

The poems in *Buffalo Gals* are similar to those in *Wild Angels* and *Hard Words*, an eclectic mixture of styles. That mythopoeia remains important to Le Guin can be seen by her decision to reprint "Mount St. Helens/Omphalos." Also, she self-consciously defines herself as engaging in re-mythopoeia. She notes that "very often the re-visioning consists in a 'simple' change of point of view. It is possible that the very concept of point-of-view may be changing, may have to change, or to be changed, so that our reality can be narrated" (75).

Reality is not what we thought it was, and so the old realism must be replaced. Similarly, in *Wild Oats and Fireweed*, her most recent collection of poetry, a number of revisionings of myth appear. "Luwit" (19-25), for example, consists of three parts written about the eruption of Mount St. Helens. This poem reinforces the spiritual significance of that volcano for Le Guin, as the first part, "The Grey Quaker" mythologizes the mountain as a Hindu goddess. Set against the "realist" second and third parts, "The Grey Quaker" suggests that the magnitude of wilderness' power requires that we approach it with awe and respect if we are to understand the manifestations of the energy web in which we participate. The latter two parts provide numerous examples of the failure to adopt the appropriate awe and reverence when looking on the face of wild nature, with destructive and self-destructive results. The eruption must be seen as not simply destructive, but part of a balancing polarity of birth and death, chaos and stabilization, part of the "circle of life."

IV

And we too are right here in the "circle of life," with Snyder and Le Guin offering themselves, through their writing, to serve as compass points in a postmodern world lacking any true or even magnetic North Pole. But beyond that world remains one in which a Pole Star may be sighted, instruments set, and courses corrected, despite whatever beliefs the pilot may hold or eschew. In Le Guin's *The Dispossessed*, a favorite slogan is "True Voyage is Return." But we may need to hyphenate and restate that as "re-turn," to turn again, as in revolution, as in pivot, toward an ecological spirituality, a new godless pantheism perhaps, that decenters and untethers us and our thought from the post of postmodernism, particularly as its radical skepticism necessitates a continuously negative counter-agentive critique.

What we see time and again in the works of these two writers, whether in their poetry or their prose, is an attempt to grapple with the complexities of human experience in the world rather than to evade those complexities by a simplistic appeal to accurate description or true naming, or finding oneself through some isolated purgative retreat to stream or pond or lake or cabin. They do not rely on naive realism. At the same time, both refuse to capitulate to the dominant images of culture and daily life. They will not accept the objectified world of global consciousness. Through fantasy, myth, "healing songs," as well as the mundane and the ephemeral, they work at encouraging a re-cognition that does not rely exclusively on the conscious, rational component of the mind, nor on sensibility separate from the sensory. As can be traced through the historiography of academic criticism of these two authors, whenever a critic analytically concludes that Snyder or Le Guin has been fixed, his or her center located, his or her essential ethos determined, each shifts stance, moving to another pivot. Two of their titles suggest their "coyote" tendencies in this regard. Snyder's latest volume of poetry is titled *No Nature*, and Le Guin labelled her recent collection of prose *Dancing at the Edge of the World*. Perhaps, then, in this postmodern moment, we can adaptively learn from these two poets—although, of course, not from them alone—how to dance with this world at the edge of no nature.

III

Chapter Ten

Let the Survivors of Contact Speak: In the Canon and in the Classroom

In Chapter Three, I briefly criticized the function of *The Norton Book of Nature Writing*, published in 1990, in regards to the problem of the codification of nature writing as a genre and its implications for the continued marginalization of women and minority writers. I also claimed that Native American texts made problematic any effort at a formal, rather than modal, definition of environmental literature. In this chapter, I would like to elaborate on these two points and to emphasize the benefits that accrue from including Native American writing, particularly by women, in nature writing and other literature courses.

I
Native Americans and Definitions of Nature Writing

The Norton Book of Nature Writing, edited by two white males from New England, will prove, regardless of any editorial self-deprecation, to be a primary mechanism for canon formation in the field of nature writing, joining a set of others which have appeared in the past few years clearly intended to be used as classroom anthologies. *The Norton* continues the same problem demonstrated by two other texts preceding it. These are *On Nature* (1987), edited by Daniel Halpern, and *This Incomperable Lande*, edited by Thomas J. Lyon, originally published in 1989, with the paperback edition appearing in 1991.

On Nature and *This Incomperable Lande* are smaller, more modest editing projects than *The Norton*, yet they have served as part of the process that has led up to the decision to edit and publish a Norton compendium on the subject. Halpern cautiously begins *On Nature: Nature, Landscape, and Natural History* with an essay by John Hay that warns against trying to define clearly and exclusively the concept of the nature writer or the subjects upon which he or she might write. Hay's four-page essay provides only a few examples of the diversity of nature writing, yet prominent among them is a spontaneously recited woman Eskimo's winter song. And Hay remarks that "if a Western reader should read this as a poem for the first time, he might find it pleasing, fragmentary, even moving, but the depth and spontaneity which occasioned it would certainly pass him by, as, I am afraid, much of the Indian experience has passed us by" (9). So, how does editor Halpern respond to Hay's warning and his including song/poetry as part of nature writing? He does so by calling on a single Native American, among the twenty-four anthologized authors, to represent not only "Indian" experience, but all minority experience in North America and the British Isles. And he includes only what would be defined as "nonfictional prose."

The Indian is Leslie Marmon Silko. Halpern does add two essays about Indians after Silko's, by white anthropologists. And while these may be accurate, they tend to reinforce an ethnocentrism that treats Native Americans more as an object of American cultural studies than as diverse speaking subjects. Silko alone is allowed, in these 300 pages, to speak as an Indian about Indians to non-Indians, in an essay, an Anglo-literary form, rather than one of her more culturally-based artistic creations. This seems particularly ironic, given that, in various oral presentations, Silko has inveighed against the formal essay.

Tom Lyon, I am afraid, does not even provide room for even a token native to speak, nor does he include anything not definable as an essay. Clearly aware of these limitations, he states in his preface:

> I have arbitrarily confined this book to materials I consider nonfictional. The selection is similarly limited to writings by the European-American "white man," though in Native American mythic narrative there is a strong sense of the power of nature, particularly the dignity and the respectability, in the literal sense, of animals. . . . For the Indian, as has often been noted, there was no wilderness here, in the sense of a dichotomous term opposed to "civilization." The literature covered in this book reveals, perhaps, something convergent to that native outlook developing. (xv)

But why, then, not include some examples of that outlook, both in its historical and its current manifestations by hundreds of Native American authors? And such examples would certainly not need to be limited to "mythic" texts.

Lyon inadvertently commits the same kind of literary genocide that mars Max Oelschlaeger's recent book, *The Idea of Wilderness: From Prehistory to the Age of Ecology*. Where do Indians fit in this volume? They appear as "prehistory" and as the object of observation by white men. The chapter on Thoreau contains the most sustained attention given Indians. Do we learn what Indians have to say about wilderness? No, we learn what Thoreau thought "Indian wisdom" was. Oelschlaeger devotes more references to this Anglo-philosophical conception of "Indian wisdom" than he does even to Indians as objects of attention. The effect of *The Idea of Wilderness* and *This Incomperable Lande* is to create the impression that Indians have had nothing to say on their own, except in "mythic narratives," and that they are saying and writing nothing today, literary or otherwise, and this I would label literary genocide. Both Lyon and Oelschlaeger would no doubt be shocked by such a charge and deny that they ever intended anything of the sort, and I would believe them. I am not speaking of the intentions of these men, but of the effects of their decisions on the perceptions and understanding of their audiences, particularly the classroom audience in the increasing number of nature writing courses that are being taught around the country. Even though few of them are limited to nonfiction, *This Incomperable Lande* is an obvious choice as a text for such courses, while Oelschlaeger's book has already been used as a supplementary/research text for some.

Clearly, the Lyon anthology will be recognized by many teachers as a collection of selected readings, modest in size. No one would expect it to be comprehensive, and Lyon clearly clarifies his own decision making and foregrounds his omissions. These are not the assumptions that people will make about Finch and Elder's *The Norton Book of Nature Writing*, which assembles more nature writing than most English professors have read in their lifetimes. This volume will be turned to as the text to use to teach a survey course. By default, it will, to a large extent, define a canon. And that canon is highly exclusionary, narrowly defined, and chauvinist. Out of 908 pages, fewer than eighteen are given over to Momaday and Silko, their Native American authors. Finch and Elder include eighteen of the twenty-two authors that Lyon chooses, frequently including the same excerpt. Looking at these two texts, one witnesses a quick convergence toward a recognized modern canon of nature writers who are, predominantly, white males.

It is amazing to me that Finch and Elder, in producing the headnote for Momaday's brief selection, can quote him as saying: "I believe that the Indian has an understanding of the physical world and of the earth as a spiritual entity that is his, very much his own. The non-Indian can benefit a good deal by having that perception revealed to him" (774), yet can disregard that observation in their editorial practice. They claim that "our primary aim was to represent, as fully as possible, the range of nature writing in English over the past two centuries" (25), and they thought it important to bring British writers before American readers. But wouldn't it be more significant to bring the insights of the original inhabitants of this continent before an immigrant population predominantly of European descent? One would think so. Why are there, then, not more Native Americans in *The Norton Book of Nature Writing*? An author must be alienated to produce good nature writing, to have that "loss of integration between society and nature" (26). The editors do claim, however, that Native American experience and thought is not excluded from nature writing: "Today, through Native American writers like Scott Momaday and Leslie Marmon Silko, as well as through non-Indian writers like Richard Nelson and Gary Nabhan who are seeking to understand the Indian way of knowing the earth, this voice flows into and amplifies the tradition" (26). Note that they do not say that this Indian voice raises questions about or contradicts the tradition.

The Native American Authors Distribution Project catalog lists approximately 500 titles by Native American authors, most but not all of them contemporary works, comprising non-fiction, fiction, poetry, and storytelling. But, of course, much of this would not qualify as "nature writing," if by this term is meant nonfictional literary prose written along "naturalist" lines. Funny, what we have at issue here is a kind of writing informed by a certain mode—an attention to human-nature relationships with frequent emphasis on observation and depiction of specific, physical details; Lyon refers to "experiences in nature"—that is limited according to a definition of genre—a form of organizing the material—which privileges a style of writing primarily practiced in the past two centuries by white males. In other words, the editors define a mode of topical attention or thematic awareness as a genre of writing according to a set of formal criteria that are considered important to and primarily practiced by white males. Then they go out looking for items to include in their anthologies, and end up with seventy-nine of their ninety-four authors being white males. Lee Schweninger points out what will be lost if anthologies continue to be organized along these lines:

> Certainly, study of Native American literature as nature writing can provide the student and scholar an acquaintance with and an understanding of Native American ecology and culture that will lead them to a better understanding of and appreciation for the culture and, by contrast, ultimately a better undestanding of the dominant Western, Euro-American culture. Acceptance of some typically noncanonical literature in typically canonical genres (such as nature writing) is crucial, because not only can we not afford to dehumanize others by accepting traditional prejudices, we can no longer afford to ignore other cultures or other eras. From outside Western tradition we must salvage ideas for both our intellectual and physical survival. (58)

Finch and Elder want an Indian voice to flow into and amplyify a white-dominated tradition—dominated not only by type of author but also by type of perception. They believe that readers need to study nature writing by alienated authors, but seem less certain about studying writings by integrated, inhabitory authors. That is to say, their model of otherness is based on the psychoanalytic/cultural model of alienation and distance, the standard Western, patriarchal, Cartesian kind of binary opposition. The Indian experience of which Momaday speaks would seriously call into question the efficacy and necessity of such an alienation model. Similarly, Lyon wants the American-European white man's consciousness to converge toward a Native American consciousness, but he does not allow his readers to have this process complicated, or to have the degree to which it is actually occurring called into question, by including that native outlook in its historical or contemporary manifestations in his collection, again on the exclusionary basis of a definition of genre.

Jimmie Durham's speech at the Tellico Dam Congressional hearings (Matthiessen 119), or a few excerpts from Geary Hobson's collection *The Remembered Earth*, might make one wonder if convergence isn't a synonym for assimilation. Similarly, Oelschlaeger is very interested in "Indian wisdom," as conceptualized by Thoreau, but apparently not interested at all in letting Indians speak about themselves, or unable to integrate such speaking into the theoretical paradigm organizing his analysis. In contrast, Brian Tokar, in *The Green Alternative*, makes a point, three pages into Chapter One, of quoting Native American environmental beliefs, as presented by Segwalise, Dhyani Ywahoo, and the Haudenosaunee, in order to demonstrate the presence of other perceptions of human-nature relationships than the dominant ones in both mainstream U.S. culture and the U.S. environmental movement.

What would happen if we included Native American authors in nature writing courses? What would happen if we started noticing that we have contemporary Native American novelists and poets and critics, and even neighbors, and included their voices in the American literature courses that we teach? As Gregory Jay argues in the March, 1991, issue of *College English*, it would be the end of American literature as it so far has been conceptualized. The canon would melt down. Generic and modal prescriptive definitions of literature would have to be critiqued and rethought. The idea of nature writing as some neurotic practice of rationalistically structured essay writing by a bunch of alienated white guys escaping to the woods, usually only temporarily, to live out some fantasy of unconscious communion—perhaps really only a displacement of the desire to return to the womb—and arguing whether or not sport hunting is ethical, would have to be completely rethought (see Vitali).

A sophomore student of mine, a white male Chemistry major, was working on the draft of an essay for Introduction to Literature, while I was drafting the conference version of this chapter section. He was working on a comparison of Mary Oliver's *Dreamwork* and Linda Hogan's *Savings*. His tentative hypothesis, which he successfully developed, was that Oliver has to go out to nature, to find herself and to establish a kinship that breaks down alienation, because she has no tradition of a healthy culture-nature relationship to draw on for understanding her place. Hogan, however, includes nature continuously in her purview, but does not distinguish it from her cultural values and practices because, as a Native American raised in her Chickasaw heritage, she comes from a nature-culture integrative tradition. Hogan is, by his definition, just as much a nature writer as Oliver, but of a very different kind. To define only Oliver as a nature writer, because she is seeking to overcome alienation, or to define neither of them as nature writers, because they write poems rather than essays, would preclude this neophyte scientist from learning some of the valuable lessons possible only through comparative analysis.

A few years ago when I taught "Man in the Natural World" (the official catalog title), an upper division majors course, some of my students had trouble deciding whether the poetry in *Songs from This Earth on Turtle's Back*, edited by Joe Bruchac, was nature writing or not, because it was not 'about' nature. Rather, nature flowed through it. (The same problem would no doubt arise with Lerner's *Dancing on the Rim of the World*.) Similarly, they debated whether or not the city poems in Hogan's *Savings* and Paula Gunn Allen's *Skins and Bones* were nature writing or even environmental literature. I did not yet have Joy Harjo and Stephen Strom's *Secrets from the Center of the World* to show them in order to deepen their quandary. It might very well have set us off in a new direction. But let us accept for the moment that we will not include poetry or multimedia in our nature writing course. Do we need then to exclude Native Americans? No, Annie Booth and Harvey Jacobs's annotated bibliography, *Environmental Consciousness—Native American Worldviews and Sustainable Reource Management* contains numerous entries that could serve. And they range from the simplistic, brief entries collected in Aline Amon's *The Earth is Sore: Native Americans on Nature*, to collections that combine essays with other forms of relating experiences in nature, such as *Between Sacred Mountains: Navajo Stories and Lessons from the Land*, Hobson's *The Remembered Earth*, and McLuhan's *Touch the Earth: A Self-Portrait of Indian Existence*.

Many of the texts Booth and Jacobs cite are collected by non-Indian editors and provide varying degrees of context for the material presented. Nevertheless, they present a greater diversity of the Native voice than most anthologizers to date seem able to locate. In particular, these works, in their volume and diversity, indicate that the Native voice is not a background melody, which "flows into and amplifies the tradition" of white male nature writing, but very much forms its own variegated tradition and projects a set of perceptions and depictions of nature that calls into question the ontological authenticity of nature writing based on Cartesian dualisms and alienation models of human-nature relationships.

Let the survivors of contact speak about nature, themselves, and the connections among nature, culture, and the various peoples that inhabit these interpenetrating domains. Let us stop excluding the original Americans from nature writing and from American literature courses in general. Across the entire range of their courses, the survivors of contact can teach our students, as well as us, about right ways to live in relation to the land and right ways to live with one another. Many Native American writers have a different understanding of an ecological, relational model of anotherness than the psychological/political alienation one. This arises both from the historic rootedness in the land of their peoples and their families, and the cultural practices they have fought and struggled to maintain, relearn, and renew. As Paula Gunn Allen remarks about the traditional and contemporary stories collected in *Spider Woman's Granddaughters*, "there are transformations occasioned by the endurance of community, of aesthetics, of vision, and of truth. . . . They are testaments to cultural persistence, to a vision and a spiritual reality that will not die" (25). And she has continued her project of renewing the understanding of "spiritual reality" through the publication of *Grandmothers of the Light: A Medicine Woman's Sourcebook*. If we are going to learn from this vision, then we need to redefine our generic boundaries and our course parameters to let those testaments appear and be heard. The end of exclusion may prove quite transformative.

II
Teaching Native American Women Writers to the Immigrants

Conceptualizing the inclusion of Native American authors, in nature writing courses in particular and American literature courses in general, as a means of teaching stories from the indigenous, inhabitory cultures to immigrants still lacking a culture appropriate to the conditions in which they find themselves, can structure such student encounters with Native Americans in a way very different from the ones to which most students are accustomed. Rather than objects of attention, the voices represented in and through these texts will have to be approached as speaking subjects, as wisdom figures, as participants in the shaping of the present-day orientation toward the developing future. And in certain courses, emphasizing the women writers will extend the dialogue across a wider range of cultural differences and contradictions than would occur with a selection of male writers or a mixed-gender selection of writers, since students would tend to view even a mixture of male and female authors as male normative.

Let us begin, then, with the recognition that Native Americans have had to survive nearly five hundred years of attempted genocide. David Rich Lewis makes the point that "the first significance of Native Americans in the twentieth-century American West is their physical and cultural persistence as identifiable ethnic individuals and communities in the face of overwhelming odds" (205). So their cultural continuity and inhabitation have had to be based on a different set of imperatives and struggles than those of other peoples currently living in the various bioregions collectively identified as the United States of

America. And this is even more intensively the case for Native American women, who have had responsibilities for bearing, nurturing, and protecting their kin in the face of a protracted effort to end Native American birth in its entirety. Added to this has been gender oppression. Patriarchy as a systematic form of women's oppression had not been experienced by many Native Americans prior to European contact, given that large numbers of tribes had been and remain based on matrilineal descent, matrilineal clans, and matrifocal spirituality with women as political leaders and wisdom figures (see Bannan). In Paula Gunn Allen's words, "male supremacy, like any other idea of one-sidedness, is uncongenial to traditional American Indian thought or social systems" ("Teaching" 135).

Yet despite this double oppression, of European colonization and patriarchal subjugation, coupled with extensive exploitation of their peoples and lands, Native American women today are celebrating not merely the survival but also the revitalization of their more than eight hundred tribal cultures.[1] An amazing number of Native American women, given that Indians comprise slightly less than one percent of the U.S. population, have become artists, to communicate the values of this continent's original human inhabitants to each other and to a horde of overwhelmingly rootless, spiritually deprived, and alienated immigrants. They have much to teach us.

Who do I mean by "us"? I mean non-Native American teachers and students, female and male. How many college professors in the United states are Native Americans, in whole or in part? How many of our students can trace back their ancestry on this continent much before the turn of the century? According to the most recent figures for my school, Indiana University of Pennsylvania, 92 percent of the students are white; 95 percent are from Pennsylvania. And in the state system of fourteen campuses, 86 percent of the students are from Pennsylvania, with the percentage of those being white pretty much the same as for IUP with one exception, the "historically black" college. We are mostly white professors teaching white students, with our faculties more ethnically diversified than our student population.

We are teaching people who for the most part have not yet learned how to inhabit their regions in an appropriate, ecologically sound way. They have virtually no experience of learning from those who have preceded them and lived far more in balance with their environment than any significant segment of European settlers have ever been able to do. And our women students, in particular, have not even been brought up to appreciate the lessons and the wisdom of their foremothers, but have been mostly educated with an androcentric concentration on European forefathers and their North American sons. This same education has also denied them an accurate portrait of the position of women in the indigenous societies that pre-existed and continue to exist alongside Anglo-American culture. As Gretchen Bataille concludes in her study of autobiographies: "The Indian woman is and has been strong within her culture. . . . The life stories of Indian women . . . support the view that the role of the Indian woman was and is defined within American Indian cultures as important and essential" (97).

For our female students especially, across the entire range of their courses, the survivors of contact have lessons to impart about right ways to live in relation to the land. They can also teach them about right ways to live with one another, since more Native Americans have had experiences of a woman's life in cultures not based on patriarchy—or at least not as solidly and historically as entrenched in patriarchy, nor based on a woman's alienation from her body, or on a woman's degradation as a result of her biological specificity—than the immigrants have had. Many Native American women writers, then, have a valuable vision to share about the ways in which the world could operate more equitably and holistically, based on their having sustained ways of living alternative to the dominant culture. And they have acquired valuable experiences in the ways to survive contact with patriarchy in its most virulent colonialist, capitalist, and individualistic forms.

For example, Patricia Clark Smith argues that much contemporary Anglo women's poetry about women relatives treats these people as being alien to the author from an individual, psychological perception of otherness which ranges from "seeing the woman as suddenly unfamiliar in some way to seeing her as a monster" ("Ain't Seen You" 112). But, Smith claims, "the image of a woman relative as an alien being simply does not appear in American Indian women's poetry" ("Ain't Seen You" 114). Instead, there is "a tendency to see conflict between women as not totally a personal matter but, rather, as part of a larger whole, as a sign that one of the pair has lost touch not with just a single individual but with a complex web of relationships and reciprocities" ("Ain't Seen You" 115). How different might our students' perceptions of their relationships with one another and their own mothers and grandmothers be, if Joy Harjo, Paula Gunn Allen, Luci Tapahonso, and Linda Hogan were used to establish the example, rather than Sylvia Plath and Anne Sexton?[2]

Paula Gunn Allen, in the introduction to *Spider Woman's Granddaughters*, declares that "it is of great importance that they be read as tribal women's literature, an old and honored literary tradition in its own right. . . . We are not so much 'women,' as American Indian women; our stories, like our lives, necessarily reflect that fundamental identity. And as American Indian women, we are women at war" (24). To become true inhabitants, immigrants must learn from indigenous peoples. Integrating Native American women writers into Women's Studies and other college courses can facilitate achieving a number of goals and developing students' recognitions of a series of cultural problems. But integration must be distinguished from assimilation. As Allen takes pains to clarify, when teaching the stories in *Spider Woman's Granddaughters* or any other native text, the differences between women of color and white women must not be ignored and their particularities must not be conflated to create some totalizing and idealist notion of Woman. Such teaching requires a "multicultural pedagogy," which, according to Gregory Jay, "initiates a cultural revision, so that everyone involved comes not only to understand another person's point of view, but to see her or his own culture from the outsider's perspective" (274).

Most of the students that most of us will be teaching the rest of our careers will be white students raised in the Judeo-Christian tradition of Western civilization. They need to realize the more oppressive aspects of that heritage, and of their subject positions as whites and as women in the world today. Introducing them to Native American women's literature can foreground the relationship of self and other in particularly beneficial ways. Native American women's experiences differ from those of other peoples of color insofar as they are the only descendants of the original human inhabitants of this continent.

Much feminist criticism has necessarily emphasized the need to overcome the alienation of women from their bodies and from their foremothers that has resulted from centuries of patriarchal oppression. The Introduction to *Rising Tides* unequivocally states that "women must learn the self-love, the self-idealizing, the self-mythologizing, that has made it possible for men to think of themselves as persons" (qtd. in Elias-Button 201). But Native American women have already been doing this for centuries. As Helen Bannan notes, "the granddaughters of the first educated generation appreciate the traditions that their grandmothers still remember and teach, and reaffirm the ancient continuity of maternal strength in their writings. . . . Native American granddaughters are following Spider Woman's advice to hold fast the web of tradition, and . . . use their power to increase that web, preserving its basic design while incorporating new materials and experiences into its structure" (276).

I am not claiming, and I would not care to do so, that Native American women are better writers than other women, or that they have necessarily suffered more as individuals than other women. Native American women do, however, have a *different* experience of the world as women than do most of our students. Native American women bring from their experiences different concerns and they propose a different set of solutions than we hear from other women writers. They have survived many of the crises currently facing other women in the United States today; their survival speaks a hope, a promise, and a success for the rest. And they have demonstrated an ability to retain and revitalize cultural and familial practices arising from matrifocal societies that conclusively point to the possibility for a nonpatriarchal society to replace this country's dominant patriarchal one. Luci Tapahonso states this quite simply: "In the Navajo society . . . it's just been equal and it's having a status that's different from the one that non-indian people have" (qtd. in Moulin-Cohen 10).

Chapter Eleven

Centering the Other: Trickster Midwife Pedagogy

"Things fall apart; the centre cannot hold." For Yeats these words pronounced a cataclysmic problem; for us today they announce a promise: patriarchy had a beginning; it will have an end. Feminism, in its various manifestations, is founded upon such a belief, and works toward that project in myriad and, at times, contradictory ways. Crucial to ending patriarchy is the effort to break open the phallocratic, androcentric ideologies that place Man at the center of the universe with Woman and Nature ever-subservient throughout a long history of political and cultural systems. Education and attendant self-consciousness have always been crucial contested terrain and remain so today. And as feminist pedagogy continues to develop in conjunction with feminist theory, the relationship between method and message in education becomes ever more sharply delineated. How we teach and what we teach cannot be artificially disengaged from one another any more than can theory from practice. Centering the other as a way of challenging patriarchy is one form of feminist praxis, based on a particular pedagogy, that of the Trickster Midwife, and a specific theoretical foundation, that of ecofeminism.

The Trickster Midwife serves as a pedagogical model for replacing the outworn banking model of a thrifty investor who fills an empty lockbox with his precious intellectual stock and gems. A Trickster teaches by story, paradox, and questioning, to help people grow up and individuate without losing their vision.[1] Ursula K. Le Guin exemplifies just such an approach in her feminist rendition of "Coyote" in the novella "Buffalo Gals." In my metaphoric conceptualization, Trickster does not chart a path or dispense a treasure map, but highlights the entanglements, whirlpools, and rocks that the dominant culture utilizes to smash individual alterity and any group solidarity or struggle for change. Such education requires that the student recognize the teacher as guide and aid, but not as monological, monolithic authority (see Bakhtin, *Problems* 81). With a Trickster Midwife as professor,[2] the student learns that the teacher is the one with the questions, and the student is the one who must discover and invent the answers, not simply guess what the teacher wants. Or, in Gloria Anzaldúa's words, "Voyager, there are no bridges, one builds them as one walks" (v). Tricksters have generally been imaged as males, but traditions exist that images them as female, as rowdy and irreverent Sophias.

In order to conceptualize a Trickster Midwife pedagogy, we need to take issue with Jean Piaget's belief that the consciousness and relationship to reality of college students have already been established because they have reached the rational stage of cognitive development. And we need to do so from the perspective that Patricia Yaeger outlines via Benjamin: "'the triumph of cognition' Piaget celebrates in the adult signals the child's 'defeat as a revolutionary subject.' However, the presence of children speaks eloquently in every generation about a new potential for emancipatory activity" (221). Rather than having attained some acme of rationality, college students are far more frequently entering a stage marked by the crystallization of half-understood received values. To reverse that process, to unsettle the sediment of an enforced passive receptivity, we must conceive of the teacher as one who can stimulate active and reflective critical thought. The Trickster Midwife allows for the possibility of engaging in such desedimentation without imposing a new set of received values, hardly better understood than the former ones, which would only replicate the patriarchal monologues of the traditional classroom. Such a teacher serves as a guide who encourages students toward self-consciousness, self-motivation, and inquiry in search of commitment.

The concern is with method-as-process rather than result, a self-conscious dialogical pedagogy that first of all recognizes and appreciates the difference between self and other. And specifically in regard to Women's Studies and women-centered courses, such as topics in women's literature or feminist theory, dialogical pedagogy enables the female student to perceive her subject position as that of self rather than other, the position she has been permanently assigned by patriarchy. Judith Fetterley has caustically noted that "as readers and teachers and scholars, women are taught to think as men, to identify with a male point of view, and to accept as normal and legitimate a male system of values, one of whose central principles is misogyny" (xx; see Schweickart 41–42); another, of course, is hierarchy. But it is not enough that a Midwife foster the birth of female subject construction as self, for the reverse also needs to be fostered: males perceiving their subject position as being constructed as precisely that of other prior to and always alongside of self. Young males must experience the object position of self as other, a status they have previously reserved for everyone and everything else. As Carolyn Shrewsbury has noted, "one goal of the liberatory classroom is that members learn to respect each other's differences rather than fear them. Such a perspective is ecological and holistic" (6). Yes, but; it is also true that some may learn respect only after having passed through the fear and discomfort that come when one's sense of self is challenged by the assertion of alterity and the legitimacy of otherness, not through some non-confrontational "I'm OK, you're OK" pluralism but through a dialogical multivocality that stresses engagement and interaction. In Audre Lorde's words, "difference must be not merely tolerated, but seen as a fund of necessary polarities between which our creativity can spark like a dialectic" (99).[3]

The professorial Trickster operates primarily in the "logosphere, that ecosystem whose prime constitutent is the utterance" (Holquist, "Surd" 153); and in that sphere dialogics needs to be foregrounded, to empower the critical habits of social beings on the brink of self-consciousness. That sphere must also be inseparably linked to the rest of the physical world with which it is interdependent, if students are to grasp a sustaining, i.e., ecological, purpose for such self-consciousness. And in this linkage they must be introduced to the idea that one's self is always someone else's other, and both are another to each other.

Consider gender balance as an example. A struggle continues to be waged to gender-balance the curriculum. And the first wave consists of balancing the subject matter, for example, the choice of literary authors or depictions of women in history. But what will it profit women to gain the teaching of their literature, if they fail to gain their voice about that literature? Inclusion in syllabi parallels the shift in patriarchal thought from viewing nature as a howling wilderness, whose inhabitants must be damned, to a resource to be utilized for man's higher purposes. In either case it is an object requiring patriarchal domination. Carole Tarantelli correctly notes that "feminist literary scholarship has rightly emphasized the fact that one of the principal triumphs of the women's literary tradition has been the recovery for visibility of the world *from the female point of view* and of the hidden and unexpressed female part of the world" (190; my emphasis). Yet men will be more than willing to teach literature by women, if they must, in the same way that they teach works by men, with a male normative audience, androcentric values, patriarchal power structures, and the monological authority of the dominant gender, thereby evading precisely the female point of view that such literature represents. And they will continue to do so, neutralizing such literature and placing it in safe canonical, suburban cul de sacs, unless their students challenge such beliefs by forcing a dialogue upon them in the classroom and their colleagues do the same elsewhere.

Barbara Johnson, in reading Moliere's *L'Ecole des femmes*, raises some crucial questions: "Are our ways of teaching students to ask *some* questions always correlative with our ways of teaching *not to ask*—indeed, to be unconscious of—others? Does the educational system exist in order to promulgate knowledge, or is its main function rather to universalize a society's tacit agreement about what it has decided it does not and cannot know?" (76–77). Such tacit agreements must be exposed and inspected in the classroom. The monological voice of received values needs to be relativized. Yaeger proposes a number of examples of such practice by women writers in *Honey-Mad Women*. She says, for example, of Charlotte Bronte's practice, that "the point is to make the dominant discourse one among many possible modes of speech" (41), and points to Mary Wollstonecraft's handling of Rousseau as exemplary of such dialogizing of authority: "Wollstonecraft removes Rousseau's language from the distanced, nondialogic zone where she finds it and makes it available for alteration. As his hierarchical stance is challenged, his prose grows open to change, disagreement, conflict: it acquires a relative, particular status" (173).

Focusing on a dialogical method with a sense of the historical development of crucial cultural debates enables the recognition that while one idea, culture, class, or value, may become dominant, it need not remain so; nor does that dominance mean that the subordinate polarity of that unity has been eradicated or discredited. Women's experience and feminist interpretations of that experience clearly do not dominate the scene of instruction campuswide, but just as clearly they are no longer so easily dismissed. The dialogical classroom organized by a Trickster Midwife will allow both the student to see that her ideas may be valid and to learn mechanisms by which not only to voice those ideas but also at times to invert the dominant power relationship. Instead of the presentation of a *correct* view of the world in a monological, authoritative, patriarchal utterance that encourages passive assent rather than active debate, the Trickster professor works with developing "internally persuasive discourse," which "makes a claim on the speaker that may carry authority but is open to questioning and modification" (LaCapra 314). The dialogical moment, then, more than providing any alternative viewpoint or answer *per se*, can serve to introduce students to alterity itself through the utilization of any range of examples, including but not limited to one's own beliefs; and, concomitantly, to internal dialogical debate as well as external dialogue over values, beliefs, and goals.

But it is crucial, as Dale Bauer notes, for the kinds of internal debates that female students undergo, particularly with their first encounters with the recognition of the validity of their own experiences, that the learning and the dialogue not remain internal. She points out that "the notion of internal polemics is a dangerous one for feminism in that it seems to argue for non-speech or silence" (5). Rather, "we acquire 'ourselves' by engaging in our own dialogue with others, and especially with texts that challenge our beliefs" (8), and people who challenge or reject them. Recognizing the importance of externalized dialogues for women, particularly those in which women get to confront men as authorities, interpreters, and answerers, requires that Trickster pedagogy attend constantly to gender differences in the classroom. While some women need to be encouraged in self-authorization, some men need to be encouraged in self-silencing. In the former case, the student needs to learn more about the self and her own authority; in the latter case, the student needs to learn more about the other and the relativity of authority.

We need to find ways to break down the position of authority awarded us as teachers from the outset, not in some pseudo-egalitarian way limited to just rearranging seats in a circle while simultaneously waving the grade book about, but in ways that clarify the importance of each student developing her or his own self-conscious critical posture. Paula Treichler points out that:

> Studies of teachers find that, at every educational level, women tend to generate more class discussion, more interaction, more give-and-take between students and teacher and among students. In direct relation to the degree to which this is true, (1) students evaluate these classes as friendlier, livelier, less authoritarian, and more conducive to learning, AND (2) students judge the teacher to be less competent in her subject matter. (86)

If we foreground Trickster Midwife methods, let the students in on the secrets of why the teacher is doing what she or he is doing, i.e., perform a meta-criticism of the pedagogy in process, engage in self-critique and group evaluation of the pedagogy and the subject matter, then we can break down the myth of competence-equals-patriarchy that Treichler finds as the only explanation for the contradictory evaluations she has summarized. Treichler's remarks also flag the gendered differences in student expectations that each teacher must confront, and that the male teacher, in particular, must discern and challenge. Men need to teach differently than their training both as teachers and as males in this society has prepared them to do. Males practicing as Trickster Midwives have a specific role to play in altering perceptions about the way women and men should and do teach and the social function of teaching in general, by challenging patriarchal stereotypes and norms.[4]

Work against patriarchy is both political and dialogical, in that the alternative to patriarchy is not matriarchy, but heterarchy. The self-recognition of otherness that exists in a Women's Studies classroom and is made explicit in the Trickster classroom encourages a dialogical conception of self and a critical self-consciousness regarding the world and one's place in it. Ellen Morgan argues that "Women's studies classrooms can't tell students how to escape the discomforts of the alienation that comes with role change. . . . But I suggest that as teachers we recognize that our students will very likely need methods to survive and thrive on the feminist madness we may wake in them. . . . I think this means that when we present materials on women to them, we should also prepare them for the possible consequences of their knowing and acting upon it" (6). Female students who experience such a classroom (in or out of Women's Studies), should be assisted in realizing the necessity to view it not only as an enclave in which to speak freely among themselves and to each other, but also as a base camp—whether they see that metaphor as originating in mountain climbing or guerrilla warfare may depend more on their level of militancy—from which to launch themselves into other classrooms, into the logosphere dominated by patriarchy, and break the conspiracy of silence with public debate, polemic, and dialogue.

Similarly, male students who encounter a classroom that is not patriarchally male-normative will be challenged to recognize the relativity of received values and the otherness always coterminous with any conception of self. Both male and female students will be presented with the premise that "alienation and mediation are conditions of agency" (Stewart 11). As Teresa de Lauretis sees it, "to envision gender (men and women) otherwise, and to (re)construct it in terms other than those dictated by the patriarchal contract, we must walk out of the male-centered frame of reference in which gender and sexuality are (re)produced by the discourse of male sexuality" (17).

But in order to establish a base camp classroom, the Trickster needs a theoretical foundation for orientation, tools, and philosophical affirmation. Negative critiques and deconstructions of existing pedagogical models, theoretical systems, and canons of texts and interpretations, are all well and good, but also fall short. As Yaeger recognizes, even as she engages in deconstructive practice, "we must also make room in a theory of emancipatory strategies for the 'positive ideology' of content and the intersubjective dimension of collective dreams" (275; see also 266), and it comes as no surprise that she chooses Mary Oliver, an ecological poet, for her exemplar of such ideology. Or, as de Lauretis expresses it, "it is power, not resistance or negativity, that is the positive condition of knowledge" (30). While it may be the case that without destruction there can be no construction, the latter produces the necessity for the former. I would like to suggest that the dialogical ecofeminist theory I have elaborated in the early chapters of this book provides a foundation for construction without a prescriptive architecture that dooms every classroom to look like the Hilton chain, with the hotel in Houston indistinguishable from the one in Boca Raton.

Susan Stewart has claimed that "when we look at the history of 'our discipline' [literary studies] . . . we see that changes in the discipline are not mere changes of topic—they are, rather, changes effecting methodology, hence reorganizing the social network of knowledge and thereby resulting in new objects of knowledge" (10–11). And Johnson argues that "the profound political intervention of feminism has indeed been not simply to enact a radical politics but to redefine the very nature of what is deemed political" (31); that politics itself remains a focus of intense debate precisely over what should constitute "the social network of knowledge" and what teachers' "new objects of knowledge" should be. Ecofeminism is a branch of feminist theory and a branch of ecological philosophy that provides a farther-reaching, more synthesizing orientation in the world for transformative pedagogy than other feminisms, because it links the self/other relationship among individuals to the self/other relationship of individual and nature, and has the potential through a dialogic method to take it beyond a perception of otherness to one of anotherness, that non-threatening interdependent difference of which Audre Lorde speaks. Ecofeminism is also based on a heterarchical preservation of difference and a radical decentering of the human that challenges the andro- and anthropocentric underpinnings of patriarchy, including its modern-day pluralistic humanism variant.

I believe that it is possible to change the world by changing consciousness; such changes, however, have often been disastrous for the world and its humanity. In contrast, to understand the world and to have knowledge of interrelationships, reciprocities, and interdependence requires the development of self-consciousness founded on dialogical debate and self/other interaction oriented toward the productive tension of continuously resolving and reforming difference. Ecofeminism provides women with a different conception of self as another, which is tremendously empowering, since it also recognizes males as mutually another in relation to the biosphere and calls for behavioral reorientation. Trickster pedagogy can serve to foster just such awareness of anotherness and action in the world because it is based on and derives value from that world. Ecofeminism provides the ground upon which the Trickster professor may walk, or even dance, in the process of encouraging students to build the bridges they need from the self to another, from the human to the rest of the world.

critical self-consciousness regarding the world and one's place in it. One immediate practical result of this recognition of the pedagogical value of feminism should be the full engagement of each teacher with gender, balancing the classroom texts to attention to the needs and interests of both genders in attendance and to attention to the representation of women within the course material. While this task and needs to be pursued at all levels, it is crucial to pursue at the graduate level because of the foregrounding of canon formation that is currently taking place.

Although it goes without saying that the arena of canon formation is the one that lends itself most readily to dialogical thought, we should be aware that the dialectic, rather than the dialogue, it is the synthesis of some shadowy dialectic that is foregrounded. The dialogic move is to open the canon for critique rather than to replace one set of icons for another. The latter seems to me the key problem in the proliferation of "nature writing" anthologies occurring in recent years. Such substitutions do nothing to disrupt the hierarchical thinking that constitutes canon formation and it should be apparent by now that often-unnamed advice, of temporal is to the mainstream only serves to reinforce the illusion of democratic freedom without challenging the rules of the game. Canon formation itself needs to be called into question at the level of one's own defining production, and at the level of classroom instruction. As a student argues that

Pedagogy, particularly in the realm of culture, need turn to like the fundamental challenge to share both the transmission of coded knowledge and the critical transmission of knowledge. . . . Learning is always, but not in the traditional positivist sense, it involves a non-synchronous requirement to in the widest sense for the discovery of new theoretic reconstructions in the process of taking possession of and transforming identities. It is a methodologically ecological act it honors the forms and ruptures of pathos and desire in forms of alternative knowledges are what Pierre Bourdieu and Jean-Claude Passeron would call "cultural arbitraries." [28]

Gerald Graff has rather persuasively suggested at the end of Professing Literature that the critical debates behind the constitution of literary studies have not been brought into the classroom, so that students are subjected to the experience of conflicting, competing alternative authorities on literary interpretation rather than attempting to the library cacophony as outrageous. Such texts are better of exposed to the possibility that the idea of truth stuck to debate rather than demonstrate leads to the true idea.

We can conceive of ourselves as teachers as Trickster figures who can emulate into the center of intellectual attention the paradox of self-conscious

Chapter Twelve

The Present is to Nature as the Past is to Culture as the Future is to Agency

The Separation Fallacy

Gregory Bateson has warned that "when you separate mind from the structure in which it is immanent, such as a human relationship, the human society, or the ecosystem, you thereby embark, I believe, on a fundamental error, which in the end will hurt you" (qtd. in Bowers 109). That fundamental error remains a pervasive one in Western thought, and consists not only of constructing reality in terms of inequitably weighted dichotomies but also of treating the entities constituted by such dichotomies as separate, oppositional, and, at times, potentially autonomous from each other. Bateson establishes three contexts of immanence for "mind" that have been repeatedly treated as dichotomies: individual mind/individual human body; individual mind/human society (collective human "body"); and, individual mind/ecosystem (world "body"). A fundamental fallacy must be assumed as a given truth if each of these dichotomies is to be conceptualized: the mind has a radical independence enabling it to be uniquely self-constituting. In U.S. culture this fallacy popularly takes the ideological forms of individualism (domestically) and American exceptionalism (internationally).

I would argue that this assumption of radical independence comprises a necessary hypostasis for the modern penchant to separate humans from the rest of nature; in contrast, a hypostasis of individual interdependence within the world body can serve to promote a conception of human agency, which I will outline here, consonant with the realization of human interconnectedness with the rest of nature. These two conflicting hypostases can be represented by the distinction between thinking in terms of the not-self as other and as another.

While in philosophy a hypostasis is defined as "the underlying principle or nature; essence; substance" of an entity, in the biological sciences it means something quite different: "the masking or suppression of a gene by one or more genes that are not its allelomorphs"[1]—that is, not its linked differential twin. In other words, one characteristic of a biological entity's physical structure is suppressed by another. I would argue that, in like manner, there are cultural hypostases: one characteristic of a culture is suppressed by another, but with an added, ideological dimension, in that the characteristic suppressed is necessarily defined as negative, evil, or undesirable, while the suppressor takes on the status of positive, good, and desirable. Although quite different, these two meanings of hypostasis meet in the "fundamental error" identified by Bateson. The continued propagation of individualism—a belief in the radical independence of human beings from all else, including each other—enables the continuation of popular dichotomies that perpetuate the opposition of nature and culture. This ideological dominant in U.S. culture serves to mask and suppress not only human origins, by denying any evolution, alteration, or natural history for the species, but also to deny all ongoing human interrelationship with the rest of nature, of which we, as individual members of a species, and the species, as a collective body, remain a part in evolutionary process.[2]

Only by denying the larger implications of genetic coding than whether a baby's eyes will be blue or brown can we imagine that we are not part of nature. Our chromosomes themselves serve as a model of differential interdependence in that the dominant or recesssive condition of genetic traits, or the presence of such hereditary diseases as sickle cell anemia, depends on *almost* identical twinned arrangements of molecules on a pair of chromosomes (see Durham 482–85), which themselves are produced by the interaction of two separate parental genetic streams. Yet, the unique characteristics of each offspring depend upon the differences that result from an identical structure of procreative genetic interactions perpetuated through thousands of years by the species. And when we then think about all of the dimensions of human societies organized around, in the service of, and resulting from, human sexual reproduction, then only by denying that the mind is formed as part of the body can we imagine that culture does not arise from nature even as nature is shaped by culture. In the Introduction to *Coevolution: Genes, Culture, and Human Diversity*, William Durham stresses this dialogic relationship of nature and culture in human existence by invoking the words of a geneticist, Theodosius Dobzhansky: "Human evolution cannot be understood as a purely biological process, nor can it be adequately described as a history of culture. It is the interaction of biology and culture" (Durham 10).

Naturalized Alienation

In common usage, "nature" is that which is nonhuman, or in terms of human nature, that which is not conscious or acculturated. In popular representations of it, nature is something fundamentally unchanging and not the product of any process or activity, except insofar as it results from biblical Creation—conceptualized as a brief period of generation followed by stasis. Rather, nature serves as an inexhaustible treasure chest of the raw materials to be managed and transformed in the production of everything human. The current promotion of nuclear power as *the* energy alternative for the future, for example, conveniently ignores that uranium supplies are as exhaustible and as geologically determined as oil or coal; also, the spotted owl debate has largely failed to convince the American public that the old growth forests are as endangered as the owls, and that a forest is more than a large number of trees located in one place. George Watts, President of the Nuu Chah Nulth Tribal Council in "British Columbia," caustically observes that "walking in the forest where the trees are spaced ten feet away from each other, exactly in the same distance in the north and south direction as in the east and west direction, that is not the same as walking in a forest that was put there by other forces!" (91).

Culture, in contrast, seems to be very much the product of the past, and this culture, like the past upon which it is established, is then viewed as finalized, reified—i.e. packaged—for public consumption. And that public is considered not to be or to become, but to remain another raw material, to be commodified and cybernated as employee, constituency, and consumer. Such reification depends upon the separation of mind from body, and individual from nature, in order to conceptualize reality by means of static models utilizing discrete components. Thoughts are static commodities that can be traded and sold long after the thinking body that has produced them has culminated its process of conscious life; board feet of timber can be traded and sold long after the forest that generated them has been clear cut and the humus eroded.

Descartes stands as the champion of such separation of mind and body, and as the point man for the Enlightenment commodification of nature, which Carolyn Merchant has documented. And as Max Horkheimer and Theodor Adorno argued nearly fifty years ago, "the Enlightenment has extinguished any trace of its own self-consciousness" (4). The crucial element of that extinguished self-consciousness was the recognition that alienation, which has been enthroned as a given of modern rational existence, is generated and continuously reproduced by Enlightenment beliefs, rather than arising as a byproduct of consciousness. Such a tautology had to be suppressed in order to justify an increasing exploitation of nature and other humans, which expanded globally through the oppression and extermination of indigenous cultures that did not practice or believe in such alienation. Modern culture as a continuation of the Enlightenment,[3] then, is represented as the crazy glue that cements past, present and future humans together in a static continuity of contradiction and alienation from the rest of the world from which they arise, in which they participate with other entities, and to which they eventually return. Yet this condition of contradiction and alienation cannot be presented as a hypostasis of Enlightenment ideology, since that would open it to critique and rejection; instead, it must be represented as a part of the natural order.

And even when such alienation, predicated upon the nature/culture oppositional dichotomy, is recognized as culturally specific, it nevertheless escapes analysis and rejection, as in the case of recent nature writing anthologies. *The Literature of Nature: The British and American Traditions*, edited by Robert J. Begiebing and Owen Grumbling is a case in point. The editors claim that, despite the limitations required by the selection process, and their acknowledgment that what they treat is "only one strain," their anthology's "selections represent, or at least suggest, the enormous field of nature writing in England and America during, roughly, the past two hundred years" (v). Curiously, neither their "England" nor their "America" includes Canada, which apparently has no specific culture—perhaps it is too natural a territory. Their representative sample includes no persons of color, no indigenous peoples, and no non-English speaking inhabitants of North America during the pre-U.S. period, that is, all of the colonized others. Their claim that the British and American "canons" of nature writing form a "common tradition," really means the codification of a few select world views established by white male writers (only three white U.S. women are included). Native Americans are apparently not defined as "Americans" by these editors, suggesting that indeed a certain kind of alienational intellect is required for nature writing. The degree to which the editors have not interrogated their own Enlightenment mindset or ideological subject construction is indicated by the following: "In its depiction of natural objects, nature literature explores how the natural world meets human needs beyond the merely physiological, economic, or technological" (viii). The world consists of "objects," for which white male authors are the subjects, and the function of the rest of the world is one of meeting "human needs" of one kind or another, which is to say that the world remains conceptualized as exclusively a thing-for-us. In no way are nature writers perceived as things-for-others, in the way that Gary Snyder, for instance, would define his obligation as a poet to let other aspects of the world speak through him in poetry.

Situated Knowledges

The historical transformation of the myriad human and nonhuman aspects of the contemporary earth's past into the coherent, homocentric Past upon which the abstract, idealized official Culture of a modern nation-state, its various canons, is founded is nothing less than the Enlightenment ideal of the scientific method made manifest in the human sciences. With a B.A. in History, I can recall no history text that I studied in my first sixteen years of schooling that included environmental change as a significant political variable. Fred Dallmayr, invoking Horkheimer and Adorno, contends that "modern epistemology is wedded to discursive logic and to universal concepts or categories to which particularities are rigidly subsumed or subordinated; in this manner the diversity and elusiveness of reality are sacrified to the primacy of general rules" (Dallmayr 35). In particular, the diversity and elusiveness of nonhuman nature are denied by contemporary nature/culture and mind/body dichotomies, in order to continue to generate an alienational model of human separation from the rest of nature, in which independence, rather than any kind of interdependence, is exalted as the ideal state of individual existence.

Yet certainly, in the United States as elsewhere, Enlightenment culture is not the only past upon which we may draw for contemporary cultural practice. And it may very well prove to be the case that the Enlightenment will one day be viewed by its cultural descendants, as it already is by many indigenous peoples, as aberrant behavior. Gary Snyder observes that "the term *culture*, in its meaning of 'a deliberately maintained esthetic and intellectual life' and in its other meaning of 'the totality of socially transmitted behavior patterns,' is never far from a biological root meaning as in 'yogurt culture'—a nourishing habitat" (15). And he suggests that we can learn from some past cultures, in order to chart a course for future cultures that will shake us loose from the alienated thralldom of the Enlightenment:

> The culture areas of the major native groups of North America overlapped, as one would expect, almost exactly with broadly defined major bioregions. . . . In the old ways, the flora and fauna and landforms are *part of the culture.* The world of culture and nature, which is actual, is almost a shadow world now, and the insubstantial world of political jurisdictions and rarefied economies is what passes for reality. We live in a backwards time. We can regain some small sense of that old membership by discovering the original lineaments of our land and steering—at least in the home territory and in the mind—by those rather than the borders of arbitrary nations, states, and counties. (37)

Snyder contends, then, that bioregional human social organization places individuals fundamentally more in relationship, and less alienated from the rest of nature, because the very criteria employed in the structures of the social body are attentive to the specific characteristics of the world's body, and, necessarily, the individual body would gain nourishment and sustain itself in terms of those specifics.

Such bioregional acculturation would foster modes of thought directly contradictory to the "modern epistemology" that Dallmayr criticizes, and which Horkheimer and Adorno, as well as Merchant, blame for the intensification of human alienation from the rest of nature, and human exploitation and oppression of other humans. It would also necessitate a recognition of the need for partial, "situated knowledges" as requisite equipment for human life in different parts of the world. In Donna Haraway's words, "I am arguing for politics and epistemologies of location, positioning, and situating, where partiality and not universality is the condition of being heard to make rational knowledge claims. These are claims on people's lives; the view from a body . . . versus the view from above" (195). Further, she argues that in addition to reversing the Enlightenment tendency toward abstract universals, "situated knowledges" also "require that the object of knowledge be pictured as an actor and agent, not a screen or a ground or a resource" (198). Such a practice would explode the mind/body and human/nature dichotomies that allow both the nonhuman and other humans to be defined as resources for exploitation.

Future Agency

Agency is the requisite concept for any strategy of affirming the future in terms of possibility. But the future itself has been reified, as Marcuse phrased it, into a "dead world of matter." Future generations of Americans are already obligated to provide for our Social Security checks on the one hand, while paying taxes to service our parents' National Debt on the other. Future studies themselves are largely a product of the Enlightenment and the triumph of industrial capitalism. What could be more utilitarian than planning for the future? In the literary and cinematic manifestations of future studies, the modern utopian genre and science fiction, the vast majority of works tend toward static projections of ideal or already existing structures and elaborate depictions of things—notice in the films *2001* and *Star Trek I*, for example, how much time and attention are given to constructed objects. In the contemporary television series, "Space Rangers," the characters open one episode complaining about personnel cutbacks and hazard pay, in dialogue that could have recently been lifted from a Pittsburgh Police locker room. In the end, such novels and films propose monological and authoritarian systems to which the people of the future will be obligated to conform.

In utopian fiction, such inevitability is usually demonstrated by the first-person narrator, who visits and observes the future or alternative world, eventually conforming for his (they are almost always male) own good, whether one reads Bellamy or Gilman, Wells or Howells. The future, then, is not depicted as a process manifesting possibilities but as the Future, abstracted and idealized into just as static and orderly a human-centered world as the Past. Such a configuration implicitly renders the specific, localized present of the reader as the Present, the necessarily dominant reality from which the Future must develop. The existence of the Soviet Union, or an equivalent "evil empire" combatting the United States, in so much science fiction, demonstrates how the short-lived Cold War era was repeatedly rendered as a naturalized, permanent condition of global and galactic political economy.

Only in recent years have we seen, particularly as practiced by such feminist authors as Joanna Russ, Ursula K. Le Guin, and Marge Piercy, the creation of open-ended, contingent eutopias in process, developing and changing. And in order to depict them as such, they cannot present ideal, finalized utopian constructs, but rather must reveal the internal contradictions that any vital society or complex system will have. In particular, they reveal the difference between dualistic and dialogic conceptions of contradiction: the former assumes a reductionist dialectic in which antitheses can always negate theses and produce a synthetic resolution of the specific contradiction; the latter assumes that some fundamental differences are unresolvable and remain in tension and dynamic alternation of proactive/reactive relationship—the human male/female dyadic structure seems to me one of these. The nonhuman life of the future is also more likely to be addressed by this kind of fiction than by traditional utopian literature, as discussed in Joanna Russ's *We Who Are About To. . . .* (Murphy, "Suicide").

Until very recently, then, at least in Anglo-American science fiction, the agency of authorial imagination has denied the agency of future peoples and future ecosystems, which are always assumed to be human-user friendly. Le Guin has criticized the utopian tradition as being "European." By this, Jim Jose believes that Le Guin means that "the language of power which assumes that the future can be created in our imagination is a language of conquest and control. . . . Those who might be inhabiting the future are written out of the 'discovery.' For the 'new world' is to be new only for the inhabitants of the old world" (184). The parallel between European colonization of the Americas and imaginative colonization of the future is, of course, not fortuitous. And this point parallels my earlier critique of the oppression and extermination of indigenous peoples by European colonizers as being necessary to naturalize Enlightenment beliefs as universal; or, to naturalize Cold War-era beliefs to justify dividing all other peoples and ecosystems, as in the case of southern Vietnam, into two categories: friendly and hostile.

Culturopoeic Agency

To break with the universalizing abstractions and concomitant alienation of modern western cultures generated by the perpetuation of Enlightenment beliefs, and to initiate cultural change that can replace the polarization constituted by dichotomies, we need to conceptualize agency not only in terms of the possibility of our own behaviors and actions in oppositional cultural practices, but also in terms of the possibility of an ecological *culturopoeia*, the creative dimension of situated knowledges. Ecologically based culturopoeic praxis could provide nascent structures, practices, behaviors, and attitudes upon which our children could build their own future with a more natured culture. By natured culture I mean a human culture that functions on the basis of harmonizing human and nonhuman interaction, rather than on the basis of maximizing human action on the nonhuman. Joseph Grange captures the sense of this in defining human homecoming as "a matter of learning how to dwell intimately with that which resists our attempts to control, shape, manipulate and exploit it" (qtd. in Evernden 69). Any one of the recent documentaries on the ecological degradation resulting from industrialization in Eastern Europe, and its effects on the health of the children in that region speaks to the necessity to redefine culture to include human-nature interrelationships, rather than nature-civilization contradictions. The multinational corporations and banking combines of the West see the former Warsaw Pact peoples as a new world, for capital investment and low-wage industrial labor without the expense of environmentally safe working conditions or health standards. The instrumental reasoning of global economics can provide these people with neither freedom—democracy—nor life, for they will not be allowed any other path than the superhighway of toxic industrial development, and only those locales most propitious for exploitation will receive the benefits of contemporary technology.

The Australian ecofeminist sociologist Ariel Salleh puts it in no uncertain terms:

> The brutalization of nature is not merely symbolic. The growing number of ecological disasters following on human intervention in natural processes demands continuing critical examination. Given the escalating plunder and misappropriation of natural and "human" resources that passes for "productivity," it is not more "reason" that is required but less: the analytic blade has wrought enough destruction. What is apposite to the human condition at this point in time is "remembrance." ("Epistemology" 137)

The remembrance of which Salleh speaks, building on its identification in *The Dialectic of Enlightenment*,[4] is that of which Snyder speaks in terms of past inhabitory practices—many of which continue today in remote regions, although daily threatened by the expansion of the technocratic global village—which have been more nature-related than the nature-alienated ones of the present. Such bioregional remembrance seems to me the only way to research behaviors that have proven appropriate in specific parts of the world, and to study how these might be adapted through culturopoeia for a larger population than the ones who have historically practiced them.

Additionally, within such a process attention must be given to sustaining peoples who continue to practice various old ways without coopting them or forcing their assimilation as a result of efforts to learn from them. Hopi, Inupiaq, Koori, Ainu, or Hawaiian peoples are not obligated to teach immigrant descendants in their regions, even if such descendants are obligated to learn from them in order to cultivate a more nature-related inhabitation. Such descendants are, however, obligated to avoid romanticizing or idealizing indigenous peoples, which denies them their own agency in the same way that utopian projections deny the agency of future peoples.

Volitional Interdependence

An ecological agency means neither autonomy nor determinism, but *volitional interdependence*. Engels claimed that "freedom is the appreciation of necessity." But in classically mechanical fashion, Marxists have interpreted that to mean one correct behavior for each perception of necessity; some postmodernists have redefined this idea to mean no freedom because of necessity—the notion of total ideological subject construction. Volitional interdependence would mean the appreciation of opportunities within increasing awareness of necessities; making choices while recognizing that no decision is completely conscious or arrived at exclusively in terms of the factors operative at that moment. The choices I make regarding the colors of my home and my wardrobe are affected by genetics—my color blindness; acculturation—raised and dressed as a boy; past experiences—coloring the only purple lake in second grade; the culture industry's dynamics—what's for sale; and, unconscious associations—identification of certain colors with people and places, pleasant and unpleasant, and so on.

Human beings are dependent on other entities—animal, vegetable, mineral and biotic—for our very existence, just as other entities are dependent on us. Interdependencies are necessities in the sense that the connections existing between us and other parts of our particular culture or our bioregion are based on reciprocations without which damage and loss are inevitable. The violation of such reciprocities, however, incurs varying degrees of consequence. We won't become extinct immediately after we've eradicated snail darters, but the Greenhouse Effect may wipe out tens of thousands of us by a variety of repercussions. We cannot rid ourself of anaerobic organisms and remain alive, but we can provide an infant with immunities through breast-feeding, until the age when the child can generate her own (La Leche 350–54), and we thereby improve the health of the human side of the anaerobic/aerobic symbiosis. Humans exercise volition in terms of our behavior in relation to ecosystemic interdependencies, with all actions producing reactions, but we do so as interpellated subjects largely ignorant of the implications of our behavior. In contrast to theories of critique based only on negation, a theory of ecological agency would say: not this present situation, no; but based on what we understand, perceive, and feel, let us seek to become something more another than other, in closer relationship to the vast array of entities constituted as alien others by patriarchy, and let us utilize a culturopoeia that affirms our interdependencies and enhances our self-consciousness of the trajectory of our volitional behaviors in terms of our children's future.

From Other to Another

A dialogical orientation to the difference of (an)other can be based on the ecofeminist recognitions of interdependence and genetic diversity, dialogue at the most basic levels of energy/information exchange, as in gene pools and cross-fertilization. Anotherness proceeds from a heterarchical sense of difference, recognizing that we are not ever only one for ourselves but are also always another for others (in the U.S. being one for oneself remains an ideal for men, while being another for others, with no regard for self, remains the operative definiton for mother). Otherness isolated from anotherness suppresses knowledge of the ecological processes of interdependency—the ways in which humans and other entities survive, change, and learn by continuously mutually influencing each other—and denies any ethics of reciprocity. The degree to which patriarchy, throughout its historical manifestations, has placed both women and nature in the category of the absolute Other attests to a continuing refusal to recognize reciprocity as a ubiquitous natural process, reflected and enacted throughout any healthy human culture. C. A. Bowers argues, for example, that

> The gender issue raises important questions about the origins of our guiding generative metaphors; for example, are the analogues for the image of both the utilitarian and expressive forms of individualism derived essentially from masculine domains of experience and metaphorical frameworks? Gilligan's study, as well as the analysis of other feminists concerned with the gender-epistemology issue, highlights another critically important point; namely, that there are metaphorical images of self as an individual that promote power through separation, and that other metaphors of self, derived from a more contextual way of understanding, foster an awareness of the more subtle and complex information exchanges that characterize relationships. (118)

It remains the case in contemporary American newspaper reporting that men are defined predominantly by their careers or craft, with no mention of their marital status or children, while women are invariably so defined, even in an article exclusively devoted to their career. For example, newspapers run articles on the family separation problems of newly elected *women* members of the United States Congress, but not on any of the men.

Iris M. Zavala contends that "what is specifically challenging in Bakhtin is precisely the lucid exploration of dialogics as a coherent epistemological conception of meaning as a responsible engaging with 'another' and the communal basis for human emancipation and freedom. . . . As a multi-leveledness visualization of forces that coexist simultaneously, dialogics is a method of thinking as a whole and a rejection of world views that recognize the right of a higher consciousness to make decisions for lower ones, to transform persons into voiceless things" (86), i.e. the objectification of both women and nature as silent objects of attention rather than agents and actors. A dialogical conception of self is fundamentally a relational analysis of subject construction, attending to the ways in which personality and psyche are shaped by interpersonal affects, rather than emphasizing individual development. An individual consists of many selves, in the sense of different personal characteristics displayed or called forth by different circumstances, included interaction with the non-human. The very conception of "vision quests" and "walkabouts" prominent in indigenous cultures reflects a sense of human/non-human dialogue in self development.

The Anothers of Bioregionalism

One problem with dominant American culture is its failure to admit the limitations of human perspective. Increasingly, in ecological circles, bioregionalism as a political organizing and human habitation base has gained credibility because the bioregion, primarily defined in terms of a watershed-based ecosystem (the Shasta river region in northern California, the Ohio River near my home, or Cornwall in England, for example), is a small enough unit of socio-ecological organization that a finite group of humans can work out interdependencies in far greater sophistication than is possible at nation-state and global levels. Gary Snyder contends that "the aim of bioregionalism is to help our human cultural, political and social structures harmonize with natural systems. Human systems should be informed by, be aware of, be corrected by, natural systems" (Plant and Plant 13). Bioregional analyses and programs also aid us in affirming the strengths and limits of particularized cultural beliefs and practices, because such programs cannot be universalized. Even the concept of the constitution of a bioregion is subject to regional specificities and irreducible random variables through time, such as rainfall, volcanic eruptions, and river course changes.

Concomitant with the ecofeminist recognition of the health of ecological diversity is the bioregional recognition of the mutual health of humans and nonhumans within specific ecosystems, in terms of their interactive configurations, such as sustainable agricultural or silviculture practices. The dialogical notion that Snyder expresses, of cultural systems being informed and corrected by natural systems, can only be fully practiced if bioregionalism is also ecofeminist, since sex and gender constitute an interaction of natural and cultural systems, and genuine dialogue requires entertaining difference as relational rather than dichotomous. Additionally, such bioregionalism also implies a dialogical conception of self, continuously developed through a lifetime in relationship with the anothers, human and nonhuman, with which one shares the bioregion.

Donna Haraway provides an illustration of the extension of the concept of anotherness beyond human/human relationships to human/other-natural-phenomena relationships, which is a necessary component of bioregional consciousness. In direct contrast to the Enlightenment's acceptance of absolute alienation and the objectification of everything other than the human subject, Haraway posits that "in a sociological account of science all sorts of things are actors, only some of which are human language-bearing actors, and that you have to include, as sociological actors, all kinds of heterogeneous entities. . . . this imperative helps to break down the notion that only the language-bearing actors have a kind of agency" (Penley and Ross 5). Many writers, women and Native Americans in particular, are countering the Enlightenment model of otherness with the questions: Is alienation really the way of the world for human beings who have self-consciousness? What if, instead of alienation, we posit *relation* as the primary mode of human/human and human/other-natural-phenomena interaction, without conflating difference, particularity and other specificities?

The Natured Culture Premise

From an ecological perspective, the crucial criterion for evaluating the health of any given culture would be the ways in which that culture defines its relationship to the rest of the natural world. From an ecofeminist perspective, such defining would, invariably, also reveal the relationship of men to women within that culture, as Susan Griffin has tellingly drawn this comparison for Western Culture in *Woman and Nature*. Only by recognizing that humans are not only things-in-themselves and things-for-us, but also things-for-others (including having a role that affects countless others within the stable evolution of the biosphere), can we begin to understand our ecological niche and attendant practices. Affirmation here involves determining how to engage biospheric responsibility on a daily and long-term basis, focusing our attention locally/bioregionally. It also involves identifying those aspects of the existing North American cultures that display some of this sense of responsibility, while fashioning new cultural values and practices to place anotherness at the heart of our construction of relationships.

To merely support and promote the various movements and practices that will stand against the cultural homogenization of the world's peoples, which seeks to reduce all things, human and otherwise, to resources for the maximization of profits and self-perpetuation of growth-model economics, will not suffice. Salleh asserts that the now-traditional utopian projection for the future is no longer a viable option: "Reorganization of productive owner-ship, or the reshuffling of status hierarchies, affords no release from the pre-sent excesses of productive imperialism . . . in short, the substitution of nat-ural human needs by manufactured needs destructive of both the human body and its eco-sphere" ("Epistemology" 135–36). Perhaps the conceptualization and implementation of the bioregional ideal of diversified natured cultures, ones that organize human activity and seek sustainable co-habitation of humans and other natural entities—as was the case throughout most of North America prior to European conquest, and as Le Guin envisions in *Always Coming Home*, and as such bioregionalists as Gary Snyder, Peter Berg, Judith Plant or Freeman House work toward today (see Plant and Plant)—might afford some release without waiting for an ecological apocalypse or economic Armageddon to clear the ground for fresh planting. That method of agricul-ture, scraping the ground bare, with the topsoil blowing away on the wind, is inefficient and profligate anyway. Much more energy-efficient is the as-of-yet little practiced cultivation of new growth within the midst of the old.

Chapter Thirteen

Simply Uncontrollable, Or Steaming Open the Envelope of Ideology

Throughout the pages of this book, when I have quoted various female theorists and critics and discussed various texts by women writers, I have not at any moment meant to speak for women, but about women, as a man attempting to learn from them and share that learning with others. Women, as Carolyn Merchant outlines in *The Death of Nature*, have been configured by male-dominated ideologies as chaos. They have been perceived as a threat unless defined as a nurturing, domesticated entity (which is what J. E. Lovelock does with Gaia in his book by that name). Yet Merchant also points out that cataclysms have been essential for the growth curve of Western expansion. European settlement of the Americas depended on quantum leaps of destructive energy and the attempted extirpation of indigenous species, and such destruction continues, in altered but accelerated forms. Yet such cataclysms are always ideologically configured as forms of order, manifest destinies, willed retribution of a master deity; all of which are considered means of controlling the alleged chaos of material life. The return of the native and of the woman as cataclysm or chaos, as uncontrollable, prefigures the end of empire, as in Leslie Marmon Silko's *Almanac of the Dead*.

At the University of California, Davis, in June, 1986, Ursula K. Le Guin, quoting Linda Hogan, stated that "the women are speaking.... those who were identified with Nature, which listens, as against Man, who speaks—those people are speaking" (*Dancing* 162). And she went on to claim that women distrust "Nature" with a capital "N" because "that Nature is a construct made by Man, not a real thing; just as most of what Man says and knows about women is mere myth and construct. Where I live as a woman is to men a wilderness. But to me it is home" (*Dancing* 162). Women's experience that has not been shared by men (because they have not been listening) becomes part of the howling wilderness that cannot be controlled by male stories of conquest, adventure and domination. In the Fall of 1993, when I drafted this chapter, I was teaching a senior-level interdisciplinary course titled "Gender, Ecology, Culture" with twenty-four students, only one of them male. And these students agreed from their experience that there were many realms of male discourse in which women were expected to participate by active listening, such as voyeuristic sports, but none of the men they knew felt a need to understand the varied realms of female discourse. Is it the nature of language, of gender, or of a particular culture that generates asymmetrical structures of understanding difference? And if so many men are unwilling to learn the discourses of the other side of their own species, what about that of other species?

But what does Le Guin want? Perhaps it is nothing more or less than the value of women's experience as a Wilderness/Nature/Home issue. Women have not been equal participants in the configuration of the thought/theory/ logic guiding or justifying cultural practice here and in many other places. But now the women are speaking. In the Summer 1993 issue of *Wilderness* magazine, Terry Tempest Williams issued "a woman's call to community," which she titled "The Wild Card." She quotes another woman, Claudine Herrmann, who claims that "all political systems . . . end up with the same singular result: that of placing life last among all their preoccupations." And Williams responds with her own idea about representing women's preoccupations, a resistance to a particular ordering of the world.

She calls on women to carry "wild cards" to demonstrate their reactions to any "act that violated the health and integrity of her community." She calls for a "General Home Stand Act of 1993, designed to inspire and initiate a community of vigilance and care towards the lands we inhabit." Williams is not really interested in wilderness, as it has been defined primarily by men in the past century, but what she is proposing is Wild "because it has everything to do with home rule," a kind of localized decolonization. "As women wedded to wilderness," she contends, speaking directly to her specific audience of other women, "we must realize that we do carry the wild card, that our individual voices matter and our collective voice can shatter the status quo that for too long has legislated on behalf of power and far too little on behalf of life." Perhaps there is a connection between the appearance of this article, and the President and Vice President of the Wilderness Society's now being women, and the formation of the society's WHEN program: Women, Health, and Environment Network?

To me, Tempest Williams' remarks represent powerful speaking, and yet we must note and attend to the resistance to such speaking. Also in 1993, *International Wildlife* dared to run an article on the empowerment of women and the restoration of the environment in the context of population control (Stranahan). Some of the subscribers were, of course, livid, seeing, or else desiring, no connection between the preservation of "wildlife" and "wilderness" with the empowerment, that is, de-domestication, of women. What was the most radical element of the article? The summary of a United Nations survey, which stated that "if those women who said they wanted no more children were given that option, the number of births would drop by 27 percent in

Africa, 33 percent in Asia and 35 percent in Latin America" (18). For all of these women and their sisters in Europe and North America, the freedom to say "no" to being a domesticated reproduction unit is a crucial component of recovering the wild within them and preserving the wild around them that yet remains. In their following issue, *International Wildlife* ran an article by Lucille Craft, titled "The Woman Who's Shocking Japan," about Reiko Amano who is organizing grassroots demonstrations to protect wild river runs because she is an avid angler. In order to participate equally in a sport that requires wild passages of rivers, rather than organized, dammed and channeled ones, she has had to address not only environmental but gender issues in male-dominated Japan, in order both to fish and to organize demonstrations to protect her freedom for that fishing.

The women are speaking, but are the men listening? Hélène Cixous, in a dialogue with Catherine Clément, notes that ideological constructs, such as the image of the manly individual fronting the rugged mountains, the woman cooking the fish instead of catching it, are a "kind of vast membrane enveloping everything. [Women] have to know that this skin exists even if it encloses us like a net or like closed eyelids. We have to know that to change the world, we must constantly try to scratch and tear it. We can never rip the whole thing off, but we must never let it stick or stop being suspicious of it. It grows back and you start again" (1250). But should steaming open this envelope be solely their responsibility?

Men have to address the refusal of other men to learn from women's speaking, from their acts of self-empowerment and their participation in acts of mutual empowerment for ecological rehabilitation. We need to see the ways by which the men who have been speaking well must learn to speak better, by attempting an understanding of that wild home Le Guin posits, and to see the ways by which the men who have been deaf to women's voices can be confronted to hear that other men are listening and will, increasingly, become a force against male resistance to women's speaking, to women's experience, to women's understandings—in their diversities and differences. Domestic violence and rape are major attacks against the recovery of the wild. Take back the night is not only a slogan trumpeting women's pro-active resistance to personal violence, but also a call for the freedom of all individuals to experience the stars while standing alone in the dark, without having to carry a can of Mace in a mad dash from the jobsite to the parking lot.

What are some of the ways in which women are speaking that need to be heard? Silko, in *Almanac of the Dead*, prophesies the coming together of diverse forces to eradicate Anglo-European domination of the Americas. She suggests that prophecy consists of envisioning the larger forces that are shaping the cataclysms that will enable a future, not determine it. Throughout her text certain women play key roles, in many ways as Medicine Women, keepers of wisdom and catalysts of change. *Almanac* depicts a multifaceted process of recovering the wild through delegitimating the ideological powers that reign.

Pat Mora, in *Nepantla*, links cultural conservation with preservation of the land and the relationships of people and place. She emphasizes a rootedness to the land that must be preserved, and a cultural heritage that must be maintained, and she specifies a necessary culling of the cultural heritage, to eradicate such regressive and destructive features as machismo. Mora's women are strong, resistant, and wild. They choose the desert over the domicile, which renders them uncontrollable and able to regain balance. Again, it is a steaming open of the envelope of ideology, particularly, in this case, of the ways in which her *mestiza* heritage colludes with the dominant Anglo heritage to oppress and subjugate women and deny them access to the wild known by *curanderas* and *brujas*, a wild wisdom based on a symbiosis with the land and its animal and vegetable inhabitants.

The reinvention of nature depends upon the recovery of the wild, the wild within people, and especially the wild within women, because in the past two centuries, as mechanization and urbanization have reduced family inhabitation of the land, women have been defined more and more in terms relating to domestication, repression, and, most recently, the control and structuring of reproduction.[1] The reinvention of nature depends upon a reinvention of the wild zone of female discourse as a productive space for human agency. For the poet Mary Oliver the movement into the world is also a movement into *jouissance*, a polymorphous ecstasy and celebration of the female body, an unleashing of an energy for transformation. And ecstasy relates to vision and to balance, the balance of the integration of the chaotic, the stochastic, into apprehensions of the dynamic processes of life and death.

We see such dynamic balancing also in the way that Gloria Anzaldúa thinks through the multiple layers of *mestiza* consciousness and the wild zone of the borderlands of the geopolitical spaces, the human body and its sexualities, and the psyche and its multiple languages. Her *Borderlands/La Frontera* is a reconfiguration of what it means to be human and to be whole—which is not unitary, singular or autotelic, but multiple and shifting, transformative and regenerative.

There are no plans that we can design today for the benefit of our children's desires. There can only be plans for ways to free our children from the desires that our actions would impose upon them. The future cannot be a colonized place, but must be generated as a possibility. But this can only occur if people are rooted in themselves and in their places, working through the dynamic tensions of life processes. If the desire for domination, the obsessive hallucination of control and order, continues to define the characteristics of American culture because men are feeling alienated—from the land, from themselves, from their emotions—it is our own fault. And it is not the responsibility of women to cure men or to help them heal their psychic splits, or to always be sure to include them in every conversation and consideration. It is the responsibility of women to seek their own forms of freedom. But I see no way that, as women recover the wildness within, recovering their own access to the wild without, they can help but reinvent the nature of female-male relationships and the nature of human participation in the world.

Afterword

A tremendous amount of rethinking concerning the field of English-language literary studies has occurred in the decade that I have been involved with the profession, first as a graduate student and then as a faculty member. While critical theory initiated this rethinking, it could not in and of itself transform the discipline. Rather, most departments and many critics and teachers attempted to ignore the theory fad. When I delivered the conference version of "Centering the Other," a long-time feminist activist, who has remained strongly anti-theoretical, responded in part by informing me that her contacts at the research universities had indicated that theory was passé. They were all writing memoirs, becoming concrete and autobiographical rather than abstract and theoretical. Either they are slow to publish, or autobiography has not replaced theory; rather, autobiography has been being theorized of late, and both are appearing side by side and mutually influencing each other.

Another approach to avoiding coming to terms with theoretical challenges to the discipline as it was constituted after World War II has been the pluralist assimilation technique. A department hires a token theorist, who is expected to do and teach only theory, while the rest of the faculty continue to practice and/or teach whatever they have always been doing, such as new critical close readings—oblivious to the degree to which American deconstruction relies on close reading and, often, the same canonical texts for its practice. When I was applying for early promotion at IUP, the faculty member reviewing my file could not understand why I was publishing "so much." It had not occurred to him that I would want to do all that writing, articulating for myself as well as for others what I thought and understood about the subjects I was teaching. He actually commented that if the university wanted publications from the department's literature and criticism graduate program we should just hire someone to do that—a token publishing scholar.

A third response has been, first, to recognize that the discipline is becoming theorized, that theory is becoming a component of whatever English professors do, and that junior faculty will engage in theory as well as criticism; and, second, to structure programs so as to minimize the impact of theory on the department for as far into the future as possible. When revising the B.A. program, the people who employ this reponse avoid any discussion of claims that English has become a world language and a world literature, that North America has sufficient literary and cultural diversity that departments no longer need to be primarily British, and secondarily American, literature departments (we still have no place for international literatures written in English, at our university and at many others). They will allow for the designing of a theory course, but then include it among an optional set of electives, with the hope that the other courses will be perceived as more immediately useful and less difficult. They attempt not to engage under any circumstances in a discussion about whether or not English Departments should continue to exist at all as they are currently structured; such discussion would require addressing the assumptions upon which their organization, or lack of it, is founded.

Theory initiated much rethinking, but that thinking has begun to have structural, pedagogical, reading list, and syllabi impact more as a result of such phenomena as new historicism and cultural studies, than theory *per se*. The differences between the first and second editions of the MLA *Introduction to Scholarship in Modern Languages and Literatures*, edited by Joseph Gibaldi, demonstrate such changes. That the shift in scholarly emphasis would be perceived as controversial is suggested by the MLA publication division's decision to sell the uncorrected proofs of the second edition months in advance of actual publication. Similarly noteworthy is the 1992 publication by MLA of *Redrawing the Boundaries: The Transformation of English and American Literary Studies*, edited by Stephen Greenblatt and Giles Gunn. The subtitle indicates a *fait accompli* in research that is just beginning to have impact at the level of disciplinary structure and course design. Both "Cultural Criticism" and "Postcolonial Criticism" have a chapter here. Yet, while the word "environmentalism" appears at least once in this volume in relation to critical reevaluation of Thoreau, the editors did not deem it a term worthy of indexing.

Unlike new historicist, postcolonial, and cultural studies, which have evolved from a theoretically informed rethinking of the discipline that has produced new scholarship, new programs and departments, and new courses, ecological criticism finds itself in a different evolution at this point in time. Courses on nature writing, such IUP's "Man and the Natural World," have been in the catalog since the 1960s at many colleges and universities. Taught frequently with high enrollments in the earlier decades, these courses often remained on the books but out of the schedule in the 1980s. But in whatever decade, they were mostly taught at liberal arts colleges and state universities, rather than research institutions, by faculty hired as specialists of a more traditional kind, who had a passion for nature or a particular nature writer, such as Thoreau, Muir, or Leopold, and/or were members of The Wilderness Society, The Sierra Club, Trout Unlimited, or even Greenpeace. Instead of theoretical rearticulations of the field, it has been the environmental movement worldwide which has brought these courses back into prominence, expanded their number, and increased the faculty teaching them and writing about the works that would be taught in them.

But as the spate of anthologies recently published, and the majority of conference papers being delivered, indicate, much of the teaching of nature writing, and the ecological criticism being practiced on the texts fitting this label, remains theoretically unsophisticated. Too often, there exists an anti-theoretical, naive, realist attitude expressed in such presentations and practices. Gender, race, and generation gaps clearly exist in ecocriticism; nevertheless, the situation is changing. Graduate students are flocking to ecological criticism and environmental literature in droves. They tend to be theoretically sophisticated, conversant with poststructuralism in its various permutations. Many of them are women and feminists. Few as yet are non-white, which is generally the case for graduate students in the Humanities regardless of the specialty. Often they find it difficult, in the Ph.D. program at their university, to write a dissertation in ecological criticism, because only one faculty member is interested, or even willing—and often no faculty member has sufficient expertise—to direct such an undertaking. They are, largely, teaching themselves, or learning their specialty from faculty at colleges without doctoral programs, who are publishing and presenting on this subject. They are out on the job market, and when they find jobs they will expect to be permitted to teach not just nature writing but environmental literature, ecological criticism, and ecological theory. Their practice will drive the transformation that must redraw the already being redrawn boundaries of "English and American Literary Studies" if the environment is not to be left out of the Humanities. I see *Literature, Nature, and Other* as serving these new faculty in their efforts, and it was an awareness of the number of graduate students looking outside their institutions for authorization for what they wanted to study that spurred me to complete this project.

As the chapters of this book attest, I have significant concerns about the state of the field of ecocriticism and nature writing. Foremost is my apprehension about the degree to which anthologies, monographs, articles, and syllabi demonstrate an apparent intent, in too many cases, to codify existing knowledge about this subject, and a resistance to the generation of new knowledge, which must necessarily include a critique of what is thought to be already known. I worry about the continuing tendency to promote universalizing and totalizing knowledge claims rather than the representation of situated knowledges. I remain fearful of the degree to which there are faculty saying something analogous to what a professor at IUP told a female student about the Romantics when she asked why he did not include any women writers in the course. He said, in effect, that she should master the Big Six and worry about the marginal figures later. Apparently he had forgotten that three decades earlier, if there were six major figures, they were not the same six he was teaching, and that a decade before that there were not six figures considered major, and not too long before that almost no one took the Romantics seriously.

I believe that today codification is an impediment to what we need to be doing in the field of ecocriticism and environmental literature. The theoretical orientation I have elaborated here is a valuable one when measured by the criteria of its challenging accepted notions, producing fruitful interpretations, and recovering neglected works, but it is certainly not *the* theory for ecocriticism. It does, however, suggest the benefits of a theoretically informed ecocriticism and a broadly inclusive approach to texts for study and teaching. And, on the one hand, while it provides an expansion of discussion of environmental literature from a gender perspective; on the other hand, it does not adequately treat race and ethnicity. A multicultural ecocriticism, and a theoretical orientation for its practice, remains to be developed. I have provided some examples here and suggested some of the directions that the theorizing of an ecological multiculturality might take. I intend to address that subject more fully in the near future, both by expanding on the discussions of American "minority" writers initiated here and by treating other authors not mentioned. One element of such expansion will surely be a consideration of urban environmentalism.

I intend, then, that this Afterword serve not as a conclusion but as a "Forward" for the theorizing and critical practice of the readers of this book, and a precursor for what I need to do next. We have bridges to build, paths to take, and camps to break.

Dialectics or Dialogics: Method and Message in the Classroom

This paper was originally presented in somewhat longer form at "The Political Responsibilities of the Critic and Teacher" conference, sixth annual meeting of the GRIP Project, May 20–22, 1988, at Carnegie-Mellon University, Pittsburgh. Although I had already been working with Bakhtinian dialogics for a couple of years, writing this paper marked an important breakthrough for me: the articulation of my disagreement with Marxism and dialectics as an ideology and a pedagogy. My ideological break with Marxism had occurred several years earlier, and so the really significant aspect arises in relationship to classroom practice, since I had not been attempting to implement Bakhtinian dialogics as a self-conscious pedagogy up until the time I wrote this polemic.

While my setting dialogics against dialectics and my criticisms of various forms of Marxism appear in the early chapters of this book, they presume rather than recapitulate the position taken in "Dialectics or Dialogics." Thinking that the working out of this difference might interest some of my readers, I wanted to include it, but, because I could not find an appropriate place for it in the body of the text, I have made it an Appendix. Some readers still have one; others have had theirs removed along the way. Please treat this one in the same fashion, as individually useful or not.

I want to focus here on the specificity of the relationship between dialectics and dialogics and how that affects our presence as teachers in the classroom and in the academy. In the theater of the contemporary classroom it is dialogics rather than dialectics that can prove more productive in carrying out the tasks of "politics." And I mean politics here in the narrow sense of social and class action and in the wide sense of world view, or ideology. This means utilizing a dialogic method for presenting and critiquing one's own ideas as they are presented in the classroom and as they structure that classroom within the larger structure of the educational institution; and, emphasizing the cultivation of a dialogical critical process as a worldly engaged intellectual method over any general political message that one might want to promote at any given time.

Before turning to the classroom, let me make a few distinctions. Dialectics as a mode of critical thinking needs to be distinguished from dialectical materialism and from historical materialism. Vulgar, or mechanical, Marxism has been beset by what Lenin once termed "rectilinearity" in a warning to himself, i.e., myths of inevitable progress and the forward march of one class replacing another in a formulaic slot, which leads conveniently to the theory of productive forces. In "On the Question of Dialectics," Lenin remarks:

> Human knowledge is not (or does not follow) a straight line, but a curve, which endlessly approximates a series of circles, a spiral. Any fragment, segment, section of this curve can be transformed (transformed one-sidedly) into an independent, complete, straight line, which then (if one does not see the wood for the trees) leads into the quagmire, into clerical obscurantism (where it is *anchored* by the class interests of the ruling classes). (363)

Michael Ryan differentiates materialist dialectics and dialectical materialism in another way: "Marxisms abound, and Alvin Gouldner argues that there are at least two major schools, the 'scientific' and the 'critical.' Scientific Marxism is grounded in the axioms of the Soviet Union's celebrated metaphysics, 'dialectical materialism.' It interprets the world in one way at all times, and, therefore, it remains closed to new advances in philosophy and critical analysis, such as deconstruction" (xiii); scientific Marxisms "set themselves up as formal dogmas or as totalizing closures" (xv).

A sophisticated dialectics, or what Ryan would call "critical Marxism," sees the struggle between theses and antitheses as promoting and developing, but not always producing foreseeable, syntheses. It also recognizes the site of that struggle as a scene for ideological development, debate, and correction. Ryan, however, has a less philosophical and more narrowly political definition of "critical Marxism" than one to which I can ascribe as a postmarxist: "Critical Marxists depart from the leninist tradition in that they call for political organization forms that are not exclusive, elitist, hierarchical, or disciplinarian. . . . Democratic socialism would further the displacement and defusion of power relations, the institution of radical democracy, and the development of forms of self-management and of self-government" (xiv). Such a definition, unfortunately, seems to remain within an economic paradigm of Western industrialization that I suspect can only reinscribe patterns of capitalist exploitation due to the regressive influence of the productive forces and the means of production on the relations and mode of production. Similarly, such social-democratic politics and the industrial-productive forces assumption appear repeatedly in the essays in *Marxism and the Interpretation of Culture.* Ecological and ecofeminist alternatives to capitalist-designed industrialization and its attendant exploitation of the environment as well as humans remain largely absent.

V. I. Lenin has a series of illuminating remarks on dialectics versus historical materialism, and they are particularly instructive because of the nature of their rhetorical form. Unlike the "phallocratic, univocal style of thinking and writing" that appears in much of Lenin's public pronouncements and theoretical polemics, which Ryan condemns (195), this series of remarks consists primarily of inquisitive and contemplative marginalia collected in *Philosophical Notebooks*. I find these particularly interesting because they are written overtly in *dialogue* with Lenin's readings, particularly of Hegel; they are thus speculative, meditative, reactive remarks for further speculation and consideration, not dogmatic, programmatic, or authoritative statements. Lenin notes that "flexibility, applied *objectively*, that is, reflecting the all-sidedness of the material process and its unity, is dialectics, is the correct reflection on the eternal development of the world" (110). One cannot achieve all-sidedness without allowing contradictory voices to speak; or, as Mikhail Bakhtin described it in relation to literary characters, without allowing the *other* to become a "speaking subject" whose own world view is presented and who is not just rendered as an object for the purposes of promoting the author's ideology or political programme (*Problems* 7, 49–53).

Further, Lenin observes that "every concrete thing, every concrete something, stands in multifarious and often contradictory relations to everything else, ergo it is itself and some other" (138). How then can a historical materialism avoid reductionism and avoid the imposition of a monological authoritative voice that precludes interrogation and debate for those who have not already embraced it, unless it presents the "self" and the "other" of the historical moment and the interpretations of that moment so that a dialogue may occur in which others may participate and from which others may draw conclusions? Applicable to the relationship of materialist dialectics to historical materialism as a theory of the world, as a method for practice, is the recognition that "causality, as usually understood by us, is only a small particle of universal interconnection, but (a materialist extension) a particle not of the subjective, but of the objectively real interconnection" (Lenin 160). The recognition of any individual's limited ability to conceptualize comprehensively causality should encourage a foregrounding of dialectical method over a reliance on historical materialism as a way of understanding the world.

I emphasize this because it is precisely "historical materialism" rather than "materialist dialectics" that Jim Merod, for example, emphasizes in the introduction to *The Political Responsibilities of the Critic*, and by means of which he defines Marxism. And yet it is precisely interpretations of "historical materialism" rather than the practice of dialectical debate that have encouraged a rush to synthesis, whether that be a voluntarist idealism—as when factions in the anti-war movement saw their struggle as the beginning of the end of U. S. imperialism—or a materialist determinism—as when individuals and organizations today await the "inevitable" imperialist economic crisis that will lead to a revolutionary crisis requiring only the "correct" leadership to enable the masses to seize political power. One also sees such an apocalyptic determinism among segments of the environmentalist movement. And it is to counter this nostalgia for immediate synthesis that Ryan invokes Derrida as an ally of Marx (52–53). But deconstruction tends to emphasize only the difference of contradiction in its own right rather than in its relation, not contradiction's unity of opposites and potential for their transformation.

Let me turn to Bakhtin for suggestions and considerations of dialogic method as a corrective to what I view as both the reductionism and dogmatism of traditional Marxisms and the incapacitation and solipsism of American deconstruction. A distinction needs to be made between materialist dialectics and historical materialism or dialectical materialism. The latter two labels privilege the opposition of a commitment to materialism rather than to idealism as a philosophical starting point over the cognitive method to be used for developing an understanding of and ability to influence reality and human perception of that reality. And, "historical" instead of "dialectical" as a modifier for "materialism" has an implicit and at times explicit assumption of inevitablity that renders for me the claim to materialism immediately suspect.

The dialogic method, then, serves here both as a proposed corrective to philosophical problems in Marxist thought, a theoretical proposition as already outlined, and as a strategy for praxis, which I will discuss here specifically in terms of the college classroom. The teacher has a choice between practicing political responsibility within the classroom's potential site of dialectical struggle as one who issues calls to action, agitates, propagandizes, or theorizes. The first three of these tasks—and one need not be self-conscious of his or her own ideological world view to practice them—although at times necessitated by the immediate situation, work against and can inhibit the development of critical thinking on the part of students. If presented monologically and utilizing the authoritative power relationship of the classroom, it can actually reinforce the hegemonic assumptions of the culture's dominant discourse, because the authoritative word is "hierarchically distanced" and implicitly patriarchal (LaCapra 313–14). For example, Richard Mohr in "Teaching as Politics" states that

> The other educational function for which the philosophic teaching of public policy issues is also uniquely suited is pedagogically more sticky—the provision of a variety of situations. For the way to do this is to push a specific line and to push the line that is, most often, at odds with the received opinions of our culture, the ones students most likely already have. . . . One needs to push a line in order to be intellectually honest and to do what philosophers indeed do. . . . If we are to teach students how to think, we must be willing to show them how to draw conclusions. One does that by playing out some line of argument to its end. . . . In classes that are allowed to be all discussion

and no conclusion, cynicism holds the reins while skepticism rides shotgun. (9)

But whose conclusions are being drawn? The professor's; and are students really learning how to draw *their own* conclusions as mutually speaking subjects in the classroom, or are they learning to receive the conclusions and the method of drawing conclusions that is being monologically and authoritatively presented to them in a way no fundamentally different from that in which the "received opinions of our culture" were presented to them? As John Brenkman pointedly notes, "the potential for uncoerced mutual understanding and recognition in any given set of language practices is, however, constrained by the social relations of domination in which those practices function" (231).

The fourth option, theorizing, has the potential for a genuinely dialectical development only at certain levels of sophistication, but can nevertheless be introduced. And in that scene of ideological and critical growth, the teacher needs, if he or she is concerned with altering and opening up for (re)examination the world views the students hold, to emphasize the dialogical engagement of contrasting theses. Focusing on dialogical action enables the recognition that while one idea, culture, class, value, may become dominant, it need not remain so; nor does that dominance mean that the subordinate polarity of that unity has been eradicated or discredited. This recognition is also a concern of much current cultural criticism as well.

The danger, though, with the emphasis on the cultural is that the individual as social being will get lost in the treatment of social forces. As Don Bialostosky highlights, "dialogics is interested in ideas as they are held by people and in people as holders of ideas" ("Reply" 832). Bialostosky's "Reply" is part of a series of exchanges printed in *PMLA* following the publication of his essay, "Dialogics as an Art of Discourse in Literary Criticism." There he heavily emphasizes the relationship of individual and ideas, not to the exclusion of social forces but as an essential component of any social network. He states: "Dialogics, in contrast, would try to re-create the image of specific persons who voice their ideas in specific texts and contexts; it would situate an utterance historically or imaginiatvely in a field of other persons' utterances rather than topically in a field of dialectical terms or rhetorical commonplaces" (790). As such, dialogics should constitute a foundational ingredient of cultural criticism. Dialogics can also serve as a corrective to pyschoanlaytic trends in criticism that would privilege the individual and individual interpretation to the exclusion of the socially constituted character of the self. And it is the individual as student, that is, a person in a specific subject formation in complement and contradiction with that person's other subject formations, that must remain the focus of attention of the teacher in the classroom; even as we attempt to render the students conscious of themselves as social beings, we must also help them to develop into people who are *active* "holders of ideas" rather than receptacles of values.

Instead of the presentation of a *correct* view of the world in a monological, authoritative, patriarchal utterance that encourages passive assent rather than active debate, the teacher works with developing "internally persuasive discourse," which "makes a claim on the speaker that may carry authority but is open to questioning and modification" (LaCapra 314). In this description of Bakhtin's concept, Dominick LaCapra recognizes that the context of discourse may very well preclude any achievement of complete heterarchy, an unavoidable situation in any classroom. And the teacher's responsibility is to establish dialogic engagements that encourage questioning and modification. But, and here's a major point, such questioning and modification cannot consist only of a critique of some other perception of the world, but must also include the teacher's world view, as well as behavior in the classroom, as fair game.

But let us assume that instead of dogmatically presenting a hierarchically distanced world view in the classroom the teacher initiates a dialectical debate between his or her beliefs and those of the students. Such a dialectical move would tend to be predicated upon the optimistic belief that students already have a thesis, a conscious world view, for which the professorial critique will provide the antithesis to raise their consciousness. It has been my experience that students for the most part have only passively received values, which they frequently have not had to articulate or defend. In this sense, they have no clear thesis upon which to initiate the antithetical debate that Mohr wants to carry on. The establishing of a contradictory, argumentative form of teaching, in which some faculty engage, pushes students toward a defensive articulation of previously only passively received values rather than toward an opening-up, a self-questioning critique. Only as they begin to articulate and query their previously inherited values will they reach out toward supplements, alternatives, and counterideologies.

Such alternatives can and ought to be entertained in the classroom, but not as if one were waging class struggle against the students themselves. The dialogical movement can serve to foreground the necessary existence of *alterity* itself through the utilization of any range of examples, including but not limited to one's own beliefs; and, concomitantly, to internal dialogical debate as well as external dialogue over values, beliefs, and goals.[1] It is not so much what people think, but how they think that is the real problem, and capitalism is one of the manifestations of this problem in recent history; patriarchy is another manifestation and one predating capitalism; but much of the problem remains that of ignorance versus knowledge, and nonantagonistic, developmental differences that cannot be worked through without individuals having a more sophisticated analytical method.

The dialogical classroom also can obviate the tendency that some teachers have to present their world view and/or the world view of other critics and authorities as isolated, equally valid alternative ways of thinking, that is, pluralism. A *laissez-faire* competitive capitalist model of ideas and world views is not an example of dialogical activity. Such a tendency suggests a value-free grab bag of ideologies from which a student may opportunistically or situationally choose. Rather, dialogical debate would not only engage divergent ideas in comparative analysis of their own merits within the confines of language games, but also dialogize the world of ideas in relation to the world of actions. The positions that students debate, whether on abortion, capital punishment, the ozone layer, or the preservation of endangered species, do not only demonstrate different thoughts about the world but also different practices in that world, and students can be encouraged to measure the validity or applicability of their ideas in relation to anticipated ensuing results. Of course, the dialogic method requires the teacher to take a gigantic risk: students may develop a contradictory world view. But this is precisely the risk that must be taken if we seek to help students develop into individuals capable of critical thought.

In the graduate classroom, the teacher is in a much different position from that of the undergraduate classroom, particularly that of general education courses. At the graduate level, the first responsibility is to be forthright about method. But here it is important to suggest that all other faculty have methods and the issue is not method or no, but unconscious of self-conscious. We need to find ways to break down our own subject position as singular "authority" in order to encourage each student to develop self-authority at the same time that he or she is exposed to the relational characteristics of "authority" itself as it is variously culturally constructed. Interdisciplinary programs, and in particular Women's Studies courses, point the way in terms of practice and in terms of the contradictions that must be confronted. Critics themselves are too often guilty of gender, racial, and rhetorical stereotyping of authority-knowledge, both because of its function as professional "capital" and because of our their own tendencies to universalize specific cultural norms. Richard Barney, for example, points out that Barbara Johnson may receive less attention as a deconstructionist because "unlike deMan or Miller, who have often tended toward authoritative declarations of theoretical principles . . . Johnson employs a candid style that is much less doctrinaire" (196).

For men and women, one of the tasks in setting up a dialogic classroom would be to emulate the best of Women's Studies practicum and turn every classroom into a feminist one. The move against patriarchal patterns in the classroom is both a clearly political one and a dialogical one, in that the alternative to patriarchy is not matriarchy, but heterarchy, even when we speak of matrifocal values. The self-recognition of otherness implicit and explicit in the Women's Studies classroom encourages a dialogical conception of self and a critical self-consciousness regarding the world and one's place in it. One immediate practical result of this recognition of the pedagogical value of feminism would be the engagement of each teacher with gender-balancing the classroom, both in attention to the needs and interests of both genders in attendance and in attention to the representation of women within the course material. While this can and needs to be pursued at all levels, it is crucial to pursue at the graduate level because of the foregrounding of canon formation that is currently taking place.

Although it goes without saying that the arena of canon formation is one that avails itself most readily to dialogical debate, we should be aware that too frequently rather than the dialogic, it is the synthesis of some shadowy dialectic that is foregrounded. The dialogic move is to open the canon for critique rather than to replace one set of icons for another. The latter seems to me the key problem in the proliferation of "nature writing" anthologies occurring in recent years. Such substitutions do nothing to disrupt the hierarchical thinking that constitutes canon formation; and it should be apparent by now that substitutions or adding of marginalia to the mainstream only serves to reinforce the illusion of democratic freedom without challenging the rules of the game. Canon formation itself needs to be called into question at the level of one's own syllabus production and at the level of classroom discussion. S. P. Mohanty argues that

> Pedagogy, particularly in the realm of culture, need then to face the fundamental challenge to escape both the transmission of coded knowledge and the coded transmission of knowledge. . . . Learning is dialogic, but not in the traditional Socratic sense. It involves a necessary implication in the radical alterity of the unknown in the desire(s) not to know, in the process of this unresolvable dialectic. . . . Teaching "meanings" is a fundamentally ideological act: it ignores the ruses and ruptures of politics and desire in favor of self-evident knowledges, of what Pierre Bourdieu and Jean-Claude Passeron would call "cultural arbitraries." (155)

Gerald Graff has rather persuasively suggested at the end of *Professing Literature* that the critical debates behind the constitution of literary studies have not been brought into the classroom, so that students are subjected to the experience of conflicting, competing alternative authorities on literary interpretation rather than alternatives to the literary critic as *authority*. And they are never exposed to the possibility that the idea of truth leads to debate rather than debate leads to the true idea.

We can conceive of ourselves as teachers as Trickster figures who can stimulate into the center of intellectual attention the potential for *self-conscious,* and hence active, reflective, critical, thought (White 9).[2] Such a professorial Trickster figure is neither the "Absurdist" critic that Hayden White defines nor the wisdom figure who engages in the socratic method in order to work the student toward a desired end by means of cunning questions. According to White, "the Absurdists attack the whole critical enterprise, and they attack it where Normal criticism in all its forms is most vulnerable: language theory" (263). I am not suggesting that we attack the entire critical enterprise, since critique forms an element of self-consciousness, and the lack of criticism and self-criticism leads only to the maintenance of the status quo, regardless under whose banner blind obedience and passive value reception is practiced. The coyote is not an absurdist precisely because in our profession this leads to the impotent play of language games, and in our culture almost invariably leads toward individualism, not individuality, and solipsism, not community. Rather, the coyote figure is a "spiritual" guide whose role is to encourage students toward self-consciousness, self-motivation, and inquiry in search of commitment. According to Michael Holquist, "in Bakhtin, the more other, the more self" ("Surd" 148). The coyote serves, to use Gary Snyder's imagery in *Myths & Texts*, as the perfect complement to "Earthmaker." Rather than the teacher attempting to win over his students to a particular world view or to a particular programme or party—to the terrain of the Earthmaker—the teacher as coyote stimulates, questions, disturbs, and goads the students toward self-knowledge, self-consciousness, and the intellectual methods that will enable them to choose which of the proclaimed Earthmakers to aid and to oppose. The coyote operates primarily in the "logosphere" and in that sphere dialogics must be foregrounded, not to seize power, but to empower the critical habits of social beings on the brink of social self-consciousness. That work in the logosphere prepares the students for their lives in the ecosphere. Our responsibility in the classroom is to practice dialogics; the students must choose the responsibility to integrate that into their own world view and world practice. Otherwise, while power may change hands, and parties trade positions, the world will look little different.

✂ Notes ✂

Preface—By Way of Memoir

1. "Ecology," according to Berg, "is the interaction of all natural systems and beings in the planetary biosphere, whereas environment is really a view of what's around us, in a fairly narrow perspective" (23).

Chapter One: Prolegomenon for an Ecofeminist Dialogics

1. This criticism of the concept of "pluralism" includes a self-critique of my use of that term in the originally published version of "Sex-Typing" in *Environmental Ethics*.

2. "Feminisms" means for me the orientation of feminist-anchored practices, including political activism, women's studies, feminist critique and gynocriticism, and feminist theory; but recognizes that there is neither a monolithic "feminism" nor "feminist theory," and that much valuable feminist critical work is non- or anti-theoretical.

3. I take up the relationship and difference of dialogics and dialectics in greater detail in "Dialectics or Dialogics" in the appendix to this volume.

4. The Deep Ecology/ecofeminist debate has been running for several years. For examples of the Deep Ecology side of it, see the works by Calicott, Devall and Sessions, Fox,and Johns; for examples of the ecofeminist side, see the essays by Doubiago, King, Salleh, Warren, and the special issue of *Hypatia* edited by Warren.

5. Although a few proponents of Bakhtin have initiated such reaching, dialogics remains primarily a method for literary criticism or rhetorical studies, for which it serves very well. But my point is not only that it need not be as limited as most adoptions of it suggest, even in the case of such broader essays as Don Bialostosky's and Charles Schuster's, or as limited as Bakhtin himself allowed it to be, but that it must not remain so limited if it is to realize its effective potential in the world.

6. In relation to this point, see Bakhtin's discussion of primary and secondary speech genres in *Speech Genres* 60–63, and the remarks on the materiality and ideological value of semiotic materials in *Marxism* 10–12.

7. Cary Nelson observes that feminism does not need men for its theoretical development (157). While I agree with this in relation to theory and to any particular critical innovation or realization, I must disagree with the idea of a lack of a "need" for men in relation to the potential for ideological and political victories on the part of feminist struggles, given the balance of forces in the world today.

Chapter Three: Voicing Another Nature

1. In a review of *Native American Literatures,* edited by Laura Coltelli, in *Studies in American Indian Literatures* 3.2 (1991): 86-89, Arnold Krupat notes that "one of the most recent cliches is the regular reference to the term 'alienation' as applicable to the situation of some of the better-known protagonists of contemporary Native American fiction, an odd term to employ, one might think, for critics who regularly point out the problems of using Western terms for Indian literatures. . . . What Tayo or Abel or Jim Lonely feel may be something like what 'alienation' in its western history tries to denote—but of course what is interesting is how that term does not quite account for what they feel."

2. Holquist, *Dialogism* 32. For readers unfamiliar with the term "transgredience," Holquist defines it as "the degree of outsidedness toward the second. . . . Transgredience is reached when the *whole* existence of others is seen from outside not only their own knowledge that they are being perceived by somebody else, but from beyond their awareness that such an other even exists. . . . there is in fact no way 'I' can be completely transgredient to another *living* subject, nor can he or she be completely transgredient to me" (emphasis in original, 32–33).

3. For example, Patricia Clark Smith argues that much contemporary Anglo women's poetry on women relatives treats these relatives as being alien to the author due to an individual, psychological perception of otherness which ranges from "seeing the woman as suddenly unfamiliar in some way to seeing her as a monster." But, Smith claims, "the image of a woman relative as an alien being simply does not appear in American Indian women's poetry." Instead, there is "a tendency to see conflict between women as not totally a personal matter but, rather, as part of a larger whole, as a sign that one of the pair has lost touch not with just a single individual but with a complex web of relationships and reciprocities" ("Ain't Seen You" 112, 114, 115).

4. Bakhtin, *Problems of Dostoevsky's Poetics,* 302. Caryl Emerson, in an editor's note to Appendix II explains Bakhtin's statement *"ja i drugoi:* "Russian distinguishes between *drugoi* (another, other person) and *chuzhoi* (alien; strange; also, the other). The English pair "I/other," with its intonations of alienation and opposition, has specifically been avoided here. The *another* Bakhtin has in mind is not hostile to the *I* but a necessary component of it, a friendly other, a living factor in the attempts of the *I* toward self-definition."

5. Bakhtin, *Problems* 47. Bakhtin was clearly not ecology-minded and never extended any of his ideas to pertain to the human-nature dialogue, even attempting in some of his early writing, to preclude it. Perhaps this reflects in part the pernicious residues of Kantian philosophy and the anti-ecological attitudes prevalent throughout Marxist thought, which constituted nature as always a thing-for-us, a raw material to be worked up, no different from the bourgeois attitude, both equally products of instrumental reason: "The multitudinous affinities between existents are suppressed by the single relation between the subject who bestows meaning and the meaningless object," as Horkheimer and Adorno argue (10). Bakhtin was unable to distinguish, as ecofemi-

nists do, between speaking subjects who exercise agency and nonspeaking subjects that exercise agency, or as Donna Haraway puts it, between "speaking subjects" and "actors."

6. Pryse points out that in line with Lydia Maria Child's *Hobomok* (1824) and Catharine Sedgwick's *Hope Leslie* (1827), Austin's writing shares a recognition for "alliance and sympathy between white women and Indian women," which is also reflected in "her lifelong recognition of the value of Indian culture" (Austin, *Stories*, xvi).

7. See the first part of this essay for Elder and Finch's treatment of Native Americans. Tom Lyon has a similar problem and ends up excluding Native Americans altogether from *This Incomperable Land* because they had no sense of nature as a "wilderness" and, apparently, for him inadequately distinguished in their storytelling between fact and fiction (xv–xvi).

8. Quite recently, the efforts of ecofeminism to work for positive critique and inclusive debate have come under attack by the social ecologist Janet Biehl, in *Rethinking Ecofeminist Politics* (Boston: South End Press, 1991). Biehl engages in an extensive negative critique of ecofeminism based on the failure of so many of the individuals who use the term to define their beliefs to meet her criterion that in order to be progressive, feminist ecologists must adopt Murray Bookchin's rationalistic theory of "social ecology" and its clearly delineated political program. Apparently, her notion of "a free ecological society" has no room for heterarchical difference and dissonance. A more helpful approach to addressing the differences between ecofeminism and social ecology can be found in an article by Mary Mellor, "Eco-Feminism and Eco-Socialism," and an interview by Valerie Kuletz with Barbara Holland-Cunz in *Capitalism, Nature, Socialism* 3.2 (1992): 43–78.

Chapter Five: Sex-Typing the Planet: Gaia Imagery and the Problem of Subverting Patriarchy

1. For evidence of this patriarchal mythology emphasis even in ecological circles, see J. Donald Hughes and the rejoinder by Richard Frank. Hughes, in supporting the adoption of the term Gaia, ignores the issue of sex-typing. Frank's rejoinder, while not addressing the issue of sex-typing, does emphasize the need to distinguish between prepatriarchal and patriarchal mythologies.

2. Certainly, the Gaia hypothesis is not the earliest instance of scientifically conceiving of the planet as a single organism, as Dolores LaChapelle points out with reference to P.D. Ouspensky and Aldo Leopold (295–96). But it is the most widely recognized scientific model, and is the one hypothesis that has produced a popular name for this organism.

3. While Lovelock falsely, although no doubt inadvertently, considers his example a universal experience for his readers, women and men alike, it does exemplify a historically common male experience. Annette Kolodny points to William Byrd's 1728 use of the same identification, but then questions its motivation: "was there perhaps a *need* to

experience the land as a nurturing, giving maternal breast because of the threatening, alien, and potentially emasculating terror of the unknown?" (9). This element of terror may also influence the contemporary male's choice of the same image, with the terror arising not from the unknown, but from the emasculating potentials of toxic pollution and nuclear devastation (See Todd 431–32 and Zimmerman 24).

4. In this regard I think it useful to distinguish between "matriarchist" authors and feminist authors who use Gaia imagery. Matriarchal refers to those authors who attempt to reverse the hierarchical patterning of patriarchal society by replacing it with a hierarchical view of women as superior to men, thus reinscribing the kind of alienating, dualistic thinking that guides patriarchal society. Feminism seeks to end patriarchy in order to end oppression, not replace it with a new culture that emphasizes hierarchical differences (see Adler; also, Warren, "Feminism," on "transformative feminism," 17–20). Jean Freer, who describes herself as a priestess of Diana, serves as an example of a matriarchist. She respells woman as "womyn," claiming that "this spelling of our name identifies our autonomous existence according to our gyn-ecology" (135 and 233n7). Such a claim of "autonomy" directly contradicts the ecofeminist recognition that all parts of an ecosystem are interrelated and interdependent, although to varying degrees. Troublingly enough, Freer invokes Gaia imagery and pre-patriarchal goddess worship in order to promote such a new gender hierarchy, suggesting that even the explicit use of pre-patriarchal Earth Mother/Goddess worship may hinder the development of genuine ecological consciousness. This problem of reinscribing patriarchal paradigms through theological valuations of feminism is strongly criticized by Luce Irigaray and Hélène Cixous, who are in turn criticized by Domna Stanton for falling prey themselve to the employment of ontotheological tropes (see Stanton).

5. Throughout Davis's essay runs an underlying tone of male nostalgia seeking reassurance that the "mother" remains all-knowing and that, if the male can somehow gain *access* to the mysterious knowledge and power of the female, he can be cured of his separation from the womb and the breast. His very title reveals the sexist nostalgia that he fails to acknowledge: "Ecosophy: The Seduction of Sophia?" Repeatedly Davis approaches and then backs away from a critical assessment of his own language and questions that his own critique raises. This retreat enables him to render the female *superior* to the male because she is more "natural": "The unifying theme of the unity of opposites suggests a generative power transcendent of the material realm. However, this spiritual power seems to be intrinsically feminine, a 'natural' characteristic of the female psyche" (155). This is precisely the kind of inverted patriarchal thinking that ecofeminists such as Ynestra King, Ariel Salleh, and Karen Warren criticize.

6. It should also be noted that even in pre-patriarchal, matrifocal cultures, the Earth Goddess was only inconsistently portrayed as hermaphroditic and, hence, potentially parthenogenetic rather than female (see Hughes 9).

7. This interdiction can be seen not only by the fact that the solitary quest is envisioned as an exclusively male undertaking in American culture but also by the situation that in American culture only men can safely undertake such a journey. Kolodny pene-

tratingly observes that "our continuing fascination with the lone male in the wilderness, and our literary heritage of essentially adolescent, presexual pastoral heroes, suggest that we have yet to come up with a satisfying model for mature masculinity on this continent; while the images of abuse that have come to dominate the pastoral vocabulary suggest that we have been no more successful in our response to the feminine qualities of nature than we have to the human feminine" (147).

8. Such a heterarchical appreciation of difference can be seen as a crucial corollary to, and a guiding orientation of, Carol Gilligan's *In A Different Voice*: "Through this expansion in perspective, we can begin to envision how a marriage between adult development as it is currently portrayed and women's development as it begins to be seen could lead to a changed understanding of human development and a more generative view of human life" (174).

9. Zimmerman suggests the difficulty in breaking free from socio-gender stereotypes: "In a non-patriarchal society, human beings would presumably manifest a healthy interplay between emotion and thinking—and moral issues would be informed by both as well. Yet, the notion that a healthy human being would be androgynous, that is a 'combination' of traits currently described as 'male' or 'female' is problematic insofar as that notion maintains the dualism between male and female. At this stage in human history, we are still groping to understand what it would mean to be a mature man or woman in a nonpatriarchal society" (35).

Chapter Six: Somagrams in An/Other Tongue: Patricia Hampl's "Resort"

1. But it must be emphasized that the conception of the pre-Oedipal can never be posited as a point of return, a nostalgically imagined site of undifferentiated origins, but only as a construct to reveal a gap in patriarchal discourse and analysis through which alterity may be voiced. In Jane Gallop's words, "we are not looking for a new language, a radical outside, but for 'the other within,' the alterity that has always lain silent, unmarked and invisible within the mother tongue" (320).

2. In regard to the speculation about a hysterectomy and its being the most problematic of the loss/absence conditions identified here, see Diane Collecott's opening remarks about her own hysterectomy in "A Double Matrix."

3. This refusal to name does not indicate an avoidance of anatomy in the way by which Alicia Ostriker distinguishes a "poetess" from a "woman poet": "One of the ways we recognize a 'poetess' is that she steers clear of anatomy. One of the ways we recognize a woman poet, these days, is that her muted parts start explaining themselves" ("Body" 248). Hampl plays a more complex game than the choice of moves identified by Ostriker's false dichotomy suggests.

4. At the same time, the glorification of mother status can also "cover over differences between feminists," as Jane Gallop has noted (318).

Chapter Seven: Ecology and Love: The Spiderwebs of Joy Harjo

1. When I presented a conference version of this chapter at the American Literature Association Meeting, San Diego, May, 1992, Lynda Koolish, also a presenter, criticized my use of this quotation as an out-of-context misrepresentation, and we had a spirited discussion about "transcendence." I have revised this section of the chapter as a result of that exchange, and would like to thank her for helpful comments.

2. Similarly, Paula Gunn Allen criticizes application of another Western, specifically Judeo-Christian, term to Native American writing: "It [*House Made of Dawn*] is not about redemption, for redemption is not a Pueblo (indeed, not an American Indian) notion" (571).

3. I should mention also that not only is there a need for critics such as myself to be cautious about application of Western-tradition terminology to other traditions, but also a need in multicultural studies to be cautious about "pan-ethnic" generalizations resulting from cross-ethnic terminology applications. The relationship, for example, of African Americans or Chicano/as to Judeo-Christian tradition is far different from that of Native Americans. Allen suggests such sensitivity in her discussion of differences among poets in her interview with Katharyn Machan Aal, "Writing As an Indian Woman."

4. Linda Hogan, a decade ago, claimed that "evolutionary communities suffered a great deal of destruction because of government practices of interference, removals, relocation, suppression of religion and the church-controlled boarding schools. In spite of this destruction tribalism is not in decline. It is in a process of transformation" (405). And Allen remarks in "Bringing Home the Fact" that "the central issue of Pueblo belief is growth and transformation" (575).

Chapter Eight: "A Mountain Always Practices in Every Place": Climbing over Transcendence

1. See, for example, Rothberg 32 and Nelson 220. Altieri argues against the application of such a term in *Enlarging the Temple* (137).

2. Rothberg argues for the Transcendentalists through Whitman lineage (28–29); Nelson for the Zen basis (209–12). In contrast, Lin emphasizes the difference between Snyder and the Transcendentalists, including Thoreau.

3. Abe quotes Dōgen on this point as saying that "to think practice and realization are not one is a heretical view. In the Buddha Dharma, practice and realization are identical" (57).

4. I have omitted *Six Sections from Mountains and Rivers without End Plus One* since it comprises only part of an unfinished longer work. Similarly, I have omitted *Left Out in the Rain* since it contains poems ranging across Snyder's entire adult life.

5. Snyder told Robertson that he had stopped writing poetry for a few years after having written "quite a bit" prior to this new burst of creativity in 1955 (Robertson 53). Yet in the 1977 "Introduction" to *Myths & Texts* Snyder quotes his own earlier remark that this poetic sequence "grew between 1952 and 1956" (vii). Snyder also includes seventeen poems in *Left Out in the Rain* that he identifies as having been written between 1952 and 1956. It would seem that Snyder had not actually given up writing poems so much as he had given up a certain *ambition*. Also, *Myths & Texts* was not actually completed until after the Yosemite experience (see Jacoby 50). As a result, the Yosemite poems can rightly be called "a new departure," and Snyder's experience could be labelled a *kensho*.

6. Later the concept of Other would become more conscious as exemplified by Robertson's quotation of Snyder: "The experience from which these Yosemite poems come is the experience of interacting with the Other—of constantly trying to be aware of the Universe as all one body, of trying not to be separate from it but recognize every part of it as part of yourself" (56; capitalization here was Robertson's transcription decision). But even here there are limitations: first, the cultural determinations that the word other carries and that contradict the very sensibility that Snyder is trying to express; second, the relationships between part/whole and other/self that are projected by the sentence structure having "yourself" rather than "Universe" as the ending point. I remain unsure of the source for Snyder and Robertson's use of Other in this context, but it is certainly the case that critics influenced by Lacan tend to overemphasize the indissolubility rather than the interpenetration of difference. Thus, one understands the difficulty Dean has in coping with the idea of a non-alienated relationship with "the Other" (58–59), which I think can be addressed through the concept of "another" that I have discussed in earlier chapters.

Chapter Nine: Pivots Instead of Centers: Postmodern Spirituality in Gary Snyder and Ursula K. Le Guin

1. Here Hutcheon is quoting from "Nancy Reagan Wears a Hat: Feminism and Its Cultural Consensus." *Critical Inquiry* 14 (1988): 223–43; specifically p. 226. See also Fraser and Nicholson 26.

2. "Involvement, identification, acceptance" are terms used by Snyder in a letter to the author, in contradistinction to the goal of "detachment" that some schools of Buddhism emphasize. Please see my discussion of this point in Chapter Eight, in relation to Masao Abe's citation of Dōgen that "to think practice and realization are not one is a heretical view."

3. There is an amazing parallel to this viewpoint to be found in certain Native American beliefs. As one Pueblo speaker has been quoted: "We are not searching—we are already there. And you don't have to join us: you are already there too. You just have to realize it" (quoted in Booth and Jacobs, "Ties" 43).

4. For a more detailed discussion of this poem and other Le Guin poetry, with an emphasis on the "fantastic," see my essay, "The Left Hand of Fabulation."

5. The rise of the ecological in Le Guin should not be seen as inducing a necessary decline in the Daoist. Ames, Cheng, and Ip, for example, argue specifically for the compatibility of Daoism and environmentalism in their essays.

6. See Ostriker for the concept of "revisionist mythmaking": "the poet simultaneously deconstructs a prior 'myth' or 'story' and constructs a new one which includes, instead of excluding, herself" ("Thieves" 72). See also my essay, "High and Low."

7. Our ephemeral and transient presence on the earth, in comparison to the continuity of stone, is summarized in her poem, "Slick Rock Creek, September," in *Hard Words*, which compares nicely with the philosophy and imagery in Snyder's untitled poem on page 51 of *Axe Handles*.

Chapter Ten: Let the Survivors of Contact Speak: In the Canon and in the Classroom

1. According to Leanne Howe, "Even after two hundred and ten years of worldwide immigration into the United States, Indians still exist, numbering two million people in some eight hundred and forty-six tribes" (253–54). About equal, she notes, to the current number of new immigrants in New York city.

2. For a comparison of Anglo and Indian approaches, see Patricia Clark Smith, "Ain't Seen You Since"; for a focus on Anglo and Black women, see Elias-Button. It is also interesting to note that in Native American writing the relationship with the muse is unlikely to be problematic for women writers who frequently look to Grandmother Spider Woman for inspiration, while it is often problematic for white women writers who may, as Elias-Button's title indicates, view the muse as Medusa or some other instance of the "Terrible Mother."

Chapter Eleven: Centering the Other: Trickster Midwife Pedagogy

1. In the past I have used the metaphor of "Coyote" as the prime embodiment of the Trickster figure, which is found throughout cultures around the world, such as the Renaissance "fool," the Chinese monkey-king, Raven in the Pacific Northwest, and Rabbit in the Midwest. It seemed appropriate to select a figure indigenous to the United States, and from my reading, as well as my observations of popular culture, Coyote seems to be the most well-known of the indigenous Tricksters. S/he is also the one most written about in Native American texts and in non-Indian North American texts. But criticism of such appropriation is increasingly being made by Native American authors and scholars, and I would prefer to refrain from using an image with specific meanings as a representation of an apparently universal cultural phenomenon, rather than have its use be considered insulting by some (see Littlefield, particularly 104–105).

My use of the Trickster here is not Jungian or psychoanalytic, although my awareness of the Trickster is influenced by reading Jung. I conceptualize Trickster as a figure arising from within any culture, just as carnivalization appears in any culture, and view Tricksters as a necessary organic part of any healthy community (see "Literature and Vicarious Experience" by Patrick H. Dust).

2. I first encountered the image of "Midwife" applied to teachers in Belenky, Clinchy, Goldberger, and Tarule's *Women's Ways of Knowing*. It seems to me that at this point the association has become so prevalent that it does not require conceptual elaboration.

3. Lorde goes on to say that "only within that interdependency of different strengths, acknowledged and equal, can the power to seek new ways to actively 'be' in the world generate, as well as the courage and sustenance to act where there are no charters. Within that interdependence of mutual (non-dominant) differences lies that security which enables us to descend into the chaos of knowledge and return with true visions of our future, along with the concomitant power to effect those changes which can bring that future into being. Difference is that raw and powerful connection from which our personal power is forged" (99). And Barbara Smith testifies: "What *I* really feel is radical is trying to make coalitions with people who are different from you" (Smith and Smith 126).

4. The particular problems and tasks of male professors addressing gender balance and feminist teaching has not yet been adequately addressed. And, while a book such as Jardine and Smith's *Men in Feminism* proves invaluable for helping to sharpen awareness of the contradictions inherent in such concepts as "feminist men" and "men in feminism," none of the essays in this collection addresses the specific problems of males practicing feminist pedagogy. Three essays in *Gendered Subjects*, edited by Culley and Portuges, do address these issues, but while helpful they are only a beginning. Utilizing the basic theoretical construct outlined here, and a portion of the same text, I have addressed some of these points in more specific detail in my essay, "Coyote Midwife in the Classroom: Introducing Literature with Feminist Dialogics."

Chapter Twelve: The Present is to Nature as the Past is to Culture as the Future is to Agency

1. An "allelomorph" or "allele" is "either of a pair of genes located at the same position on both members of a pair of chromosomes and conveying characteristics that are inherited alternatively in accordance with Mendelian law"—Webster's New World Dictionary.

2. I use the term "evolutionary" here devoid of any Enlightenment sense of "progress" or "development," although inclusive of complexity. I concur with William Durham when he observes that "evolution, popular usage to the contrary, is *not* progress or improvement (it is simply cumulative and transmissible change)" (21).

3. I think it instructive here to note that Janet Biehl, in her social ecologist attack on the alleged "incoherence" of ecofeminist philosophy, finds it necessary to defend the modern philosophical, cultural, and political benefits of the Enlightenment against various "mystical" and "superstitious" segments of the ecofeminist movement, without in any way noting the degree to which this involves the representation of a specifically Anglo-European mode of thought as a universal good (see 94). Such universalizing

contradicts some of the fundamental aspects of the Bookchinian political program that she promotes, a contradiction that seems possible only because she has naturalized the hypostases of the Enlightenment, as in her uncritical invocations of "truth and rationality" (96). It is precisely to counter such universalizing that Donna Haraway posits the need for "situated knowledges" (184–201).

4. Salleh lays claim to the Critical Theory project of Horkheimer, Adorno, and Marcuse—with significant emendation and recognition of limitiations—for ecofeminism: "the School offers a sophisticated critique of the Nature versus Culture dichotomy; one which leads them to reject traditional gender prescriptions. Further, their epistemology and substantive analysis both point to a convergence of feminist and ecological concerns, anticipating the more recent arrival of eco-feminism" ("Epistemology" 131).

Chapter Thirteen: Simply Uncontrollable, Or Steaming Open the Envelope of Ideology

1. This chapter was first delivered, in slightly different form, at the "Reinventing Nature, Rediscovering the Wild" Conference at the University of California, Davis, October, 1993; hence the particular phrasing employed here.

Appendix

1. See Penley on this point in relation specifically to psychoanalytic learning and its implications for the classroom: "Taking her lesson again from Lacan, [Felman] shows that psychoanalytic learning (which constantly serves as her pedagogical model) is always *dialogic*" (136).

2. This choice of the Trickster figure arises primarily from my reading of such writers as Gary Snyder and Ursula K. Le Guin and the terrain of the ecological critique of capitalism, and its indebtedness to Native American tradition, one of the places from which the Trickster figure, particularly as "coyote," arises. But it also occurred to me when I gratifyingly read Michael Holquist's "The Surd Heard" in which he refers to "that other Trickster, Bakhtin" (140), comparing Bakhtin with Derrida. See Natoli on the Bakhtinian carnivalization of theory as an anti-canonical, heterarchical, dialogical move.

⌁ Bibliography ⌁

Aal, Katharyn Machan. "Writing As an Indian Woman: An Interview with Paula Gunn Allen." *North Dakota Quarterly* 57 (1989): 148–61.

Abe, Masao. *Zen and Western Thought.* Ed. William R. LaFleur. Honolulu: University of Hawaii Press, 1985.

Adams, Hazard, and Leroy Searle, eds. *Critical Theory Since 1965.* Tallahassee: Florida State University Press, 1986.

Adler, Margot. "Meanings of Matriarchy." In Spretnak, *Politics* 127–37.

Aerol, Meg. "Joy Harjo & Poetic Justice." Review. *The Circle: News from a Native Perspective* (Minneapolis) (November 1992): 19.

Allen, Paula Gunn. "Bringing Home the Fact: Tradition and Continuity in the Imagination." In *Recovering the Word: Essays on Native American Literature.* Ed. Brian Swann and Arnold Krupat. Berkeley: University of California Press, 1987. 563–79.

———. *Grandmothers of the Light: A Medicine Woman's Sourcebook.* Boston: Beacon Press, 1991.

———. Introduction. In Allen, *Spider Woman's* 1–25.

———. *The Sacred Hoop: Recovering the Feminine in American Indian Traditions.* Boston: Beacon Press, 1986.

———. *Skins and Bones: Poems 1979–1987.* Albuquerque: West End Press, 1988.

———. "Teaching American Indian Women's Literature." In Allen, *Studies* 134–44.

———. "The Woman I Love Is a Planet, The Planet I love Is a Tree." In Diamond and Orenstein, *Reweaving* 52–57.

———, ed. *Spider Woman's Granddaughters: Traditional Tales and Contemporary Writing by Native American Women.* 1989. New York: Fawcett Columbine, 1990.

———, ed. *Studies in American Indian Literature.* New York: Modern Language Association, 1983.

Allsopp, Bruce. *Ecological Morality.* London: Frederick Muller, 1972.

Althusser, Louis. "Ideology and Ideological State Apparatuses." Trans. Ben Brewster. In Adams and Searle, *Critical Theory* 239–50.

Altieri, Charles. *Enlarging the Temple: New Directions in American Poetry During the 1960's.* Lewisburg, PA: Bucknell University Press, 1979.

Ames, Roger T. "Taoism and the Nature of Nature." *Environmental Ethics* 8 (1986): 317–50.

Anderson, Lorraine, ed. *Sisters of the Earth: Women's Prose and Poetry about Nature.* New York: Vintage, 1991.

Anzaldúa, Gloria. *Borderlands/La Frontera.* San Francisco: Spinsters/Aunt Lute, 1987.

———. "Foreword to the Second Edition." In Moraga and Anzaldúa, *This Bridge* iv–v.

Atwood, Margaret. *Surfacing.* 1972. New York: Fawcett Crest, 1987.

———. *The Handmaid's Tale.* 1985. New York: Fawcett Crest, 1987.

Austin, Mary. *The Land of Little Rain.* 1903. New York: Penguin, 1988.

———. *Stories from the Country of Lost Borders.* Ed. Marjorie Pryse. American Women Writers Series. New Brunswick: Rutgers University Press, 1987.

Bakhtin, Mikhail. *The Dialogic Imagination: Four Essays by M. M. Bakhtin.* Trans. Michael Holquist and Caryl Emerson. Ed. Holquist. Austin: University of Texas Press, 1981.

———. *Problems of Dostoevsky's Poetics.* Trans. and ed. Caryl Emerson. Theory and History of Literature 8. Minneapolis: University of Minnesota Press 1984.

———. *Speech Genres & Other Late Essays.* Trans. Vern W. McGee. Ed. Caryl Emerson and Michael Holquist. Austin: University of Texas Press, 1986.

———. *Toward a Philosophy of the Act.* Ed. and Trans. Vadim Liapunov. Austin: University of Texas Press, 1993.

[Bakhtin] / V. N. Vološinov. "Discourse in Life and Discourse in Art." In [Bakhtin]/ Vološinov, *Freudianism* 93–116.

———. *Freudianism: A Marxist Critique.* Trans. I. R. Titunik. Ed. Titunik and Neal H. Bruss. New York: Academic Press, 1976.

———. *Marxism and the Philosophy of Language.* Trans. Ladislav Matejka and I. R. Titunik. Cambridge: Harvard University Press, 1986.

Bannan, Helen M. "Spider Woman's Web: Mothers and Daughters in Southwestern Native American Literature." In *The Lost Tradition: Mothers and Daughters in Literature.* Ed. Cathy N. Davidson and E. M. Broner. New York: Ungar, 1980. 268–79.

Barney, Richard A. "Uncanny Criticism in the United States." In Natoli, *Tracing* 177–212.

Bataille, Gretchen. "Transformation of Tradition: Autobiographical Works by American Indian Women." In Allen, *Studies* 85–99.

Bauer, Dale M. *Feminist Dialogics: A Theory of Failed Community.* Albany: State University of New York Press, 1988.

Begiebing, Robert J., and Owen Grumbling, eds. *The Literature of Nature*. Medford: Plexus, 1990.

Belenky, Mary Field, Blythe McVicker Clinchy, Nancy Rule Goldberger, and Jill Mattuck Tarule. *Women's Ways of Knowing: The Development of Self, Voice, and Mind*. New York: Basic Books, 1986.

Benhabib, Seyla. "Epistemologies of Postmodernism: A Rejoinder to Jean–Francois Lyotard." In Nicholson, *Feminism/Postmodernism* 107–30.

Berg, Peter. "Bioregional and Wild! A New Cultural Image. . . . " In Plant and Plant, *Turtle Talk* 22–30.

Berry, Wendell. *Collected Poems, 1957–1982*. San Francisco: North Point Press, 1985.

———. "The Gift of Good Land." In *The Gift of Good Land*. San Francisco: North Point Press, 1981. 267–81.

———. "A Secular Pilgrimage." *The Hudson Review* 23 (1970): 401–24.

Bialostosky, Don. "Dialogics as an Art of Discourse in Literary Criticism." *PMLA* 101.5 (1986): 788–97.

———. "Reply." *PMLA* 102.5 (1987): 831–32.

Biehl, Janet. *Rethinking Ecofeminist Politics*. Boston: South End Press, 1991.

Booth, Annie L., and Harvey M. Jacobs. *Environmental Consciousness—Native American Worldviews and Sustainable Natural Resource Management: An Annotated Bibliography*. CPL Bibliography 214, April 1988. Chicago: Council of Planning Librarians, 1988.

———. "Ties That Bind: Native American Beliefs as Foundation for Environmental Consciousness." *Environmental Ethics* 12 (1990): 27–43.

Bowers, C. A. "A Batesonian Perspective on Education and the Bonds of Language: Cultural Literacy in the Technological Age." *Studies in the Humanities* 15.2 (1988): 108–29.

Brenkman, John. *Culture and Domination*. Ithaca: Cornell University Press, 1987.

Bruchac, Joseph. "The Story of All Our Survival: An Interview with Joy Harjo." In *Survival This Way: Interviews with American Indian Poets*. Ed. Bruchac. Tucson: Sun Tracks and the University of Arizona Press, 1987. 87–103.

———, ed. *Songs from this Earth on Turtle's Back: Contempoary American Indian Poetry*. Greenfield Center: Greenfield Review Press, 1983.

Bruss, Neal H. "V. N. Vološinov and the Structure of Language in Freudianism." In [Bakhtin]/Vološinov, *Freudianism* 117–48.

Caldecott, Léonie, and Stephanie Leland, eds. *Reclaim the Earth: Women Speak Out for Life on Earth*. London: The Women's Press, 1983.

Callicott, J. Baird. "The Case Against Moral Pluralism." *Environmental Ethics* 12 (1990): 99–124.

Campbell, Sue Ellen. "The Land and Language of Desire: Where Deep Ecology and Post–Structuralism Meet." *Western American Literature* 24 (1989): 199–211.

Capitalism Nature Socialism no. 14 (June 1993).

Cather, Willa. *The Song of the Lark.* 1915. Boston: Houghton Mifflin, 1983.

Charnas, Susy McKee. *Walk to the end of the world.* New York: Ballantine Books, 1974.

———. *Motherlines.* 1978. New York: Berkeley, 1979.

Cheney, Jim. "Postmodern Environmental Ethics: Ethics as Bioregional Narrative." *Environmental Ethics* 11 (1989): 117–34.

Cheng, Chung–ying. "On the Environmental Ethics of the *Tao* and the *Ch'i.*" *Environmental Ethics* 8 (1986): 351–70.

Chowka, Peter Barry. "The Original Mind of Gary Snyder, Interview and Photographs." *East/West Journal* (June 1977, July 1977, and August 1977). Edited version reprinted in Snyder, *The Real Work* 92–137.

Chrystos. *Not Vanishing.* Vancouver: Press Gang Publishers, 1988.

Cixous, Hélène. "The Laugh of the Medusa." *Signs: Journal of Women in Culture and Society* 1 (1976). Reprinted in Adams and Searle, *Critical Theory* 309–20.

———, and Catherine Clément. "A Woman Mistress." Trans. Betsy Wing. In *The Rhetorical Tradition: Readings from Classical Times to the Present.* Ed. Patricia Bizzell and Bruce Herzberg. Boston: St. Martin's Press, 1990. 1245–51.

Collecott, Diane. "A Double Matrix: Re–reading H.D." *Iowa Review* 16.3 (1986): 93–125.

Coltelli, Laura. "Joy Harjo." In *Winged Words: American Indian Writers Speak.* Lincoln: University of Nebraska Press, 1990. 55–68.

Cornell, Drucilla, and Adam Thurschwell. "Feminism, Negativity, Intersubjectivity." In *Feminism as Critique.* Ed. Seyla Benhabib and Drucilla Cornell. Minneapolis: University of Minnesota Press, 1987. 143–62.

Craft, Lucille. "The Woman Who's Shocking Japan." *International Wildlife* (July–August 1993), 12–16.

Crawford, John, and Patricia Clark Smith. "Joy Harjo." In *This Is About Vision: Interviews with Southwestern Writers.* Ed. William Balassi, Crawford, and Annie O. Eysturoy. Albuquerque: University of New Mexico Press, 1990. 171–79.

Culley, Margo, and Catherine Portuges, eds. *Gendered Subjects: The Dynamics of Feminist Teaching.* Boston: Routledge, 1985.

Dallmayr, Fred. *Between Freiburg and Frankfurt: Toward a Critical Ontology*. Amherst: University of Massachusetts Press, 1991.

Davis, Donald. "Ecosophy: The Seducation of Sophia?" *Environmental Ethics* 8 (1986): 151–62.

Dean, Tim. *Gary Snyder and the American Unconscious*. New York: St. Martin's Press, 1991.

De Koven, Marianne. "Gertrude Stein and Modern Painting: Beyond Literary Criticism." *Contemporary Literature* 22 (1981). Reprinted in *Critical Essays on Gertrude Stein*. Ed. Michael J. Hoffman. Boston: G. K. Hall, 1986. 171–83.

de Lauretis, Teresa. *Technologies of Gender: Essays on Theory, Film, and Fiction*. Bloomington: Indiana University Press, 1987.

Delphy, Christine. "Protofeminism and Antifeminism." In Moi, *French Feminist Thought* 80–109.

Devall, Bill, and George Sessions. *Deep Ecology: Living as if Nature Mattered*. Salt Lake City: Peregrine Smith, 1985.

Diamond, Irene, and Gloria Feman Orenstein, eds. *Reweaving the World: The Emergence of Ecofeminism*. San Francisco: Sierra Club Books, 1990.

Díaz–Diocaretz, Myriam. "Bakhtin, Discourse, and Feminist Theories." *Critical Studies* 1.2 (1989): 121–39.

Dōgen. *Moon in a Dewdrop: Writings of Zen Master Dogen*. Ed. Kazuaki Tanahashi. Trans. Robert Aitken, *et al*. San Francisco: North Point Press, 1985.

Doubiago, Sharon. "From Mama Coyote Talks to the Boys." *Upriver/Downriver* #11 (1988): 1–5.

DuPlessis, Rachel Blau. "Breaking the Sentence; Breaking the Sequence." In *Writing Beyond the Ending: Narrative Strategies of Twentieth–Century Women Writers*. Bloomington: Indiana University Press, 1985. Reprinted in *Essentials of the Theory of Fiction*. Ed. Michael J. Hoffman and Patrick D. Murphy. Durham: Duke University Press, 1988. 472–92.

———. "The Critique of Consciousness and Myth in Levertov, Rich, and Rukeyser." In *Shakespeare's Sisters: Feminist Essays on Women Poets*. Ed. Sandra Gilbert and Susan Gubar. Bloomington: Indiana University Press, 1979. 280–300.

Durham, William H. *Coevolution: Genes, Culture, and Human Diversity*. Stanford: Stanford University Press, 1991.

Dust, Patrick H. "Literature and Vicarious Experience: The Imagination as Trickster and Midwife." *Journal of Mental Imagery* 5 (1981): 143–56.

Ehrlich, Gretel. *The Solace of Open Spaces*. New York: Penguin, 1985.

Elias–Button, "The Muse as Medusa." In *The Lost Tradition: Mothers and Daughters in Literature*. Ed. Cathy N. Davidson and E. M. Broner. New York: Ungar, 1980. 193–206.

Erdrich, Louise. *Tracks*. New York: Harper & Row, 1989.

Estes, Caroline. "Consensus and Community." In Plant and Plant. *Turtle Talk* 94–101.

Evernden, Neil. *The Natural Alien: Humankind and Environment*.

Toronto: University of Toronto Press, 1985.

Faas, Ekbert. *Towards a New American Poetics: Essays & Interviews*. Santa Barbara: Black Sparrow, 1979.

Farah, Cynthia. *Literature and Landscape: Writers of the Southwest*. El Paso: Texas Western Press, 1988.

Fetterley, Judith. *The Resisting Reader: A Feminist Approach to American Fiction*. Bloomington: Indiana University Press, 1978.

Finch, Robert, and John Elder, eds. *The Norton Book of Nature Writing*. New York: Norton, 1990.

Flaherty, Doug. "*Road Apple* Interview with Gary Snyder." *Road Apple Review* 1.4/2.1 (1969/70): 59–68. Reprinted in Snyder, *The Real Work* 15–22.

Fowler, Gene. "Gary Snyder," *Literary Times* [Chicago] 4.2 (December 1964): 22. Reprinted as "The Landscape of Consciousness" in Snyder, *The Real Work* 3–6.

Fox, Warwick. "The Deep Ecology–Ecofeminism Debate and its Parallels." *Environmental Ethics* 11 (1989): 5–25.

———. *Toward a Transpersonal Ecology: Developing New Foundations for Environmentalism*. Boston: Shambhala, 1990.

Frank, Richard. "Commentary." *Environmental Review* 6.2 (1982): 105–6.

Fraser, Nancy, and Linda J. Nicholson. "Social Criticism without Philosophy: An Encounter between Feminism and Postmodernism." In Nicholson, *Feminism / Postmodernism* 19–38.

Freer, Jean. "Gaea: The Earth as our Spiritual Heritage." In Caldecott and Leland, *Reclaim* 131–35.

Fuss, Diana. *Essentially Speaking: Feminism, Nature and Difference*. New York: Routledge, 1989.

Gallop, Jane. "Reading the Mother Tongue: Psychoanalytic Feminist Criticism." *Critical Inquiry* 13 (1987): 314–29.

Gearhart, Sally. *The Wanderground: Stories of the Hill Women*. Boston: Alyson Publications, 1979.

Gendler, Everett E. "The Return of the Goddess." In *Ecology: Crisis and New Vision*. Ed. Richard E. Sherrell. Richmond: John Knox Press, 1971.

Geneson, Paul. "An Interview with Gary Snyder." *The Ohio Review* 18.3 (1977): 67–105. Edited version reprinted in Snyder, *The Real Work* 55–82.

Gibaldi, Joseph, ed. *Introduction to Scholarship in Modern Languages and Literatures*. 1st edition. New York: MLA, 1981.

———, ed. *Introduction to Scholarship in Modern Languages and Literatures*. 2nd edition. New York: MLA, 1992.

Gilligan, Carol. *In A Different Voice: Psychological Theory and Women's Development*. Cambridge: Harvard University Press, 1982.

Glotfelty, Cheryll Burgess. "Toward an Ecological Literary Criticism." Unpublished.

Graff, Gerald. *Literature Against Itself: Literary Ideas in Modern Society*. Chicago: University of Chicago Press, 1979.

———. *Professing Literature: An Institutional History*. Chicago: The University of Chicago Press, 1987.

Greenblatt, Stephen, and Giles Gunn, eds. *Redrawing the Boundaries: The Transformation of English and American Literary Studies*. New York: MLA, 1992.

Griffin, Susan. *Made from this Earth: an Anthology of Writings*. New York: Harper & Row, 1982.

———. *Woman and Nature: The Roaring Inside Her*. New York: Harper and Row, 1978.

Halpern, Daniel, ed. *On Nature: Nature, Landscape, and Natural History*. San Francisco: North Point Press, 1987.

Hampl, Patricia. *Resort and Other Poems*. Boston: Houghton Mifflin, 1983.

Haraway, Donna. *Symians, Cyborgs, and Women: The Reinvention of Nature*. New York: Routledge, 1991.

Harding, Sandra. *The Science Question in Feminism*. Ithaca: Cornell University Press, 1986.

Harjo, Joy. *In Mad Love and War*. Middletown, Conn.: Wesleyan University Press, 1990.

———. *She Had Some Horses*. New York: Thunder's Mouth, 1983.

———. *What Moon Drove Me To This?* New York: I. Reed Books, 1979.

———, and Stephen Strom. *Secrets from the Center of the World*. Tucson: Sun Tracks and the University of Arizona Press, 1989.

Hartsock, Nancy. "Foucault on Power: A Theory for Women?" In Nicholson, *Feminism / Postmodernism* 157–75.

Hassan, Ihab. The Dismemberment of Orpheus: Toward a Postmodern Literature. New York: Oxford University Press, 1971.

―――. *Paracriticisms: Seven Speculations of the Times.* Urbana: University of Illinois Press, 1975.

Heath, Stephen. "Male Feminism." In Jardine and Smith, *Men* 1–32.

Henderson, Hazel. "The Warp and the Weft: The Coming Synthesis of Eco–Philosophy and Eco–Feminism." In Caldecott and Leland, *Reclaim* 203–14.

Hertz, Uri. "An Interview with Gary Snyder." *Third Rail* 7 (1985–86): 51–53, 96.

Hicks, Jack. "Poetic Composting in Gary Snyder's *Left Out in the Rain.*" In *Critical Essays on Gary Snyder.* Ed. Patrick D. Murphy. Boston: G. K. Hall, 1990. 247–57.

Hobson, Geary, ed. *The Remembered Earth: An Anthology of Contemporary Native American Literature.* Albuquerque: Red Earth Press, 1979.

Hogan, Linda. *Daughters, I Love You.* Denver: Loretto Heights College Publications, 1981.

―――. *Savings.* Minneapolis: Coffee House Press, 1988.

―――. "The Transformation of Tribalism." *Book Forum* 5 (1981): 403–409.

Holquist, Michael. *Dialogism: Bakhtin and His World.* New York: Routledge, 1990.

―――. "The Surd Heard: Bakhtin and Derrida." In *Literature and History: Theoretical Problems and Russian Case Studies.* Ed. Gary Saul Morson. Stanford: Stanford University Press, 1986. 137–56.

Hopkinson, Deborah, and Susan Murcott. "The Kahawai Koans." In Hopkinson, Hill, and Kiera, *Not Mixing* 30–35.

Hopkinson, Deborah, Michelle Hill, and Eileen Kiera, eds. *Not Mixing Up Buddhism: Essays on Women and Buddhist Practice.* Fredonia: White Pine Press, 1986.

Horkheimer, Max, and Theodor W. Adorno. *Dialectic of Enlightenment.* Trans. John Cumming. 1972. New York: Continuum, 1990.

Howe, Leanne. "An American in New York." In Allen, *Spider Woman's* 245–55.

Hughes, J. Donald. "Gaia: Environmental Problems in Chthonic Perspective." *Environmental Review* 6.2 (1982): 92–104.

Hutcheon, Linda. *The Politics of Postmodernism.* New York: Routledge, 1989.

Ip, Po–Keung. "Taoism and the Foundations of Environmental Ethics." *Environmental Ethics* 5 (1983): 335–43.

Irigaray, Luce. "Sexual Difference." In Moi, *French Feminist Thought* 118–30.

———. "This Sex Which Is Not One." In *New French Feminisms*. Ed. Elaine Marks and Isabella Courtivron. 1981. Reprinted in *This Sex Which Is Not One*. Trans. Catherine Porter with Carolyn Burke. Ithaca: Cornell University Press, 1985. 23–33.

Jacoby, John. "Interview with Gary Snyder." *Espejo* 12.2 (Spring 1974). Reprinted as "Knots in the Grain" in Snyder, *The Real Work* 44–51.

Jardine, Alice A. "Gynesis." *Diacritics* 12 (1982). Reprinted in Adams and Searle, *Critical Theory* 560–70.

———. "Men in Feminism: Odor di Uomo or Compagnons de Route?" In Jardine and Smith, *Men* 54–61.

———, and Paul Smith, eds. *Men in Feminism*. New York: Methuen, 1987.

Jay, Gregory S. "The End of 'American' Literature: Toward a Multicultural Practice." *College English* 53 (1991): 264–81.

Johns, David M. "The Relevance of Deep Ecology to the Third World: Some Preliminary Comments." *Environmental Ethics* 12 (1990): 233–52.

Johnson, Barbara. *A World of Difference*. Baltimore: Johns Hopkins University Press, 1987.

Jose, Jim. "Reflections on the Politics of Le Guin's Narrative Shifts." *Science–Fiction Studies* 18 (1991): 180–97.

Jung, Hwa Yol. "The Way of Ecopiety: Ethics as if the Earth Really Matters." Unpublished.

Keller, Evelyn Fox. *Reflections on Gender and Science*. New Haven: Yale University Press, 1985.

King, Ynestra. "The Eco–Feminist Imperative." In Caldicott and Leland, *Reclaim* 9–14.

———. "Toward an Ecological Feminism and a Feminist Ecology." In *Machina Ex Dea: Feminist Perspectives on Technology*. Ed. Joan Rothschild. New York: Pergamon Press, 1983. 118–29.

Kolodny, Annette. *The Lay of the Land: Metaphor as Experience and History in American Life and Letters*. Chapel Hill: University of North Carolina Press, 1975.

Koolish, Lynda. "The Bones of This Body Say, Dance: Self–Empowerment in Contemporary Poetry by Women of Color." In *Critical Challenges in Contemporary American Poetry*. Ed. Marie Harris and Kathleen Aguero. Athens: University of Georgia Press, 1987. 1–56.

Krauss, James W. "Gary Snyder's Biopoetics: A Study of the Poet as Ecologist." Diss. University of Hawaii, 1986.

Kristeva, Julia. *Desire in Language: A Semiotic Approach to Literature and Art*. Ed. Leon S. Roudiez. Trans. Thomas Gora, Alice Jardine, and Roudiez. New York: Columbia University Press, 1980.

————. *Revolution in Poetic Language.* Trans. Margaret Waller. New York: Columbia University Press, 1984.

————. "Women's Time." *Signs: Journal of Women in Culture and Society* 7 (1981). Reprinted in Adams and Searle, *Critical Theory* 471–84.

Kuletz, Valerie. "Eco–Feminist Philosophy: Interview with Barbara Holland–Cunz." *Capitalism, Nature, Socialism* 3.2 (1992): 63–78.

Lacan, Jacques. "The Agency of the Letter in the Unconscious or Reason Since Freud." In *Ecrits.* Trans. Alan Sheridan. New York: W. W. Norton, 1977. Reprinted in Adams and Searle, *Critical Theory* 738–56.

————. "The Mirror Stage." In *Ecrits.* Trans. Alan Sheridan. New York: W.W. Norton, 1977. Reprinted in Adams and Searle, *Critical Theory* 734–38.

LaCapra, Dominick. *Rethinking Intellectual History: Texts, Contexts, Language.* Ithaca: Cornell University Press, 1983.

LaChapelle, Dolores. "Systemic Thinking and Deep Ecology." In *Ecological Consciousness: Essays from the Earthday X Colloquium.* Ed. Robert C. Schultz and J.Donald Hughes. Washington: University Press of America, 1981. 295–323.

La Leche League International. *The Womanly Art of Breastfeeding.* 1958. 4th Rev. Ed. Franklin Park, IL: La Leche League International, 1987.

Lang, Nancy. "Through Landscape Toward Story/Through Story Toward Landscape: A Study of Four Native American Women Poets." Diss. Indiana University of Pennsylvania, 1991.

————. "'Twin Gods Bending Over': Joy Harjo and Poetic Memory." *MELUS* 18 (1993): 41–49.

Leclerc, Annie. "Parole de femme." In Moi, *French Feminist Thought* 73–79.

Le Guin, Ursula K. *Always Coming Home.* New York: Bantam, 1986.

————. *Buffalo Gals and Other Animal Presences.* 1987. New York: New American Library, 1988.

————. *Dancing at the Edge of the World: Thoughts on Words, Women, Places.* New York: Harper & Row, 1989.

————. *The Dispossessed.* New York: Harper & Row, 1974.

————. *Hard Words and Other Poems.* New York: Harper and Row, 1981.

————. Talk and Reading (taped). Places on Earth series. University of California, Davis, June 4, 1986.

————. *Wild Angels.* Santa Barbara: Capra, 1975. Reprinted in *The Capra Chapbook Anthology.* Ed. Noel Young. Santa Barbara: Capra, 1979.

———. *Wild Oats and Fireweed*. New York: Harper and Row, 1988.

Lenin, V. I. *Philosophical Notebooks*. Vol. 38 of *Collected Works*. Trans. Clemens Dutt. Ed. Stewart Smith. 4th ed. 45 vols. Moscow: Foreign Languages Publishing House, 1961.

Leopold, Aldo. *A Sand County Almanac*. 1949. New York: Ballantine, 1970.

Lerner, Andrea, ed. *Dancing on the Rim of the World: An Anthology of Contemporary Northwest Native American Writing*. Tucson: Sun Tracks and the University of Arizona Press, 1990.

Lewis, David Rich. "Still Native: The Significance of Native Americans in the History of the Twentieth–Century American West." *The Western Historical Quarterly* 24 (1993): 203–27.

Lin, Yao–fu. "'The Mountains Are Your Mind': Orientalism in the Poetry of Gary Snyder." *Tamkang Review* 6–7.1–2 (1975–1976): 357–91.

Littlefield, Daniel F., Jr. "American Indians, American Scholars and the American Literary Canon." *American Studies* 33 (1992): 95–111.

Lord, Audre. "The Master's Tools Will Never Dismantle the Master's House." In Moraga and Anzaldúa, *This Bridge* 98–101.

Lovelock, J[ames] E. *Gaia: A New Look at Life on Earth*. New York: Oxford University Press, 1979.

———, and Michael Allaby. *The Greening of Mars*. New York: Warner Books, 1985.

———, and Sidney Epton. "The Quest for Gaia." *New Scientist* 65 (6 Feb 1975): 304–6.

Lyon, Thomas J., ed. *This Incomperable Land: A Book of American Nature Writing*. 1989. New York: Penguin, 1991.

Mao Zedong (Mao Tsetung). "On Contradiction." In *Selected Readings from the Works of Mao Tsetung*. Peking: Foreign Language Press, 1971. 85–133.

Marini, Marcelle. "Feminism and Literary Criticism: Reflections on the Disciplinary Approach." In *Women in Culture and Politics: A Century of Change*. Ed. Judith Friedlander, et al. Bloomington: Indiana University Press, 1986. 144–63.

Martin, Julia. "Coyote–Mind: An Interview with Gary Snyder." *Triquarterly* 79 (Fall 1990): 148–72.

———. "The Pattern Which Connects: Metaphor in Gary Snyder's Later Poetry." *Western American Literature* 22 (1987): 99–123.

———. "Practising Emptiness: Gary Snyder's Playful Ecological Work." *Western American Literature* 27 (1992): 3–19.

Matthiessen, Peter. *Indian Country*. New York: Viking, 1984.

McDaniel, Jay. "Physical Matter as Creative and Sentient." *Environmental Ethics* 5 (1983): 291–317.

McKenzie, James. "Moving the World a Millionth of an Inch: Gary Snyder." In *The Beat Vision: A Primary Sourcebook.* Ed. Arthur and Kit Knight. New York: Paragon House, 1987. 1–27.

Meeker, Joseph W. *The Comedy of Survival: Studies in Literary Ecology.* New York: Scribner's, 1972.

Mellor, Mary. "Eco–Feminism and Eco–Socialism: Dilemmas of Essentialism and Materialism." *Capitalism, Nature, Socialism* 3.2 (1992): 43–62.

Merchant, Carolyn. *The Death of Nature: Women, Ecology and the Scientific Revolution.* 1980. New York: Harper, 1989.

Merod, Jim. *The Political Responsibility of the Critic.* Ithaca: Cornell University Press, 1987.

Michie, Helena. *The Flesh Made Word: Female Figures and Women's Bodies.* New York: Oxford University Press, 1987.

Mohanty, S. P. "Radical Teaching, Radical Theory: The Ambiguous Politics of Meaning." In Nelson, *Theory* 149–76.

Mohr, Richard. "Teaching as Politics." *Report from the Center for Philosophy & Public Policy* 6.3 (1986): 8–11.

Moi, Toril, ed. *French Feminist Thought: A Reader.* Oxford: Basil Blackwell, 1987.

Molesworth, Charles. *Gary Snyder's Vision: Poetry and the Real Work.* Columbia: University of Missouri Press, 1983.

Momaday, N. Scott. "A First American Views His Land." *National Geographic* 150 (1976): 13–19.

Mora, Pat. *Chants.* Houston: Arte Publico Press, 1984.

———. *Nepantla: Essays from the Land in the Middle.* Albuquerque: University of New Mexico Press, 1993.

Moraga, Cherríe, and Gloria Anzaldúa, ed. *This Bridge Called My Back: Writings by Radical Women of Color.* 2nd ed. New York: Kitchen Table: Women of Color Press, 1983.

Morgan, Ellen. "The One–Eyed Doe." *Radical Teacher* 10 (1978): 2–6.

Morson, Gary Saul, and Caryl Emerson. "Introduction: Rethinking Bakhtin." In *Rethinking Bakhtin: Extensions and Challenges.* Eds. Morson and Emerson. Evanston: Northwestern University Press, 1989. 1–60.

Moulin, Sylvie. "Nobody is an Orphan: Interview with Luci Tapahonso." *Studies in American Indian Literatures* 3.3 (1991): 14–18.

Moulin–Cohen, Sylvie. "Modern and Traditional Women's Issues in the Poetry of Luci Tapahonso." Unpublished.

Murcott, Susan. "The Original Buddhist Women." In Hopkinson, Hill, and Kiera, *Not Mixing* 11–23.

Murphy, Patrick D. "Beyond Humanism: Mythic Fantasy and Inhumanist Philosophy in the Long Poems of Robinson Jeffers and Gary Snyder." *American Studies* 30 (1989): 53–71.

———. "Coyote Midwife in the Classroom: Introducing Literature with Feminist Dialogics." In *Practicing Theory in Introductory College Literature Courses*. Ed. James M. Cahalan and David B. Downing. Urbana: National Council of Teachers of English, 1991. 161–76.

———. "De/Reconstructing the 'I': PostFANTASTICmodernist Poetry." *Journal of the Fantastic in the Arts* 1.4 (1988): 39–48.

———. "The High and Low Fantasies of Feminist (Re)Mythopoeia." *Mythlore* 60 (Winter 1989): 26–31.

———. "The Left Hand of Fabulation: The Poetry of Ursula K. Le Guin." In *The Poetic Fantastic: Studies in an Evolving Genre*. Ed. Murphy and Vernon Hyles. New York: Greenwood, 1989. 123–36.

———. "Mythic and Fantasic: Gary Snyder's 'Mountains and Rivers without End.'" *Extrapolation* 26 (1985): 290–99.

———. "Suicide, Murder, Culture and Catastrophe: Joanna Russ's *We Who Are About To. . . .*" In *State of the Fantastic: Studies in the Theory and Practice of Fantastic Literature and Film*, ed. Nicholas Ruddick. Greenwood Press, 1992. 121–131.

Natoli, Joseph. "Tracing a Beginning through Past Theory Voices." Natoli, In *Tracing* 3–26.

———, ed. *Tracing Literary Theory*. Urbana: University of Illinois Press, 1987.

Neate, W. D. "Rewriting, Rereading Ethnicity: The Lesson of Contemporary Chicana Poetry." Unpublished.

Nelson, Cary. "Men, Feminism: The Materiality of Discourse." In Jardine and Smith, *Men* 153–72.

———, ed. *Theory in the Classroom*. Urbana: University of Illinois Press, 1986.

Nelson, Rudolph L. "'Riprap on the Slick Rock of Metaphysics': Religious Dimensions in the Poetry of Gary Snyder." *Soundings* 57.2 (1974): 206–21.

Nicholson, Linda J., ed. *Feminism/Postmodernism*. New York: Routledge, 1990.

O'Connell, Nicholas. *At The Field's End*. Seattle: Madrona, 1987.

Oelschlaeger, Max. *The Idea of Wilderness: From Prehistory to the Age of Ecology*. New Haven: Yale University Press, 1991.

Ohmann, Richard. "In, With." In Jardine and Smith, *Men* 182–88.

Oliver, Mary. *American Primitive*. Boston: Little, Brown, 1983.

———. *Dream Work*. New York: Atlantic Monthly, 1986.

———. *Twelve Moons*. Boston: Little, Brown, 1979.

Ortner, Sherry B. "Is Female to Male as Nature is to Culture?" In *Woman, Culture, and Society*. Ed. Michelle Rosaldo and Louise Lamphere. Stanford: Stanford University Press, 1974. 67–87.

Ostriker, Alicia. "Body Language: Imagery of the Body in Women's Poetry." In *The State of the Language*. Ed. Leonard Michaels and Christopher Ricks. Berkeley: University of California Press, 1980. 247–63.

———. "The Thieves of Language: Women Poets and Revisionist Mythmaking." *Signs: Journal of Women in Culture and Society* 8 (1982): 68–90.

Paul, Sherman. *In Search of the Primitive: Rereading David Antin, Jerome Rothenberg, and Gary Snyder*. Baton Rouge: Louisiana State University Press, 1986.

Penley, Constance. "Teaching in Your Sleep: Feminism and Psychoanalysis." In Nelson, *Theory* 129–48.

———, and Andrew Ross. "Cyborgs at Large: Interview with Donna Haraway." In *Technoculture*. Ed. Penley and Ross. Minneapolis: University of Minnesota Press, 1991.

Perloff, Marjorie. "Postmodernism and the Impasse of Lyric." *Formations* 1.2 (1984). Reprinted in *The Dance of the Intellect*. New York: Cambridge University Press, 1985. 172–200.

Piercy, Marge. *Woman on the Edge of Time*. 1976. New York: Fawcett Crest, 1977.

Plant, Christopher, and Judith Plant, eds. *Turtle Talk: Voices for a Sustainable Future*. Philadelphia: New Society Publishers, 1990.

Probyn, Elspeth. "Travels in the Postmodern: Making Sense of the Local." In Nicholson, *Feminism / Postmodernism* 176–89.

Quigley, Peter. "Rethinking Resistance: Environmentalism, Literature, and Poststructural Theory." *Environmental Ethics* 14 (1992): 291–306.

Rich, Adrienne. "Notes Toward a Politics of Location." In *Women, Feminist Identity and Society in the 1980s: Selected Papers*. Eds. Myriam Díaz–Diocaretz and Iris M. Zavala. Philadelphia: John Benjamins, 1985. 7–22.

Robertson, David. "Gary Snyder Riprapping in Yosemite, 1955." *American Poetry* 2 (1984): 52–59.

Rodman, John. "The Dolphin Papers." In Halpern, *On Nature* 252–80.

Rolston, Holmes, III. *Philosophy Gone Wild: Essays in Environmental Ethics.* Buffalo: Prometheus Books, 1986.

Rooney, Ellen. *Seductive Reasoning: Pluralism as the Problematic of Contemporary Literary Theory.* Ithaca: Cornell University Press, 1989.

Ross, Andrew. *The Failure of Modernism: Symptoms of American Poetry.* New York: Columbia University Press, 1986.

Rothberg, Abraham. "A Passage to More than India: The Poetry of Gary Snyder." *Southwest Review* 61.1 (1976): 26–38.

Ruether, Rosemary Radford. *New Woman/New Earth: Sexist Ideologies and Human Liberation.* New York: The Seabury Press, 1975.

Ruoff, A. La Vonne Brown. "Woodland Word Warrior: An Introduction to the Works of Geral Vizenor." *MELUS* 13 (1986): 13–43.

Ruppert, Jim. "Paula Gunn Allen and Joy Harjo: Closing the Distance Between Personal and Mythic Space." *American Indian Quarterly* 7.1 (1983): 27–40.

Russ, Joanna. *We Who Are About To. . . .* London: The Women's Press, 1987.

Ryan, Michael. *Marxism and Deconstruction: A Critical Articulation.* Baltimore: Johns Hopkins University Press, 1982.

Sagan, Dorion. *Biospheres: Reproducing Planet Earth.* New York: Bantam, 1990.

Salleh, Ariel. "Deeper than Deep Ecology: The Eco–Feminist Connection." *Environmental Ethics* 6 (1984): 339–45.

———. "The Eco–Feminism/Deep Ecology Debate: A Reply to Patriarchal Reason." *Environmental Ethics* 14 (1992): 195–216.

———. "Epistemology and the Metaphors of Production: An Eco–Feminist Reading of Critical Theory." *Studies in the Humanities* 15.2 (1988): 130–29.

Schuster, Charles I. "Mikhail Bakhtin as Rhetorical Theorist." *College English* 47 (1985): 594–607.

Schweickart, Patricino P. "Reading Ourselves: Toward a Feminist Theory of Reading." In *Gender and Reading: Essays on Readers, Texts, and Contexts.* Ed. Elizabeth A. Flynn and Schweickart. Baltimore: Johns Hopkins University Press, 1986. 31–62.

Schweninger, Lee. "Writing Nature: Silko and Native Americans as Nature Writers." *MELUS* 18 (1993): 47–60.

Sessions, George. "Ecocentrism and the Greens: Deep Ecology and the Environmental Task." *Trumpeter* 5.2 (1988): 65–69.

Shafer, Ingrid. *Eros and the Womanliness of God.* Chicago: Loyola University Press, 1986.

Showalter, Elaine. "Critical Cross–Dressing: Male Feminists and the Woman of the Year." In Jardine and Smith, *Men* 116–32.

Shrewsbury, Carolyn M. "What Is Feminist Pedagogy?" *Women's Studies Quarterly* 15 (1987): 6–14.

Silko, Leslie Marmon. *Almanac of the Dead: A Novel.* New York: Penguin, 1991.

———. *Ceremony.* New York: New American Library, 1977.

———. "Landscape, History, and the Pueblo Imagination." In Halpern, *On Nature* 83–94.

Smith, Barbara, and Beverly Smith. "Across the Kitchen Table: A Sister–to–Sister Dialogue." In Moraga and Anzaldúa, *The Bridge* 113–27.

Smith, Patricia Clark. "Ain't Seen You Since: Dissent Among Female Relatives in American Indian Women's Poetry." In Allen, *Studies* 108–26.

———, with Paula Gunn Allen. "Earthly Relations, Carnal Knowledge: Southwestern American Indian Women Writers and Landscape." In *The Desert Is No Lady: Southwestern Landscapes in Women's Writing and Art.* Ed. Vera Norwood and Janice Monk. New Haven: Yale University Press, 1987. 174–96.

Smith, Paul. *Discerning the Subject.* Minneapolis: University of Minnesota Press, 1988.

Snyder, Gary. *Axe Handles.* San Francisco: North Point Press, 1983.

———. *The Back Country.* New York: New Directions, 1968.

———. *Earth House Hold: Technical Notes & Queries to Fellow Dharma Revolutionaries.* New York: New Directions, 1969.

———. Foreword. *Songs of Gods, Songs of Humans.* Donald L. Philippi. Berkeley: North Point Press, 1981, vii–ix.

———. *He Who Hunted Birds in His Father's Village: The Dimensions of a Haida Myth.* Bolinas: Grey Fox Press, 1979.

———. *Left Out in the Rain: New Poems 1947–1985.* San Francisco: North Point Press, 1986.

———. *No Nature: New and Selected Poems.* New York: Pantheon, 1992.

———. *The Old Ways.* San Francisco: City Lights Books, 1977.

———. *Passage Through India.* 1972. San Francisco: Grey Fox Press, 1983.

———. "Poetry, Community, & Climax." In *A Field Guide to Contemporary Poetry and Poetics.* Eds. Stuart Friebert and David Young. New York: Longman, 1980. 86–101.

————. *The Practice of the Wild: Essays by Gary Snyder.* San Francisco: North Point Press, 1990.

————. *The Real Work: Interviews & Talks, 1964–1979.* Ed. Wm. Scott McLean. New York: New Directions, 1980.

————. *Regarding Wave.* New York: New Directions, 1970.

————. *Riprap & Cold Mountain Poems.* 1959. San Francisco: North Point Press, 1990.

————. *Turtle Island.* New York: New Directions, 1974.

Spanos, William V. *Repetitions: The Postmodern Occassion in Literature and Culture.* Baton Rouge: Louisiana State University Press, 1987.

Spivak, Gayatri Chakravorty. *In Other Worlds: Essays in Cultural Politics.* New York: Methuen, 1987.

Spretnak, Charlene. "Dinnertime." In *Gary Snyder: Dimensions of a Life.* Ed. Jon Halper. San Francisco: Sierra Club Books, 1991. 359–61.

————. Introduction. Spretnak, *Politics* xi–xxx.

————, ed. *The Politics of Women's Spirituality.* Garden City: Doubleday, 1982.

Stanton, Domna C. "Difference on Trial: A Critique of the Maternal Metaphor in Cixous, Irigaray, and Kristeva." In *The Poetics of Gender.* Ed. Nancy K. Miller. New York: Columbia University Press, 1986. 157–82.

Steuding, Bob. *Gary Snyder.* TUSAS 274. Boston: Twayne, 1976.

Stimpson, Catharine R. "The Somagrams of Gertrude Stein." *Poetics Today* 6 (1985). Reprinted in *Critical Essays on Gertrude Stein.* Ed. Michael J. Hoffman. Boston: G. K. Hall, 1986. 183–96.

Stranahan, Susan Q. "Empowering Women." *International Wildlife* (May–June 1993), 12–19.

Tapahonso, Luci. *A Breeze Swept Through.* Albuquerque: West End Press, 1987.

Tarantelli, Carole B. "And the Last Walls Dissolved: On Imagining a Story of the Survival of Difference." *Women in Culture and Politics: A Century of Change.* Ed. Judith Friedlander, et al. Bloomington: Indiana University Press, 1986. 177–93.

Tepper, Sheri S. *The Gate to Women's Country.* 1988. New York: Bantam, 1989.

Todd, Judith. "On Common Ground: Native American and Feminist Spirituality Approaches in the Struggle to Save Mother Earth." In Spretnak, *Politics* 430–45.

Todorov, Tzvetan. "Postmodernism, a Primer." *The New Republic* (21 May 1990): 32–35.

Tokar, Brian. *The Green Alternative: Creating an Ecological Future.* San Pedro: R. & E. Miles, 1987.

Treichler, Paula A. "Teaching Feminist Theory." In Nelson, *Theory* 97–128.

Vitali, Theodore R. "Sport Hunting: Moral or Immoral?" *Environmental Ethics* 12 (1990): 69–82.

Waage, Frederick O., ed. *Teaching Environmental Literature: Materials, Methods, Resources.* New York: MLA, 1985.

Walker, Alice. *Living By the Word: Selected Writings 1973–1987.* New York: Harcourt, Brace, Jovanovich, 1988.

———. *The Temple of My Familiar.* 1989. New York: Pocket Books, 1990.

Warren, Karen J. "Feminism and Ecology: Making Connections." *Environmental Ethics* 9 (1987): 3–20.

———. "The Power and the Promise of Ecological Feminism." *Environmental Ethics* 12 (1990): 125–46.

Watts, George. "Working Together: Natives, Non–Natives and the Future." In Plant and Plant, *Turtle Talk* 86–92.

Weedon, Chris. *Feminist Practice and Poststructuralist Theory.* Oxford: Basil Blackwell, 1987.

White, Hayden. *Tropics of Discourse: Essays in Cultural Criticism.* 1978. Baltimore: Johns Hopkins University Press, 1985.

Wiget, Andrew. "Nightriding with Noni Daylight: The Many Horse Songs of Joy Harjo." In *Native American Literatures.* Ed. Laura Coltelli. Pisa: Servisio Editorial Universitario, 1989. 185–96.

Wilhelm, Kate. *Juniper Time.* 1979. New York: Pocket Books, 1980.

Williams, Terry Tempest. "The Wild Card." *Wilderness* (Summer 1993), 26–29.

Wyatt, David. *The Fall into Eden: Landscape and Imagination in California.* New York: Cambridge University Press, 1986.

Yaeger, Patricia. *Honey–Mad Women: Emancipatory Strategies in Women's Writings.* New York: Columbia University Press, 1988.

Yamazato, Katsunori. "Kitkitdizze, Zendo, and Place: Gary Snyder as Reinhabitory Poet." *ISLE: Interdisciplinary Studies in Literature and Environment* 1 (1993): 51–63.

Zavala, Iris M. "Bakhtin and Otherness: Social Heterogeneity." *Critical Studies* 2.1–2 (1990): 77–89.

——. "Bakhtin and the Third: Communication as Response." *Critical Studies* 1.2 (1989): 43–63.

Zimmerman, Michael E. "Feminism, Deep Ecology, and Environmental Ethics." *Environmental Ethics* 9 (1987): 21–44.

⌇ Index ⌇